A Man for Antarctica
The Early Life of Phillip Law

P. G. Law, Acting Officer-in-Charge Antarctic Division (1949).

A Man for Antarctica

The Early Life of Phillip Law

Kathleen Ralston

HYLAND HOUSE

First published in 1993 by
Hyland House Publishing Pty Limited
Hyland House
387–389 Clarendon Street
South Melbourne
Victoria 3205

© Kathleen Ralston 1993

Published with the assistance of the Monash University Publications Committee.

National Library of Australia
Cataloguing-in-publication data

Ralston Kathleen, 1938–
A man for Antarctica: the early life of Phillip Law.

Bibliography.
Includes index.
ISBN 1 875657 13 4

1. Law, P. G. (Phillip Garth), 1912– . 2. Australian National
Antarctic Research Expeditions. 3. Explorers – Antarctic Regions –
Biography. 4. Explorers – Australia – Biography. 5.Australian
Antarctic Territory (Antarctic regions). – Exploring expeditions.
I. Title.

919.8904

Typeset by Rob Cowpe Creative
Printed in Australia by Brown Prior Anderson, Melbourne

Contents

List of Illustrations

Acknowledgements

I would like to extend my thanks and very highest regard to Dr Phillip Law who helped, in every possible way, to make this study of his life such an enjoyable experience. Working with him has, for me, been a lesson in stimulating leadership and scrupulous administration.

Also I extend thanks to all those people who gave their time, shared their reminiscences, showed and loaned me photographs and allowed me to read diaries and letters that touched on Dr Law's life. Particular thanks to Tim Bowden of the ABC Social History Unit who so willingly allowed me to tap into the Unit's Antarctic archival material. A special thanks to Richard Thompson who not only gave me much valuable information for this study in the form of interviews and personal letters, but also read and commented on the drafts of the sections on the Antarctic Division. Thank you also to those staff members of the Antarctic Division who cleared the way for me to delve into the files of the early years of the Antarctic Division.

Thanks also to Dr Peter Gronn of the Faculty of Education, Monash University, for his intellectual stimulation during the period of this project.

To my husband, David, thanks for all the listening, the questioning, and the ever constant care and support.

Prologue

In 1947 the Australian Government announced their intention to establish scientific stations at the sub-Antarctic Islands of Heard and Macquarie and to carry out systematic reconnaissance of the coast of the Australian Antarctic Territory, with a view to establishing a permanent scientific station on the Antarctic continent.

The establishment of Heard and Macquarie Islands went ahead as planned during 1948. But the setting up of the Antarctic continent base was not achieved until six years later.

Finally, on 13 February 1954, the Australian flag was raised on what has been called the 'coldest, windiest, most inhospitable land on earth, Antarctica'[1] and the station was named 'Mawson' after the Australian Antarctic explorer, Sir Douglas Mawson.

The major driving force behind these achievements was the Director of the Antarctic Division and Leader of the Australian National Antarctic Research Expeditions, Phillip Garth Law.

1. Stuart Harris (ed.), *Australia's Antarctic Policy Options*, CRES Monograph 11, Australian National University, 1984, p. 2.

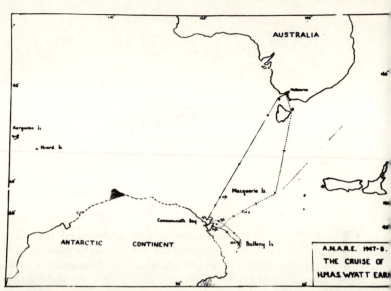

Track chart of
Wyatt Earp
voyage.

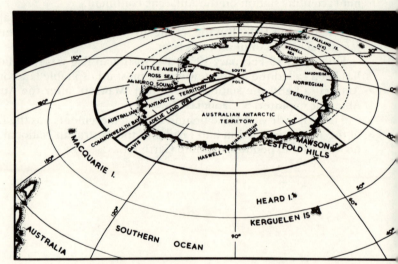

Map of
Antarctica.

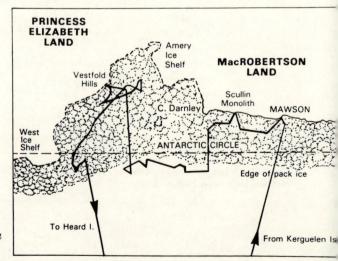

The route taken by *Kista Dan* on 1954 voyage.

1. *Little Phil, 1912–1921*

1.

PHIL LAW'S EARLIEST MEMORIES ARE WHEN HE WAS ABOUT THREE YEARS old and the Law family were living at Mitta Mitta. The first is of him and Geof, his older brother then nearly five years old, stealthily piling a heap of small stones outside the open door to the classroom where their father was teaching. Geof whispered to Phil, 'one, two, three', then they hurled the stones at their father. Off they ran with the Grade 8 boys after them. Geof escaped by climbing a tree and crawling out onto a thin branch where the heavier school boys were not game enough to follow. But Phil was easily caught and taken back, whimpering, to his father for just punishment.

The second memory is more pleasant. Phil recalls one night being taken outside by his mother to see snow flakes that had settled on an enamel dish in which the water had turned to ice.

Neither of these earliest memories is in any way remarkable and it is difficult to gauge either their importance or accuracy. Nevertheless, together they highlight threads that are consistent throughout Phil's childhood: a small, timid boy overshadowed and influenced by a rebellious older brother. The second theme, of a caring mother and a cold, unbending father also stays constant in Phil's life.

Phillip Law's parents, Lillie Lena Chapman and Arthur James Law, met in 1906 when they began studying for their Trained Teacher's Certificate at the Training College, Melbourne. Both were born in 1885 and had each gained their Merit Certificate in 1898. By 1901 they were both working as school monitors and later became probationary teachers. Their teaching careers began well, with Inspectors' reports describing Lillie as 'capable, promising, active and useful'.[1] Arthur was described as 'active, bright, useful, very intelligent and very good'.[2] Both were ambitious and both successful in the competitive examination for entrance to the Training College, Melbourne.

The similarities between the early events of their lives must not mask their personal differences. Although they were both physically small, Lillie was slim, fun loving, vivacious and an Irish Catholic, whereas Arthur was wiry, serious, intense and an Anglican.

During that first year at the College the quality of Lillie's teaching deteriorated, or her report may simply reflect the differing expectations,

1

at that time, of male and female trainees. Whatever the reason, Lillie was described as 'rather crude in her general manner' and was consequently awarded only 70 marks.[3] Arthur, on the other hand, was 'a very effective teacher ... very exact and has good control over the class' and was awarded 82 marks.[4]

By 16 December 1907 Lillie, having apparently knocked some of the edges off her crudity, had 'developed wonderfully during the year in her manner. She has worked ably and well. (82 Good)' Arthur's report on the same day read, 'A teacher of great firmness and determination. He has entered well into College. He is a conscientious and thoughtful student. (86 Very Good).'[5]

Arthur had embraced College life and taken on an official role as first Treasurer of the newly formed Training College Club. The club was presided over by the Principal, Dr John Smyth, and amalgamated the cricket, football, tennis and magazine clubs of the College.[6]

By the end of 1907 Arthur and Lillie had each been awarded a Trained Teacher's Certificate and become part of a talented minority of teachers with such a qualification.

In February 1909 Arthur was appointed as Head Teacher at the Mitta Mitta School, 40 miles from Tallangatta, where he had grown up and where his parents and other members of his family still lived. This appointment in a remote township did nothing to quell his ambitions. He had gained his Matriculation Certificate and already showed signs of the enthusiasm and dedication to education that would lead him later to become the Principal of the Melbourne Teachers College. His Inspector's Report for that year read:

> An energetic and intelligent teacher of very good ability, full of enthusiasm. Takes very great interest in his school and its work. Is employing very good up-to-date methods in his work with good results.[7]

For her part, after leaving the Training College, Lillie spent a few weeks during 1908 at Woodend and was then appointed Head Teacher at Noorongong, where she stayed until 10 December 1909, when she married Arthur. She was forced to resign from the Education Department because, at that time, married women were not allowed to be permanent teachers. This ruling meant Lillie not only had to leave her profession but also broke her bond with the Education Department and she had to repay £32.[8]

Lillie and Arthur were married on Christmas day in 1909 at St Mark's Anglican Church in Brighton. Lillie did not officially renounce her Catholic faith, but her decision to marry in the Church of England caused a furore in the Chapman family. Lillie's mother, a tiny, domineering woman, brought pressure to bear on the other members of the family to ostracise and disown Lillie. Although distressed by their treatment, Lillie stood her ground. Throughout her life she regularly attended the Church of England with her children and never returned to the Catholic faith.

The first two years of Lillie's and Arthur's married life were spent in the beautiful, rugged township of Mitta Mitta, surrounded by rivers and deep ravines. It was a tough, timber cutting and mining community where the favourite game of the school children was 'kick the tin' which entailed kicking around, barefoot, a Treacle or a Golden Syrup tin.[9]

Geoffrey, known as 'Geof', the first of the Laws' six children, was born in 1910. In the same year Arthur passed the first year of the Diploma of Education, which he had continued studying by correspondence, at the University of Melbourne.

Arthur's determination to succeed was noticed. In 1911, his Inspector's report included the statement, 'A very good teacher progressive and anxious to excel. ... A very earnest and industrious young teacher. Evidently he has determined teaching his life work.'[10] Indeed he had.

There is little evidence that Arthur's ability in educational matters extended to practical issues. In fact, stories of his ineptness became part of family lore, as Geof recalls, 'Hopeless. He was just an academic ... in a dream, always reading.' Nevertheless, Arthur was one of the few people capable of rendering medical assistance to the members of Mitta Mitta community. He was untrained for this service, but was able to gain any needed advice via the telephone from medical staff at Tallangatta. Major injuries were often sustained by the timber cutters and miners. The injured men were usually brought to the Laws' house, but sometimes Arthur had to go to where they lay, and his incompetence with horses led to him being 'stuck half-way in a dam, unable to back the horses out.'[11] He did, however, carry out this medical service with all the diligence, if not the ability, he applied to his teaching.

On 21 April 1912, their second son, Phillip, called 'Phil' throughout his life, was born in Tallangatta. It is likely that Arthur was not with Lillie during her confinement for, during the previous month, he had been appointed to a school in the Melbourne suburb of North Fitzroy. With no motor vehicle, it is probable that he took Lillie and Geof the 40 miles to Tallangatta by gig, on his way from Mitta Mitta to Melbourne, so she could spend the intervening weeks before the birth with his parents at Tallangatta.

Phil's first two years were spent in Carlton where Arthur taught at the North Fitzroy School, whilst continuing with his study for his Diploma of Education, which he was awarded in April 1914. During 1914 the Laws' third child, Marjorie, known as 'Marj', was born and Arthur was again appointed Head Teacher at Mitta Mitta.

During the following two years at Mitta Mitta, Arthur spent the evenings studying for his Bachelor of Arts degree. When, years later, Geof asked him how he had managed to achieve this whilst in a house with three children under five years of age, Arthur responded 'I didn't waste the midnight oil. My children went to bed at half past six or seven and I studied till 11pm and went to bed.' It can only be assumed that Lillie worked equally diligently to allow Arthur the freedom from interruptions to pursue his study.

2.

In 1916 Arthur was offered a post at the Faraday Street Training School and the Law family moved to the Melbourne suburb of Gardenvale. The beautiful mountains, rivers and valleys of the Mitta Mitta district were replaced with paddocks, swamp lands and market gardens. Gardenvale, originally so named because of the proliferation of market gardens,[12] was, in 1916, undergoing a transformation from a gentle rural setting to one of suburban subdivision. Telephone poles stalked down the streets and the train line between Melbourne and Sandringham was soon to be electrified. The area was popular, particularly because of the closeness of the railway, and demand for housing was high.

Arthur bought an Edwardian house in Lantana Road on a new subdivision, Gardenvale Estate. The area, originally known as Lempriere's Paddock, had previously been a popular polo ground, and after eight years of haggling between various bodies about the drainage problems that plagued Gardenvale and its surrounding suburbs, the land was finally subdivided in 1916.[13] The Laws' house was small, red brick, and nostalgically named 'Mitta'.

Phil's early life, as he recalls it, was 'violently masculine,' made up of fighting, climbing, running, hut building, canal walking, football and cricket. Like the 'Boys Own' and 'Chums' Annuals which he read, his childhood memories are sprinkled with bullies, juvenile athletes, cruel teachers, poor dirty children, faithful friends, mobs, gangs and few females.

Gardenvale, although less exciting than Mitta Mitta, seemed vast in scale to the young Phil. The paddocks surrounding the sparsely scattered houses were covered in gorse and bracken and offered the local children an adventure playground of burrows, tunnels and hide-outs. The local boys cleared one of the paddocks near their home and it became their private reserve where they played cricket and football, flew kites and ran their dogs, and was jealously guarded from 'mobs of kids' from outer areas.

Although Phil's early formative years coincided with the First World War, there is little evidence of its effect, and there are few memories of wounded veterans, even though he lived only a short distance from the Australian General Military Hospital in Kooyong Road. The stately mansion 'Glen Eira' had been turned into a hospital during the middle of the war and it became home, sometimes a permanent home, for wounded Anzacs, shipped back from Britain, France and Belgium. As the number of maimed and wounded escalated, they overflowed the grand old home and the surrounding grounds took on the effect of a city of tents and military huts to accommodate the medical and administrative staff.[14]

This absence for Phil of any jolts from the Great War is stark contrast to George Johnston, the author of *My Brother Jack*. Johnston, born only three months after Phil, and living within a mile of the Law home, vividly describes the troubling effects of the war on him as a young boy. The differences between them are explained by the roles their parents played in the war. Johnston's parents were both in active war service and, after the war, convalescing veterans stayed at the Johnston home.[15] Arthur Law, on the other hand, had been refused War Service because of his poor eyesight and there is no indication to show that the family was in any way involved with the war.

When Phil was 4 years old he attended the kindergarten in the nearby Protestant Church hall. His first day there was a short one, 'I vividly recall my bitter tears when I was led with Geof, by my Mother, to enrol and how I bolted home again as soon as she had gone.' He settled in well, but recalls, 'there were the usual unhappy memories of wetting my pants because I was afraid to ask could I leave the class [and] of bullying by older boys.' Kindergarten brought with it his 'first real acquaintance with strange girls'. One he particularly remembers, Bernice, an older girl of five, who 'attracted yet terrified' him. She was 'handsome, bold and "sophisticated". ... she had some vague sex appeal which attracted yet terrified me.'

When he was promoted to 'primers', as it was known, in the middle of 1917, his Aunty Totty, from Tallangatta, sent him a shirt and a school-bag for his new adventure. He wrote and thanked her. 'Dear Totty' he began, 'I am in primers and I do very hard work.'

Phil attended the Elsternwick State School and the trip to school, about a mile and a half from home, was fraught with dangers, both real and imagined. The market gardens, remnants of the large population of Chinese of the early history of the area, had to be run past, very fast, for the fear of the unknown they held. This fear was given substance once when a Chinese boy, brandishing a tomahawk, waylaid Phil on his way home from school. Perhaps already having learned the small boy's ingenuity for getting himself out of dangerous situations, Phil talked the Chinese boy into using the tomahawk to form a trap in a nearby short-cut path. He had succeeded in diverting the immediate danger but had strengthened the fear.

Passing by the Catholic Convent, situated near the embankment of the railway line, was also something he dreaded. A primary school was attached to the Convent and the Catholic children, for reasons Phil did not know and never really understood, had to be fought by the non Catholic children. At first these were fist fights, later the boys used stones and bows and arrows. No matter how fierce and bloody the fights between the gangs of Protestants, they were all united in their hatred against the Catholic mobs.

Another danger, this one self-imposed, was to steal a lift on the back of the market gardeners' wagons. These wagons, on their way from the outer suburbs to the Melbourne market, travelled along tracks set into the road down one side of Brighton Road. The horses walked on a bluestone path which had been laid between flat iron tracks, a little below the level of the road along one side. The tracks gave the well trained horse almost automatic guidance and a safe passage for the driver, who tended to doze off.[16] Phil and other boys would filch rides by hanging on to the backs of the wagon, with legs up on the axles and heads hanging back, or by sitting on the single step which some wagons had at the rear. Invariably other boys would raise the cry 'Whip behind' and the driver would waken from his doze and lash behind him with a long thong or, alternatively, stop the wagon and curse the boys.

All these fears could be overcome by running fast, or diverting the danger in some way or other. But one fear, which was more difficult to cope with, gripped Phil. He was afraid his mother would die and he worried inordinately about it. Lillie described this in a letter to Tot:

Phil is always thinking of some new way of dying, so that he can finish himself off, as soon as I die. His latest is to copy the cat that died of grief, and to go to my grave and stay there. Isn't he weird?

Weird he may have been, but Lillie was proud of him as the same letter affirmed:

Phil always does [writes] his [letters] alone. He just calls out if he comes to a big word that doesn't sound the right way. ... He reads well. ... Phil could read all those night and morning prayers in the back of the Album. ... Tonight he read the whole of that Jack and the Beanstalk book. His work-book at school is nothing but ticks and Passes all through it—he never gets anything wrong, too careful.

This same letter also draws attention to another significant feature of character. Lillie thought there was an enormous difference between her two sons:

Teacher says Phil is smart, and of course we know it. Geof is smart too, but lazy and careless. Phil loves work—at home or at school. He is always happy and nothing puts him out! Geof admires Phil's attitude, but can't adopt it.[17]

Phil himself recalls the differences, 'I was a thin, weedy little kid, timid, conformist, amenable and biddable.' But Geof, who was 17 months older, was a larger boy than Phil and, Phil maintained, was 'a creative innovator, a genius, ... a non conformist, in many ways a loner, completely against established authority'.

Similar contrasts are evoked by their three younger sisters who remembered Phil as their parents' 'good boy', the one who could be relied on, whereas Geof was their parents' 'enfant terrible'.

Reliability and goodness, however, are not the stuff of stories, and it was Geof's exploits which came easily to the mind of the Law sisters. Incidents were recounted with unconcealed pride and with a fluency that comes from numerous tellings. 'Geof was the hero ... more bizarre ... a non–conformist, anarchical, more colourful.' Stories of Phil as a child were harder to recall and more restrained and hesitant in the telling: 'Phil was more academic, logical scientific, smaller. ... run-of-the-mill, straight academic, high achiever, conservative.'[18]

It also appears that he was a follower and spent much of his time during those early years trailing behind Geof's questionable lead. Phil recalls that Geof was:

the rebel, mercurial, fast and inventive, always in trouble, screaming at our father 'I'll shoot you, I'll chop your head off', and retiring, fearless and defiant after a strapping, to plot more mayhem. I stumbled along in his wake, innocent-eyed, timid and apprehensive, sharing a number of his punishments and being bullied and teased into participating in fresh mischief.

The relationship wasn't always the older leading and the younger following. Sometimes, despite their differences in age, they set challenges and competed between themselves. Trying to jog-trot the mile-and-a-half from home to school without stopping was one example. 'This was sort of an athletic challenge at the earliest level ... It took quite a lot of practice before you could make it work.' It became a competition between him and Geof as to who could last the distance.

But that particular instance was amicable compared with the other clashes that occurred between the two of them. When Phil began at Elsternwick School in the second half of 1918, Geof was in Grade 3, and constantly in trouble with the teachers. Phil was placed in Grade 2. During the 1919 Spanish Influenza epidemic many of the buildings in the area, including the school, were used as temporary hospitals and the school did not re-open until April 11.[19] Despite the loss of two months schooling, Phil successfully completed Grades 3 and 4 during the remainder of the year. But Geof, defiant as ever and refusing to work at his school studies, failed the year. 'Why can't you work like Phil' his parents admonished him.[20]

Although Arthur taught education and psychology in his new position as Master of Method, Primary at the Teachers' College, he seemed unable to use that knowledge in a practical way with his own children. He constantly held up the well-mannered Phil as a model to Geof. This further aggravated the problem between the two boys and, as Geof recalls, 'of course, I hated Phil.'[21]

Geof's enmity, combined with his violent temper—'he'd go white with fury'—culminated in frightening scraps between the two boys. 'We used to have fights to the death. I used to have a fight with him on the average of about once every two days. Real go in fights.'

Despite this quarrelsome behaviour, a high value was set in the Law household on traditional middle-class values of hard work, respectability, cleanliness, sobriety, thrift, punctuality and manly independence.

Schools also held these values in high regard but they were reinforced with a brutality not encountered at home. Pupils at Elsternwick State School, like pupils in every State School throughout Australia, assembled every Monday in the bare asphalt school-yard studded with the ubiquitous peppercorn trees for the patriotic ceremony. The boys saluted the flag and the girls stood to attention with right hand on left breast, reciting 'I love God and my country' and pledged to honour the flag, obey parents, teachers and the law. The School Papers of the period encouraged children, especially boys, to be active and if a task was worth doing, to do it well, to do it now, and be busy and industrious.[22] They also warned children of the dangers of people who were seen loafing in every town, the 'no timers' and 'near-enoughs'.[23] The virtues of goodness, thrift and cleanliness were espoused, with cleanliness being next to godliness, whilst 'grubby teeth and grubby hands were seen as possible indicators of an early slide to moral ruin.'[24]

Teachers were instructed to instil patriotism into the hearts of the young. Children were told they were not to be simply citizens of Australia, but also citizens of the great Empire. 'It should be impressed upon pupils', the *Education Gazette* advised, 'that the greatness and the stability of the Empire depends upon the production of a fine type of citizen, fit of body, fit of mind, and fit of soul. They should be so directed and encouraged as to fit them for the part they had to play.'[25]

This sort of direction and encouragement was given by the Headmaster at the Elsternwick State School during Wednesday afternoon 'drill' and was feared by Phil more than either the Chinese market gardens or the Catholic Convent and with far more cause:

The Headmaster was a choleric old ex-Colonel called Dean. He was hated and feared by us all. ... Mr. Dean took 'drill' himself and every boy above Grade 3 had to attend for an hour each Wednesday afternoon. Some 200 boys would be lined up in the playground and put through a series of military manoeuvres which, at their simplest, involved 'forming fours' and, at their most complicated, consisted of 'squad drill' as then used in the Australian Army.

I would line up trembling, amongst the other boys, with my brain paralysed with fear at the sight of the grizzled Mr. Dean, long strap in hand gazing fiercely along the lines of boys. Concentrate as I would, it was only a matter of time before I made some simple mistake, then to be dragged forth, strapped on the extended hands, and ignominiously returned to the ranks.

Not only the Headmaster, but other teachers, both male and female, also strapped the children, presumably in the belief that in doing so they were preparing them for the part they were to play in the wider world. The personalities of these teachers, Phil later maintained were 'imprinted on my memory':

> 'Charlie' Charlesworth in charge of Grade 6 or 7, had a jovial humour, a 'gammy' leg and a sarcastic edge to his floggings. Miss D'Arcy, on the other hand, had a grand manner, hair which we considered either a wig or dyed, great chunky rings on her fingers and absolute autocracy.

Learning to be an Australian male meant learning to cope with violence. But physical violence and cruelty were not only confined to the teaching staff, they also occurred between mobs that formed within the school and roamed the streets at that time. Many of these were the outcome of juvenile high spirits and swagger, but some had criminal elements. The worst of the mobs, the 'Bouverie Street Mob' lurked around Carlton, near the Teachers' College where Arthur lectured. The 'Rowena Parade Rats', and later the 'Hill Mob' of Richmond, often caused physical harm both to themselves and innocent residents.[26] These larrikin pushes were widespread and not just in the inner suburbs. George Johnston, too, in his book *My Brother Jack*, refers to large feuding gangs of young hooligans that roamed everywhere around Melbourne looking for trouble. He recalls the two big rival gangs in the Kooyong Road area, where both his family and the Laws lived, as the 'Grey Caps and the Bludgers, each of them sixty to eighty strong and always attended by satellite groups of much smaller boys'.[27]

Looking back, Phil has come to the conclusion that the Elsternwick State School was a very tough school. It drew pupils not only from Gardenvale, but also from northern Elsternwick and Prahran and many of the children came from very poor families.

The savage warfare of the mobs formed by the pupils at the school was a constant reminder to Phil of both brutality and injustice. 'It was never eight or ten kids against eight or ten,' he complained, 'It was always four to one, if you could fix it.'

> The game was dirty and cruel and fought along guerilla lines. The two main bodies of contestants rarely clashed. The tactics were for six or eight of one side to try to isolate two or three of the others from their friends and then deal with them ... Decoying and ambushing were widely practised. The victim of a lunch-time

ambush would be taken to the nearby Elsternwick Golf Links and there would be tied to a tree to await release after 4pm when his mates learned of his predicament. He would then be punished at school for being absent for the afternoon.

The boys also tortured one another. One popular form was to use a magnifying glass to focus the sun and burn the victim's skin. When they ran out of ideas they even went as far as consulting books on medieval torture and experimented with some of the simpler forms.

Another part of learning to be male were the fights behind the cypress trees in the reserve opposite the school. These were fought according to strict rules. Two boys would be matched to fight bare-fisted and when blood was drawn, or when one of the contestants lay down and could, or would, not rise, the fight was over. The mob would then push another boy forward to take on the winner. The winner of this second bout would then have to face another, and so on. 'They'd just pick you and say "you fight so and so" ... I was such a little kid ... I used to be in fear of my life of those damned things.' But refusal to fight meant goading and rough handling by the assembled group, so there was seldom a shortage of contestants. One afternoon Phil was made to fight three bouts. Exhausted after the third fight, he was beaten by the fourth boy.

While the boys fought, ambushed and tortured each other, the Victorian School Papers published platitudinous poems and articles that encouraged children to show concern for animals as a desirable extension of their concern for others, as evidenced by the following poem:

> Don't kill the birds, the little birds
> That sing about your door
> Soon as the joyous spring has come
> And chilling storms are o'er.[28]

Victorian State schools issued Pledges and Certificates of the League of Kindness, in which member children pledged 'I will be kind to all living creatures and will protect them as far as I can from cruelty.'[29] The poems and pledges seemed to have little effect and the espoused values were at odds with the reality of the boys' activities. One rather perplexed writer of the time reported that 'Australian boys do not seem able to restrain themselves from chasing, catching, annoying, or hurting every living thing they see and are not afraid of.'[30]

The boys in the neighbourhood were obsessed with huts, tree houses and dug-outs. Innocent looking vacant allotments of thick brown gorse were transformed into 'hides' comprising a maze of false and true leads which would confuse any enemy mobs from adjacent districts. Boys could stay there for hours undetected, in a private, rather cramped, central chamber. They used the time to experiment with cigarette smoking.

Not having any direct access to cigarettes, the Law boys collected every butt that they could find in the streets, carefully took out the tobacco, dried it in the sun on top of corrugated iron sheets and rolled it in brown paper for secret smoking. But, for Phil, it was a short lived vice. Even chewing scented lollies and onions did not disguise the smell of smoke from his non-smoking parents. 'Phil, you've been smoking,' his mother would say as he came in the back door, 'I can smell you yards off', and he would then be strapped by his father. The guilt Phil felt was stronger than the illicit thrill smoking evoked and he gave it up for 40 years.

The Elwood Canal was a local feature which fascinated the boys and Phil, 70 years later, could still recall the pervading aromas of wet concrete, semi-clean drain water and stale urine. Arthur repeatedly warned his children against going up the canal and backed these warnings with vivid stories of young children being drowned and washed down to the sea during sudden cloudbursts. Despite these dire warnings, or perhaps because of them, exploration of the canal was irresistible. In addition, it was proof of maturity: 'one was not a full member of the senior school until one had been "up the canal".'

Invitations to 'come for a roll in the canal' took on a new meaning to Phil, sometime between grades 6 and 7, when he became aware that sexual exploits were going on in them. Small for his age and two grades ahead of his own age group, Phil was never invited to join in, 'although I would be told what went on by one of the boys at some stage'. Sexual matters intrigued him little at Elsternwick School, although he and his mates spent hours discussing the subject and 'learned in a smutty fashion about copulation but could not see any reason for it.' At that time, he was far more interested in developing other elements of male physical prowess.

The games the boys played required little, or only makeshift, equipment for there was little money to be spent on non essential items. A kerosine tin for a wicket, a straw broom for a bat and a tennis ball sufficed as a cricket set. Other games were 'marbles, shanghais, whirly-propeller sticks and hoops, which came and went according to some irregular and unpublished calendar each year'.

The one game which did have a predetermined date at which to begin and end was Cherry Bobs. It was Phil's favourite game. Cherry Bob time began on Melbourne Cup day in November of each year and finished on the break-up day for the Christmas holidays. Children collected the cherry stones from those they had eaten at home, placed them carefully on the rim of the plate, later dried them in the sun and kept them in a calico bag with running thread round the top. Gambling added excitement to this popular game and, at this time each year, the playground resembled a casino, where every possible method of betting that could be devised took place. It was a time of excitement and Phil found it difficult to concentrate on lessons while figuring out how to make a fortune in cherry bobs at the next recess. Nonetheless, it appears that Phil did concentrate on lessons and, although his classes were large, Phil, already an avid reader, soon found that he was easily able to be near the top of his grade.

His interest in reading was strengthened by a homelife that centred around Arthur's study. Family evenings were sombre with Arthur at the table studying and demanding that there be absolute quiet, Lillie knitting and the three children sitting on chairs or lying on the floor with a cushion reading books. Arthur and Lillie were not a sociable couple and seldom entertained. When they did they used the front room where the piano was kept. This room was always immaculate and, like many of the era, the children were never allowed to enter it, unless they were practising the piano or there were visitors.

Lillie had been brought up, as had many women of that time, to play a musical instrument. But she was not really a musical person, Phil relates, and played the piano in a mechanical fashion with no deep appreciation of artistry for the instrument. When Phil was about 6 years old she decided to teach her two boys to play the piano. So for some months she struggled to get them to practise scales and to learn fingering, but they resented the time away from their outside exploits and after a few months she gave up.

Money was scarce in the Law household. Teaching was not then held in high esteem and Arthur's salary was very low. With a wife and three young children to support, he supplemented his salary with lecturing one evening a week at the Postal Institute. But still there was little left over for special outings. Arthur, never free with his money, allowed the children the necessary pennies to attend the Saturday afternoon Matinee at the Elsternwick Theatre where they watched 'violent, adventure things, always "to be continued". You'd wait till next week till you could hurry back to see how they got out of the predicament.'

3.

During each long Christmas vacation, the Law family would return to Tallangatta where Phil's paternal grandparents lived. It was a place he loved, not just for its beauty and the excitement of the surrounding countryside, but because of the love and attention that was showered on him by all the relatives whenever he was there.

Tallangatta, in the far north-east of Victoria was set in a beautiful mountainous area with wide valleys drained by great rivers, the Murray, the Mitta Mitta, the Dart and the Kiewa Rivers and the Tallangatta and Koetong Creeks. In 1912 Tallangatta was a well established pastoral town with provisions brought in by rail, buggy, the biweekly mail service and by Indian hawkers. The Fire Brigade was then being established and funds raised to build the Cottage Hospital. There was plenty of self-made entertainment in the valley: bazaars, plain and fancy dress balls and concerts, sports meetings, cricket, racing, horse racing and cycling events, tennis and football clubs and a rifle club. This was the heyday of brass bands throughout Australia, and Tallangatta had its own band which travelled round the valley and played host to other bands.

It is of Tallangatta that young Phil has his happiest and most nostalgic memories, the most exciting one being when he travelled alone on the long train trip from Melbourne to Tallangatta when he was about 7 or 8 years old. He recalls:

> I was sent alone on the Albury Express to Wodonga where Auntie Em met me and put me up for the night, sending me on next day by train to Tallangatta. My love of trains is due, I am sure, to the nostalgia of my memories of the excitement, adventure and freedom of those early journeys on my own.

But memories can lie. At the time, the train trip seemed long and he was homesick, as evidenced in a letter he wrote in reply to Lillie's letter to him:

> Dear Mother, I got here safely, but I was wishing I'd hurry up and get to Wodonga. At last got there and just had some pudding for dinner. ... I missed you too very much at bedtime when I had to go to bed without that little X on my cheek. Goodnight darling. Your little mate Phil.

Written on the back of this same letter was a note from his Aunty Totty to Lillie:

> Phil was so pleased at getting your letter. While he was reading it he was blinking to keep tears back and when he was writing to you last night his eyes were shining a bit with tears. But we didn't say anything to him about it. The dear little kid. We are all so fond of him.[31]

The 'dear little kid' could not escape his smallness; it seemed to be part of his name. He signed his own letter to his mother as 'your little mate' and letters addressed to him always included the word 'little' in the salutation. 'Dear little Phil' was Geof's greeting and Lillie addressed him as 'My dear and beautiful little man'.

Phil's much loved grandfather, John James Law, owned the local newspaper, *The Upper Murray and Mitta Herald*, where he was editor, journalist, typesetter, proof-reader and correspondent all rolled into one.

John Law was born in Richmond in the 1850s and, when he was about fourteen, had been apprenticed to a printer in Carlton. At eighteen he became foreman of a newspaper in Benalla and, in 1881, he married Edith Phillips of Benalla, the daughter of a carpenter. Four years later he went to Tallangatta, where he was appointed Assistant Editor for the local Tallangatta paper. He was the sole proprietor from 1890 to 1940. The *Herald* played an important communicative role in the extensive

Shire of Tallangatta and its printing and editorial standards were held in high esteem.

John Law was a withdrawn, shy man, and considered eccentric in the town for his unusual ways and his severe manner of dress. He always wore black, with celluloid stiff collars, black tie and black hat, glasses, moustache and a walking stick. He would walk through the town, seldom looking at anyone and, even less, speaking to anyone. But in his paper a whimsical quality crept in,[32] a quality that he also revealed to his grandchildren.

The Law family's quiet existence in Gardenvale changed to one of merriment and boisterous affection in Tallangatta. Apart from Phil's grandfather, there was his grandmother, Edith Law, 'portly and placid and devoted to good works and kindness to afflicted people'. There were also a great uncle and his wife, other aunts and uncles and numerous cousins. Both Geof and Phil remember Tallangatta as the place where they were incredibly spoiled with love and kindness. Phil recalls:

> Stories, laughter, music, sweets, ice creams, pictures, rowdy parties, gangs of children screaming and chasing around the Herald office, swimming in the creek and the Mitta River, trips to the country in a horsedrawn 'gig', life on a dairy farm, horse riding, snake hunting, rabbiting, and lots of reading of many years collections of 'Munsey' magazines. When at Tallangatta we never wanted to return home again—ever.[33]

John Law, who had been a severe and unsympathetic father to Arthur, was, both Geof and Phil agree, a perfect grandfather. 'Dop', as his grandchildren affectionately called him, opened up to them a world of illusion and fantasy. Having lived in the Kelly country during the Kelly gang's reign of terror, he regaled the boys with real tales of Ned Kelly. If he didn't have true stories, he made up stories of adventure and intrigue involving whichever grandchildren were with him at that moment. He taught Geof and Phil to play the bones and the spoons, and they would improvise as Negro Minstrels for the other members of the family.

Dop often wrote letters to his grandchildren and great-grandchildren and these were fondly kept by most of them. His letters were either filled with ingenious tales, or written as if he were illiterate with the pages cluttered with grammatical or spelling errors, or sometimes both. When Phil was five years old he received the following letter from Dop:

Dear Phil
Jones is mad. We took a German presoner's little dog and sold it to Mrs. McGrath. Mr. Haire made German Sosidges out of the dog, and hung them in the window. One day Jones marched the presoners out for exercise and they 'stood easy' in front of the Butcher's

Shop. The German what owned the pup he began to cry and called
out,
'O vere O vere is my leedle dog gone?
O vere, O vere can he be?'
Presently the German Sossidge jumped off the hook and ran out
into the street, jumped up on the weeping Hun—he was
Hun–gry!—and snuggled into the German's overcoat pocket. (etc.)
Now our new aeroplane we brought down last week is nearly all
painted blue and gold. If you come up here in September you can
have a fly around in her. She is called the Skyscraper. Dop, F.C.[34]

His obvious love for his grandchildren, his ingenuity with words and
stories created a world of fantasy for the boys as together they invented
imaginary situations. Phil's favourite one was 'being in the Army'. Dop
would give the boys names and rank. Phil was usually 'Captain Hickey'
and they would stage a battle, fighting for the Empire or fighting the
Germans. Many letters to Phil from Dop were addressed to 'Captain
Hickey'.

Dop took them for a day's outing up 'The Hill' that rose almost
straight out of their backyard at Tallangatta. They would climb half way
up the hill to where there was a flat terrace and they would build a fire
and cook sausages. Dop made gravy and boiled the billy for tea. They
would stay there for hours, talking, playing, telling stories, and then
clamber down, tired out, late in the afternoon. These excursions
cemented Phil's love for both his grandfather and the mountains and
they added another dimension to his strong affinity for a physical outdoor life.

He ['Dop'] introduced us to the Jews Harp and the mouth-organ
and our first mouthful of beer. He breathed cigar smoke over us
and I am sure this nostalgic memory led me, in later life, to take up
cigar smoking. He created for us a dreamworld of adventure and
encouraged our first actual steps in that direction.

Phil's exploits at Tallangatta were different from those at Gardenvale
and more dangerous. To survival in the suburban street through relying
on his wits, he now added stamina and learned to test the limits of his
endurance.

The [Mitta] River was dangerous and exciting and adventurous. I
remember once there had been a flood and it smashed the swimming pool there and the big diving board had come loose. We
found we could lie on this diving board and get out into the current
and be swept down the river. Normally you couldn't allow yourself
to be swept down the river because of the snags, which might rip

your guts out if you got caught on them. But on this board you'd
feel the snags sort of sliding on the underside and you'd sweep in
under the willow trees and go round curves and you'd go about five
miles down the river and haul yourself out, walk back through the
thistles in a temperature at about a hundred degrees.

It is now well established that a boy's early experiences, whilst not
determining precisely the future form he will take as an adult, do play a
substantial role in shaping the personality. They influence the kind of
environment later sought out by an individual.[35] This early 'active, virile
life' already reflected the man Phil was to become; an energetic, outdoor
individual proud of his fitness, whose work and leisure were invariably
spent in the company of males.

4.

By 1920, Phil was in grade 5 and Geof in the grade below him. The
resentment this must have caused Geof can only be surmised but one
sister later maintained that Geof had never forgiven Phil for the insult it
represented.[36] At mid-year Geof was moved up into grade 5, but by now
he hated even being at the same school as Phil and managed to persuade
his parents to send him to the Caulfield Central School. Both the Law
brothers now believe that this was one of the few occasions when Arthur
Law ever made a psychologically sensible decision in regard to his children.

If Geof resented the 'prissy' Phil, Phil was constantly made aware of
his own creative limitations by the evidence of Geof's inventive and artistic talents. Even at the age of three Geof had apparently delighted his
parents with his ability in sketching and painting. During his primary
school years he made models of aeroplanes, guitars, violins and other
stringed instruments. Even Phil's letters home to his mother, written
when the two boys were holidaying in Tallangatta, are crammed with references to what Geof had made: 'a raft with pad[d]les and sails and
rudder' or 'a pirates flag and hoisted it on the mast'.[37] Later family mem-
orabilia attest to the differences between the boys' creative talents, with
at least 100 sketches, plans, maps, paintings, letters and cartoons by Geof
to one letter by Phil.

But it was not only Geof's creative abilities that impressed Phil, Geof
had many other qualities as well, as Phil describes:

> He was the acknowledged leader in any group that he joined. Noth-
> ing he did was normal or ordinary and his flair for the unusual was
> to enrich my young life and stimulate me to fight against my inher-
> ited traits of caution and conventionality. He invented games and
> group activities; he defied authority and led us children into every
> possible scrape; his inexhaustible energy and fiery personality
> flogged us into a level of activity we should never have attained with-
> out him.

Phil, on the other hand, had taken on what has been termed by psychologists as the 'defensive style' typical of males with short stature: with 'excessive reliance on rational and analytical skills with a parallel devaluation of the body world'.[38] Phil described the situation somewhat differently when he recalled, 'I was a prig.' He was articulate and well able to converse with adults about issues that were usually not expected of a child, and soon developed a reputation as a 'know all'. 'I had no sensibility, in those days,' he later recalled, 'to the ignorance of others. If they were wrong I told them so and corrected them.'

Phil's precocious manner was irresistible fuel for Geof's acerbic ingenuity. 'He'd think up little chants and he'd chant these things. Some ... were so infuriating, I'd fly at him and scream at mother to make him stop it, which of course she couldn't.' Apart from squabbles with Geof, Phil recalls his home life at that time as 'a mixture of discipline and warm loving care', with the discipline from Arthur and the loving care from Lillie.

Although both parents were trained teachers, their style of parenting contrasted sharply. Lillie showed a natural aptitude, a love of and a wish to teach her own children, whereas Arthur's interest was in the academic study and practice of education, and he showed little interest in teaching his own children, except to occasionally try out psychological tests on them. Phil recalls them both in this way:

> My father was a stern man, working long hours by day and studying late at night. My mother, a warm, tender and loving woman, shielded him [Arthur] from our attentions while he worked and enfolded us in her love and kindness while he was away. She read to us, poetry and stories, in the evening and played to us on the piano while we sang. She taught us manners and dress and housework and helped us with our homework ... It was mother who really taught us and encouraged us with her active, vigorous intelligence and broad range of interests.

Lillie was also an efficient and well organised woman:

> Mother would rush through everything and have all the housework done by about ten o'clock. Apart from cooking lunch, she'd have the rest of the morning free. And she'd have most of the afternoon free to do her own things. She read, she played the piano, she knitted, she cooked. Very feminine sort of things.

With her children, Lillie was a happy person, and her children remember her as 'full of fun and life.' During the day, with Arthur at work, she would play games, read, play the piano, sing and laugh with them.

Arthur, on the other hand, was an unrelenting man with strong beliefs, a passionate interest in education and unworldly in many ways.

Puritanical in character, he neither drank nor smoked and insisted that other members in his household abstained as well. He carried out his role as father with a rectitude, laced with a righteous anger, which put fear into the hearts of his young children. Arthur's needs and wants dominated the household and, when he was at home, Lillie was subservient and arranged the household in accord with his demands.

By 1921, after a break of seven years, a fourth child, Dorothy, later to be known as 'Noel' was born to Arthur and Lillie. She was to be the eldest of the Laws' 'second' family. The next year Phil transferred into seventh grade in the recently completed Gardenvale Central School, but his stay there was short for, a few months later, Arthur was appointed as District Inspector in the Hamilton District.

Notes

1. Lillie Chapman, EDR, EDM.
2. Arthur Law, EDR, EDM.
3. Lillie Chapman, EDR, EDM.
4, Arthur Law, EDR, EDM.
5. Ibid.
6. Don Garden, *The Melbourne Teacher Training Colleges*, Heinemann Educational Australia, 1982.
7. Arthur Law, EDR, EDM.
8. Ibid.
9. Geoffrey Law to author, 27 July 1988.
10. Arthur Law, EDR, EDM.
11. Geoffrey Law to author, 27 July 1988.
12. Peter R. Murray and John C. Wells, *From Sand, Swamp and Heath ... A History of Caulfield*, City of Caulfield, 1980, p. 264.
13. Murray and Wells.
14. Ibid.
15. George Johnston, *My Brother Jack*, Collins, London, 1964.
16. Murray and Wells, p. 102
17. Lillie Law to Emily Law, undated, LP.
18. Law's sisters to author, 6 May 1988.
19. '*100 Not Out*' Elsternwick Primary School, No. 2870, 1888–1988.
20. Geoffrey Law to author, 27 July 1988.
21. Ibid.
22. Brian McKinlay, *School Days*, Robert Andersen and Associates, Melbourne, 1985, p. 120.
23. *The School Paper*, 1917.
24. McKinlay, p. 119.
25. Education Gazette and Teachers' Aid, 1914, quoted in *School Days*, p. 15.
26. Janet McCalman, *Struggletown*, Penguin Books Australia Ltd, 1984, p. 132.
27. Johnston, pp. 39–40.
28. *The School Paper*, 1917, in McKinlay, p. 123.
29. Ibid.
30. The Children's Hour, South Australia, in McKinlay, p. 123.
31. Law to Lillie Law, undated, LP.
32. Swan, Keith, *The Shire of Tallangatta, A History*, 1987, p. 115.
33. Autobiographical Notes, LP.

34. John Law to Law, 15 July 1917, LP.
35. M. Kets de Vries and D. Miller, 'Narcissism and Leadership: An Object Relations Perspective', *Human Relations*, 38, 1985, pp. 583–601.
36. Law's sisters to author, 6 May 1988.
37. Law to Lillie Law, 28 December 1920, LP.
38. Leslie F. Martel and Henry B. Biller, *Stature and Stigma, The Biopsychosocial Development of Short Males*, Lexington Books, Toronto, 1987, p. 40.

2. 'Squib' Law, 1922–1928

1.

HAMILTON WAS A PLEASANT, SOLID TOWN WITH A POPULATION, IN 1922, of approximately 4,500, and viewed itself as both the 'capital' of Victoria's Western District and the 'Wool Capital of the World'. It was surrounded by thousands of acres of undulating plain that comprised the pastoral land where sheep graze. Within a radius of 15 miles of Hamilton are the cones of extinct volcanoes: Mount Napier, Mount Pierrepoint, Mount Bainbridge and Mount Rouse. In the north-west a set of sandstone ridges, the Grampians, dominate the skyline with a range of serrated, spectacular peaks.[1]

The people of Hamilton have always taken pride in their town with its church spires, attractive public buildings, pleasant public gardens, and gracious homes. It was, and still is, a town which had an aura of 'respectability, solidity, potentiality'.[2]

Arthur's Western District inspectorate covered a vast area and, reluctantly, he bought himself a car and transferred his incompetent driving of a horse and buggy to a new T Model Ford tourer. Arthur admitted that, when the salesman tried to explain to him the starting mechanisms and the gears, he impatiently retorted 'never mind all that, I just want to know how to stop it' and the salesman replied 'both feet down'. Marjorie Law remembered one of Arthur's anxious passengers turning to her and saying 'You know your father should never do that—you can't pass people when you are going up a hill.'[3] But Arthur apparently could. Although he was involved in many skirmishes—hitting a stump when backing out of a school, backing into a farmer's house, getting stuck in the driveway of a school and careering into a gutter and breaking the front spoke wheels,—he never had a serious accident. Geof maintained that this was only because 'there is a special providence that looks after the helpless and inept.'[4] Inept Arthur may have been, but he always looked the part when he 'went for a blow', hood down, immaculately dressed in overcoat, goggles, cap and leather gauntlets.

Arthur drove alone to Hamilton, leaving Lillie to attend to the arrangements of shifting the household, including herself and the four children, from Gardenvale.

The Australian economy had stabilised after the Great War and the early twenties were buoyant times, reflected in Hamilton by flourishing businesses and a rich social life. The interests of Hamiltonians were catered for by numerous societies, sporting clubs, concerts, serials on the wireless and the latest craze of dancing. Silent movies, showing stars such as Charles Chaplin, Mary Pickford, Lillian Gish, Rudolph Valentino and Tom Mix, with locally produced music as an accompaniment, were also popular. By the mid-twenties there were some 1 250 cinemas in Australia.[5]

Transport facilities were changing. Railway services declined in popularity as motor cars and trucks deprived them of their former patronage. The car enabled people to enjoy more travel, picnics and socialising. The car was a symbol of what was later to be known as the 'Jazz Age'. To have a car was to be 'up-to-date' and 'modern'[6] and more and more cars began to be seen around Hamilton. Each of the Laws' neighbours had cars: on one side a Buick, and on the other side, a Dodge. A speed limit was set for cars in the town of 15 miles per hour and 8 miles per hour at intersections. Keen interest was shown in aeroplanes and the residents of Hamilton could take joy flights and see demonstrations of these fascinating new machines.[7]

The Laws' Hamilton house was spacious compared to the Gardenvale home. It was a Victorian weather–board house, owned by the Education Department, of pleasant proportions with a verandah in the front and extending down the side, later to be a bedroom for Geof and Phil when the Law family expanded. The grounds around the house were larger than those at Gardenvale and there were stables in the backyard and rose bushes down the sideway.

The Law children's playground was now the Hamilton Gardens opposite their house. At that time the Gardens were a 'wilderness of uncultivated trees and bushes and a lake, immediately inside'. They could enter the gardens by squeezing through the wire fence and there the Law children and their friends 'ran and played and fought and climbed and screamed' during the following seven years.

Hamilton's respectable, industrious citizens were frequent churchgoers to Hamilton's nine churches. The Law family attended the fine bluestone Church of England. At first the Law children went to Sunday School on Sunday afternoons, but a new vicar, Canon Jessup, arrived and with a thoughtfulness for either his own or children's dislike of spending Sunday afternoons in church, he introduced a ten o'clock, half-hour, morning service for the older children: 'By 11 a.m. on Sundays we were free, having rushed home, changed out of our good clothes and dived through the fence into the gardens.'

During 1922, their first year in Hamilton, Geof, Phil and Marjorie attended the Hamilton State School. Phil was placed in the 7th grade and continued to apply himself to his studies, which was no hardship. He enjoyed the stimulus of learning and set himself the targets he wanted to achieve. Studying left him little time for other activities and, during the first year at Hamilton, he made few friends. Although Arthur and Lillie never put pressure on him to succeed, he knew they were proud of his scholastic ability and this, too, spurred him on. He loved reading and he had a plentiful supply of books. As a District Inspector, Arthur received copies of all the supplementary readers and paperback copies of the semi-classics. Phil began a habit of waking at six in the morning and spending the next hour in bed reading.

The extra effort quickly paid off and during the year he was promoted to the 8th grade. He was now 10 years old and in a grade with children of 13 or 14 years of age. Geof remembers the thin, tiny Phil casting a comical figure among the big adolescents. It was at this stage that Phil began to be called 'Squib'. Although contemporary usage of 'squib' is frequently understood to mean 'coward', Geof recalls that, at that time, it meant 'a little bit of a cracker that wouldn't go off, a small thing'.[8] Like many nicknames, it was appropriate. Nevertheless, Phil hated it. But it stuck and, for some years after, he was 'Squib' Law.

His extreme smallness did have one advantage, for the other boys treated him as a mascot for the class. Although this position held low social power within the group, Phil was happy to have a special status with the older and bigger boys. Being a mascot also protected him from ever being terrorised or bullied.

At the end of the year he was awarded the Merit Certificate at the early age of 10. He had hoped to be dux of the school, but was beaten by a few marks by the son of a farmer.

The next year, 1923, he attended the recently built Hamilton High School. Because of his excellent results he expected to be moved into form D (grade 9). But Arthur and the Headmaster of the High School decided that he was too young to be promoted to the higher form and he was kept down in the E form. Phil bitterly resented Arthur's decision. 'Looking back, I consider that my father, for all his learning, made a grave psychological mistake in not allowing me to proceed at my own pace.'

However, there were compensations in being in Form E. The students were told that, at the end of the year, the top 10 students were to be promoted directly to Form C. This was just the sort of stimulus that Phil revelled in and at the end of the year he was thrilled to finish in the top 10. His pleasure was short-lived. Again Arthur and the Head Master decided to keep him back and he was only allowed to move up the normal one grade, into Form D, the form he had expected to go into two years earlier.

Arthur's reasons for this decision, which were to have such a deep and lasting effect on Phil, are not known. Throughout his study and teaching of psychology, Arthur expressed his belief that, though there were innumerable methods of teaching children with learning difficulties, 'heaven help the bright child!'[9] He viewed true education as a 'gradual development towards maturity, physical as well as mental'.[10] With this

Arthur Law (*circa* 1920).

Phil Law (1915).

'Squib' Law (1925).

Lillie, Geof, Marj and Phil at Gardenvale (1917).

Geof (with musical instruments made by him), Marj holding Noel and Phil with bow and arrow (1922).

The Laws'
Hamilton house.

Phil, Australian
University Boxing
Championships,
Brisbane (1936).

Marj, Phil and Nel
(1939).

educational philosophy it is likely he saw Phil's single-sided development in intellectual activities as unhealthy and hoped, in some way, to balance it by placing him in a class of students nearer his own age. Whatever his reasons, Arthur took away the intellectual stimulus of competition that Phil thrived on and Phil never forgave him for it.

Phil was 'utterly disillusioned'. His intellectual friends had passed him by and he still believes the delay of the year had a profound effect upon his whole life. 'It was to spell the end of what might have been a bright scholastic career,' he later wrote. Arthur's decision had also taken away the image Phil had previously had of himself as being special. In Form D there was little that was distinctive about him. Even the basis of his mascot image had been stripped from him for he was now merely a small boy amongst slightly bigger contemporaries. The only thing that remained was the hated 'Squib' nickname.

Feeling helpless and thwarted by his father, Phil fought back in the only way he knew how; he decided to '"chuck" learning and studying'. He deliberately joined a group of, in his words, 'carefree loafers'. They were the non-academic boys, the boys who played sport, and Phil knew that, intellectually, he could keep up with them without any effort. The ramifications of this quiet rebellion would reverberate throughout his life, and marked the beginning of his later concentration on physical as well as intellectual pursuits.

Once he had joined this particular group of athletes, he became at first intrigued, and later stimulated, by their sporting ability and prowess. His competitive spirit was aroused and very soon he aimed to be 'up with the best'. The 'supreme athlete' was Reginald (Reg.) Stewart who excelled in swimming, diving, football, cricket, shooting, cycling and was the under 14 schoolboy athletics champion in Victoria. 'He was a marvellous model to emulate', Phil later wrote. As methodically as he had approached his studies, Phil set about developing skills in many areas of sport: swimming, tennis, football, athletics and cricket. But they were not as easily gained as his academic skills:

> I struggled along determinedly, always striving to attain a standard a little higher in most cases than I was capable of reaching, training fiercely, practising, cultivating style and proficiency.

His sisters too remember his determination to excel:

> He took up sports with the same enthusiasm that he took up learning. And he had to work at sport. He studied books and practised and became a swimmer, an athlete and a footballer.[11]

His previous habit of reading for an hour upon wakening, was replaced by rising at 6 a.m. to go down to the Grange Burn Weir to train for swimming, or to be first to get a bat from the sports store to practise cricket. School recesses, lunch and after-school hours were spent practising football in winter and cricket in the summer.

Even bicycle riding was competitive. Arthur had bought Geof a bicycle whilst they were in Gardenvale and he now bought Phil a 20-year-old bicycle from the Head Master of Casterton State School. The bicycle, though old, was well made, light and able to travel fast. Best of all it had a fixed wheel, free wheel being spurned by the fast cyclists at that time. The local boys developed skills and speed on the bicycles and proudly showed off to the local girls by 'standing still' and riding backwards.

Bicycles were the boys' passports to adventure. Rabbiting was a favourite pastime and they would ride 12 to 15 miles out of Hamilton on Saturdays to a suitable area. At first the rabbits were caught with dogs and ferrets, but later the boys graduated to using shotguns. They would leave early in the morning, ride out along the gravel roads, then ride miles through paddocks, park the bikes and walk. At the end of the day, their bikes laden with rabbits with their heads dangling down and jamming in the spokes of the wheels, they would arrive home exhausted, often late and in the dark to find Lillie anxiously waiting at the gate, peering through the darkness up the road.

Lillie put few restrictions on the Law boys, although she never ceased to worry when they were late returning, particularly when they were out with their guns. Looking back, Phil regards his mother as a remarkably placid woman, for he and Geof gave her plenty of reason for concern, but at the time he wondered why she worried.

Although the mid 1920s was a time when consumer goods were plentiful and women were able to buy many domestic labour-saving devices to give them unparalleled leisure,[12] this was not the case for Lillie. There were six children in the Law family now that Peter had been born in 1923 and Wendy in 1926, and Lillie's life was a hard one. Little time was available for reading or playing piano with her children. But the Law children and their friends remember the Law home as a happy one, with lots of kids and Lillie always welcoming. 'Phil's mother was a very cheery person, bubbly personality,' recalled a childhood friend, Harry Walter. 'Very good to the kids that went to the house.'[13] But on one point Lillie was resolute; she would not allow Phil to be called 'Squib' in the Law house. One day when a group of boys came and asked Lillie 'Is Squib in?', she is said to have retorted 'We call him Phil here.'[14]

Arthur's demands now impinged on his family's life very little. As a School Inspector he spent most weekdays away travelling around the district, staying in dreaded pubs with toilets outside that, to the abstemious Arthur, 'stank of regurgitated beer'.[15] He would return home only on weekends, and sometimes would be absent for two weeks. So the Law children would spend, Phil recalls, 'a lovely week with my mother, who was a tremendous person, and we just dreaded the re-introduction of the old man over the weekend again.'

One of Phil's sisters also recalls Arthur's weekend return:

> Dad was away all the week so mum had to bring us up. When dad
> got home he would have to punish us for what we had done ... He'd
> do it with a strop, hung behind the door of the bathroom. And we
> just got it. If it was minor, it was on the hand, but if it was worse it
> was on the bottom ... We used to dread his coming back.[16]

Arthur was viewed by Phil's childhood friends with a mixture of fear
and awe. His role as District Inspector contributed to this, but it was
more his stern, reserved manner that they found intimidating. 'Phil's
father never appeared to relax,' recalled Harry Walter, 'He was an
unbending man with a piercing look.'[17]

Phil, in later years, summed up Arthur's qualities in these terms:

> He had a good mind, a lawyer's mind—analytical, logical, discrimi-
> nating and direct. He hated humbug and hypocrisy. In his teaching,
> and in his writing, he would cut through to the essentials and
> express them simply and concisely. In manner he was dignified,
> punctilious, fastidious, courteous and reserved. He was cautious by
> nature—one might even say over-cautious—and very conservative.
> His private life was a model of rectitude and conformism. His
> extreme shyness and lack of small talk made even casual social con-
> tacts difficult for him, although in his later years he became far
> more relaxed. Those close to him at that time were often surprised
> by his sense of humour. In this respect it can be said that his role as
> a father was quite different in relation to Dorothy, Peter and Wendy
> from what it was to the three older children.

Phil, as he had done at Gardenvale, continued to set himself challenges, particularly if he felt he had a weakness. One of these perceived
weaknesses was an inability to be fully aware immediately upon waking
up and he trained himself to 'instantly be awake and instantly be responsible ... So, if mother would touch me and say "Time to get up Phil", I'd
say "Yes mum, right" and I would make some comment immediately to
show that I was really awake.' He never really understood why he did this,
but later reasoned 'I think it was a matter of being a more effective
person. That somehow there might be occasions where it may be important to suddenly awaken and if I trained myself I'd cope with it better.'
In fact, it was a skill that proved useful on later Antarctic voyages when
he would be woken throughout the night to make urgent decisions
about crucial issues.

Phil was still his parents' 'good boy'; cautious, evaluating everything
before attempting it and highly responsible. Lillie relied on him to do
the jobs around the house; to run the messages, to pay the bills and she
would boast that 'Phil was never a halfpenny out'.[18] He was still held up

as a model to the rebellious Geof, and Geof still continued to hound him with bullying, and to tease him with ditties. When Lillie, exasperated, would tell Geof to stop singing, he would move out of her earshot, and whistle the same tune, which infuriated Phil even more than the words.

As the two of them grew older their differences became even more marked. Phil was conservative and conformed, if reluctantly, to all the rules laid down by his parents and schoolteachers. Geof continued to break them. Phil worried about others' opinions of him and tried to live up to the expectations of his parents and teachers. But Geof was contemptuous of what other people thought about him; he resented Lillie's admonishing and was antagonistic to Arthur, constantly defying him and any other authority figures, including teachers. He would skite about his exploits and, Phil recalls, 'was continually being flogged by his parents and his teachers, but without any apparent effect.'

Geof enjoyed being alone, spending his time on creative pursuits; making musical instruments, or painting and drawing cartoons that were featured each year in the Hamilton High School newspaper 'The Grange'. Phil enjoyed the company of other boys, practising, competing and joining in all the team sports. His name featured regularly under the 'sporting activities' column in 'The Grange'. Geof was afraid of physical harm whereas Phil, Geof believed, was 'fearless. Never frightened in his life. Small. A brave fellow.'[19]

Geof tried to disown the Law family, never admitting that Arthur was his father or Phil his brother. 'I detested family life,' he later maintained. 'I was the eldest of six. I didn't want kids, bloody kids bawling, bathing them, sick children.'[20] Phil, on the other hand, showed concern for the family, particularly Lillie. On one particular occasion, when the younger children had whooping cough, Phil arranged a scheme that would stop the children vomiting in the bed, which had been causing Lillie to have lots of laundry. 'I'll put my sand-shoes on' he told Lillie, 'and when the babies start coughing, I'll run them out to the back and let them vomit.' He would swoop them up and rush to the back landing and up-end them over the rails.[21]

The Law household itself was dominated by Geof's exploits and the stories of the Law siblings are stories in relation to Geof. Whatever his feats were, they were watched and admired by Phil. Having such an older brother, his sisters remarked, 'could have crippled someone else, but with Phil, he was determined to succeed.'[22] This trait was also noticed by a school friend, Harry Walter, who recalls Phil at this time:

Whatever he approached he did very thoroughly. His build was slight and wiry and he did very well academically. He was intent on everything he did whether it was studying, a game or a musical instrument—he had the ability to give it all his attention. He wanted to win, never trifled, took things seriously but had a sense of fun.[23]

Phil added boxing to his growing list of sports, and his ability here helped him to defend himself during the constant fights that still continued between Geof and himself. And it was not just Phil who was the object of Geof's physical violence, especially when Geof was in one of his furious tempers:

> I've seen him go mad and throw kids around, suddenly go berserk and in a fury he'd just grab people and whirl around and throw them. He could sort of dominate five kids of his own age, just a whirlwind of activity.

Even Geof later admitted that he was 'a bit of a bully in those days'.[24] Despite this treatment, the local boys were always willing to help Geof with whatever project he was working on, whether it was building a boat in the backyard or preparing exhibitions for the annual Hamilton fete.

> Geof didn't try to lead people [Phil alleged]. People followed him because he added colour to their otherwise drab lives. He made interesting things happen. He didn't elicit followers, they just came.

And Phil was one of his most ardent followers, caught up, as he recalls it, in 'Geof's strange magnetism'. But Harry Walter remembers the situation somewhat differently:

> Phil seemed to be preparing himself for leadership. As a kid Phil was overshadowed by Geof, but Geof was not a leader, he would only get the kids into trouble. They both [Geof and Phil] had a sense of adventure. But Phil had more capacity to apply himself. Geof was quite clever but didn't have the same application. Geof had a temper and would 'go off the handle', but not Phil, he would treat things calmly.[25]

Despite their differences and the continual antagonism between them, Phil and Geof shared a love of the bush and spent many of their weekends and most of their school holidays together in the nearby Grampians.

2.

The Grampians form the western end of the Great Dividing Range that runs along the eastern edge of Australia. The highest peak in the Grampians, Mt William, is only a little over 3 300 ft but the range consists of a bewildering array of rock structures and jagged peaks. The rugged beauty of the area impels bushwalkers to return again and again and Geof and Phil, during their adolescent years, were no exception.

Their first trip to the range was during their first Christmas holidays at Hamilton. Arthur arranged for the two boys to be part of a three-week camping trip into the area, led by Jock MacKenzie, the Head Teacher at Portland State School. With them travelled another five or six adults and six children. They set off with two wagons, stacked full with chaff, people and gear and each hauled by three draught horses to the almost deserted gold mining town of Mafeking. Mafeking had sprung up in 1900 when 10 000 hopeful unemployed people were given free rail passes by the Government to prospect for gold. In its heyday the town had 20 hotels and wine saloons, sly-grog shops, a theatre, billiard halls, churches, seven policemen and its own newspaper.[26] But the town had had only a short gold boom life and by the 1920s it was deserted. Only two families and an old bachelor hermit still lived there, working the sluices and eking out a living. Phil recalls the fascination of the place:

> We explored, searched through rubbish and old kitchen utensils and furniture, played hide and seek through the ruins, swam in the dam, ate enormously and sang around the camp fire at night. We slept under the stars when it was fine and in large tents when it was not.

From there they travelled along an overgrown track, unused for years, until they reached the junction of the Wannon River and Jimmy's Creek where they stayed in a single-roomed wooden hut—Jimmy's Hut.

> We stayed there for a week, rock climbing, bushwalking, fishing for blackfish, surrounded by ferns, grasses and shrubs. Kangaroos hopped through the bush and emus trotted away in flocks, while wild cattle bellowed and crashed through the undergrowth.

The trip was to cement the Law boys' love, already established in Tallangatta, of being in the Australian bush.

Later in the following year a friend of Arthur's, Professor Charles Fenner, a geologist from Adelaide University, took Geof and Phil up Mt Sturgeon. This trip held a different fascination for Phil:

> He gave us a lecture as we went along, explaining all the plants and bushes and the botany and zoology and geology, and that was an eye-opener to me. I had never had any knowledge of the intimate detail of a countryside and to have the bush pointed out to me in detail in this fashion was a wonderful experience.

The boys would ride their bicycles the twenty miles from Hamilton to Dunkeld and then out to Mt Abrupt and clamber up the cliff faces and roam along the old bullock tracks in the area. Their favourite place remained the hut they had stayed in during their first trip with Jock Mackenzie, Jimmy's Hut:

It was just a hut made of slabs of timber hewn with an axe, with the fireplace at one end and a tin roof. We sheltered in it quite frequently and camped there in style on a number of occasions. From there we had access to all the peaks rising on each side of the valley.

Their bush walking equipment was primitive compared with that available today. They had no sleeping bags, just blankets, and just as swagmen did in those days, they wrapped their utensils up in their blankets and strapped them on their backs. To relieve the weight they had to carry they sometimes rode their bicycles or hired a pack-horse.

At first Phil's concentration on sport and outdoor activities had little effect on his academic ability and, in 1924, he passed nine subjects and came 8th in the class. Although his early morning reading had been replaced with sporting practice, he continued to read avidly. One of his jobs was to change Arthur's library books, so Phil developed the habit of borrowing some books for himself as well.

I rapidly developed a taste for serious novels and when I was doing Intermediate year I was clever enough not to have to do much homework and I used to do an immense amount of reading. I'd get through about three novels a week.

In 1925 he gained his Intermediate Certificate, passing eight subjects. But, during the following year, his involvement in sport began to affect his study and he found that he could no longer easily achieve the high standards he had previously gained. He struggled through the year and at the Leaving Certificate examinations he failed three subjects, only passing in two.[27] Coming after his previous successes, this failure could have been a major disappointment in his life, but it seems to have had little effect, except for the realisation that he had 'hit an intellectual barrier' and that he could no longer just 'breeze along'.

In 1927 he studied, and passed, three Leaving Certificate subjects and Honours English. By now, Geof had caught up with him and, consequently, the two Law boys were awarded their Leaving Certificate in the same year.[28] They both did well at swimming too, each coming second in the school championships; Geof behind Reg Stewart, in the Boys' Senior Swimming Championship, and Phil behind Harry Walter in the Intermediate Boys' Swimming Championship.[29]

3.

It was the Jazz Age, the era that became associated with a form of 'syncopated and skilfully improvised music',[30] usually consisting of various combinations of trumpet, banjo, piano, saxophone, clarinet, trombone, violin, drums and flute. Geof's and Phil's first musical training had begun with Dop teaching them the bones and the spoons and, when Phil was at primary school, he had learned the mouth-organ and the tin whistle. At Hamilton Phil was given a piccolo by a young man who was groom for a wealthy family in Hamilton. Phil practised on this piccolo, delighted that he could now get the sharp and flat notes he had been unable to on the tin whistle.

The local jazz band leader persuaded Geof to take up the banjo and have lessons in basic harmony and chords. Soon Geof began to play the banjo in the local orchestra, and later one of the other players, seeing Phil's equal enthusiasm for musical instruments, gave him a clarinet.

Geof decided to form a jazz band at the High School consisting of himself on piano, a violinist, a trumpeter and a saxophone player. But they had no drums and these were necessary to complete the band. Phil found that there was a foundation in Melbourne which was interested in providing musical instruments to schools, so he asked the headmaster to write to it and explain their need for drums. The money was provided, the drums bought and Phil became the drummer for the Hamilton High School Jazz Band.

The town itself had two bands—one the professional jazz band which played for the dances and the other the High School band, which was called in if two events were held on the one evening. And so began Phil's sideline career as a professional musician.

During this Jazz era, entertainment was no longer simply confined to the home. Young men and women went out as never before, to the cinema, picnics, parties, spectator sports and dancing. Dancing was the rage and courting couples would meet to dance the Foxtrot and the Charleston at local halls.

Moral standards were changing. Contraceptive aids were available at pharmacies and there was a falling-off in Church attendance. Women began to use make-up and reveal more and more of their bodies as bathing suits became briefer. Hemlines not only rose up to, but above, the knee. Many women cut their hair in a 'bob' or a 'shingle' and some even began to smoke, including the Laws' next-door neighbour who could be seen smoking in her garden. Lillie was disgusted. No one seemed able to know how to 'check this revolution in dress, conduct and morals'[31] and many of the residents of Hamilton were profoundly concerned about the new emphasis on pleasure and believed it to be a symptom of moral decline.[32] Hamiltonians also expressed their concern in the *Spectator* about the decline in the birth rate in Western societies. The Law family must have presented the image of a model family to such concerned residents with its non-smoking, non-drinking parents, its regular Church-going and its six children.

Phil, too, was changing. He began to grow. 'Between fourteen and sixteen', he recalled 'I suddenly grew about six inches, which made me finish up being normal.' He was still not tall, but was 'lean as a whip ... broad shouldered and as tough as nails'. Coupled with this change in physique, came a change in name. No longer was he called 'Squib'. He had, to his delight, outgrown the nickname.

At this time he became interested in girls. Adult morals may have been changing to what one commentator calls 'unbridled sex',[33] but these changes had little effect on the adolescents of Hamilton:

> You would never hold hands with a girl in public. You would never let anyone see, if you could avoid it, that you were interested in a girl or that she attracted you. You certainly wouldn't be seen walking with a girl. You could take her home from a dance, that was all right, anything in the darkness.

'Adolescent sex in those days', another commentator recalled 'was a frantic, funny, pathetic farce.'[34] Thoughts of sex certainly plagued Phil, day and night, during his time at Hamilton and he recalled that: 'Sex drove me crazy [but] you couldn't do much about it.' Playing in the band should have given him plenty of opportunities to meet and take girls home after dances had finished, but being the drummer had disadvantages. 'At the end of the dance the other chaps would rush off', he explained, 'often grabbing a girl on the way, and I'd be last out of the hall whilst I dismantled my drums and stacked them all up and stowed them in a car.' Within a short time he had discarded the drums and had become a clarinetist instead. The clarinet could be packed up very quickly.

He did, however, meet girls on other occasions and the repercussions of one of the incidents may have cost him his Hamilton High School prefectship. During his last year at the High School, when he and Ron Stewart were both prefects, they went by train to Ararat to play football against Ararat High School. After the football match, followed by a dinner and a dance, Ron and Phil 'picked up a couple of Ararat High School girls and decided to spend some quiet time with them in some dark place.' First they checked the train's departure time for Hamilton and found they had 45 minutes to themselves. They put their bags on the train, and went back with the girls, whom they had left hiding outside the station, to a nearby dark lane. When they returned to the station they saw the red lights of the train disappearing down the track. The porter had told them the wrong time. 'We were appalled', Phil recalls, 'because we knew that if we turned up the next day and the story got round that we'd missed the train because we'd been out with girls we might be expelled. We'd certainly lose our prefectships.'

Some of the boys from the Ararat High School football team came to their aid and loaned them two brand new Malvern Star racing bikes and, at 11.00 p.m., they started on their sixty mile ride back to Hamilton. After taking a wrong turn, which added an extra 12 miles to their trip, they arrived back in Hamilton, utterly exhausted, at six o'clock the following morning, having ridden 72 miles. After half an hour's sleep they arrived at school at the normal time and were met by an incredulous crowd of school mates. But they had anticipated some disbelief and they had ridden the Malvern Star bikes to school to prove their story. They told the headmaster that the porter had told them the wrong time, but they made no mention of girls. The headmaster believed them and not only did they retain their prefectship, but the ride gave them, for a few days at least, hero status. That year the Hamilton High School's Newsletter 'The Grange' included a cryptic sentence that read 'The Ararat–Hamilton road is very popular with some of the School footballers, especially at night time.'[35]

During that same year, Geof, now 18, left home, 'glad to get out' to go to Melbourne to attend the Melbourne Teachers' College. This was not because he had any particular aspirations to be a teacher, but because he could not think of anything else to do. When he first suggested teaching to Arthur, his father had indignantly told him 'You're not fitted for a teacher. You are not temperamentally suited. What about the bank?' But Geof insisted on teaching because 'in the bank you only get three weeks holiday not ten weeks like a school [teacher].' Arthur was disgusted and retorted 'You can't base a career on holidays.' But Geof could and did. He managed to combine teaching with a musical career for the rest of his life. 'I never let teaching interfere with my music' he remarked after retiring as Headmaster of a large city school.[36]

Geof had influenced, and in many ways dominated, Phil throughout childhood and adolescence. With Geof now gone, Phil made a decision that he later thought had a profound effect on his life:

At the age of about sixteen I made a transition from being this over-cautious deliberate calculating slow to act person, because I said to myself 'Geof's having a hell of a lot more fun in life than I am'. I could see that if I occasionally plunged without first measuring the depth I'd have a lot more fun and for about eighteen months or two years I deliberately went into things without the cautious evaluating approach. And suddenly found I was having more fun.

Phil later believed this to be a definite and important transition point in his life, one 'which changed my personality, so much as you can change a person's personality.'

At sixteen he was certainly an 'all rounder', involved in many aspects of school life, as a member of the Student Council and the Library Committee, and as a School Prefect. Later he was able to boast:

I became Vice Captain of my House and played for the school in cricket and football. I was narrowly beaten as School tennis champion. I was Intermediate School swimming champion and was the best boxer in the school (although no competitions were held). I played senior cricket with success in the Hamilton adult competition. At swimming carnivals around the Hamilton district I won numerous events in adult competitions in swimming and diving.

No matter how successful he was in his sporting activities, Phil could never gain the approval he hankered after from Arthur. If Arthur's reason for holding Phil back in his academic study had been the hope that Phil would develop his physical ability, he went about it in a strange way. He gave Phil no encouragement in sporting activities, in fact he was more likely to show 'disinterest or even disparagement. He never once bought me a tennis racquet or cricket bat. I used to be very hurt.' On the other hand, Lillie was always proud of Phil's achievements, in any area, and would ask him about the race, or the match, and show her pleasure at his successes.

At the end of his final year at Hamilton High School Phil's involvement in the other aspects of school life gained him an 'A' for Attendance, Games, Physique, Intellectual Qualities, Moral Qualities, Conduct, Public Spirit and Influence in School.[37] He was also awarded the General Proficiency prize[38] and the School Scripture prize.

Phil's ambition for many years had been to become a surgeon and he enjoyed reading articles about medicine. Chemistry was the subject he particularly loved and he passed Leaving Algebra and Geometry and gained a Pass in Honours Chemistry, but failed Honours Physics.[39] By the end of his High School years Phil had realised that becoming a surgeon, which entailed him attending University, was out of the question. Arthur, with five children still at home, could not afford the fees and living expenses for University and Phil's marks were not good enough for him to be awarded a scholarship. Phil had to re–assess his career aspirations. His interest in Chemistry and his intense desire to 'find out a reason for things' led him to choose his second love, science. 'I used to be frequently asking questions of "why this" and "why that". I had no great desire for technical things. I was much more interested in the theoretical aspect of experiences.'

Arthur persuaded Phil to pursue his science career through secondary teaching. This suggestion seemed reasonable and Phil agreed. The decision meant that Phil had to attend Melbourne Teachers' College. But he was only 16 and the entrance age to Teachers' College was 18. For two years he marked time, waiting for the opportunity to begin his scientific career.

Notes

1. Don Garden, *Hamilton, a Western District History*, Hargreen Publishing Company, Victoria, 1984.
2. *Argus*, 28 March 1885, cited in Don Garden.
3. Law's sisters to author, 6 May 1988.
4. Geoffrey Law to Law, March 1989, LP.
5. L. L. Robson, *Australia in the Nineteen Twenties, Commentary and Documents*, Thomas Nelson, Aust., 1980, p. 48.
6. Robson, p. 52.

7. Garden, op. cit.
8. Geoffrey Law to author, 27 July 1988.
9. Geoffrey Law to author, 1988.
10. L. J. Blake (ed.), *Vision and Realisation*, Education Department of Victoria, 1973, vol. 1, p. 372.
11. Law's sisters to author, 6 May 1988.
12. Robson, p.60.
13. Harry Walter to author, 7 July 1988.
14. Geoffrey Law to author, 27 July 1988.
15. Ibid.
16. Law's sisters to author, 6 May 1988.
17. Harry Walter to author, 7 July 1988.
18. Law's sisters to author, 6 May 1988.
19. Geoffrey Law to author, 27 July 1988.
20. Ibid.
21. Law's sisters to author, 6 May 1988.
22. Ibid.
23. Harry Walter to author, 7 July 1988.
24. Geoffrey Law to author, July 1988.
25. Harold Walter to author, 7 July 1988.
26. Jane Calder, *The Grampians, a Noble Range*, Victorian National Parks Association, 1987, pp. 123–4.
27. Official Hamilton High School, Public Examination, Leaving Certificate records, 1926.
28. Official Hamilton High School, Leaving Certificate and Honors records, 1927.
29. *The Grange*, December 1927, p. 14.
30. Robson, p. 42.
31. Robson, p. 43.
32. Garden.
33. Robson, p. 44.
34. James McClelland, *Stirring the Possum*, Penguin Books, 1989, p. 24.
35. *The Grange*, December 1928, p. 18.
36. Geoffrey Law to author, 27 August 1988.
37. Official Hamilton High School, Phillip Garth Law's individual record.
38. Official Award, LP.
39. Law, Official Hamilton High School record, LP.

3. The Young Pedagogue, 1929–1938

1.

I[T WAS 1929, LAW WAS SEVENTEEN YEARS OLD, AND THE STARK SIGNS OF] recession were already evident. Unemployment was rising from its 1927 level of six per cent and, as one historian records, 'Saddest of all was the plight of young people leaving school. Many had to go on for years living at home on their parents or "on the susso".'[1] This fate did not befall Law for he had been appointed 'Junior Teacher, 2nd Grade on probation', Hamilton High School.[2] But 1929 was an inopportune time for any young person, particularly an ambitious one, to enter the teaching profession. Teachers were being forced to accept cuts in salaries and their opportunities for promotion were curtailed as State expenditure on education dropped by a third from £3.37 million in 1927–1928 to £2.53 million in 1932–1933.[3]

Law's vision of himself as a scientist was slow to materialise. The term 'Junior Teacher', as it applied to a high school teacher, was a misnomer, as no classroom responsibilities were allocated. Instead, Law acted as secretary to the Headmaster, filing school correspondence, running errands and learning to type. It was hardly the career he had envisaged for himself. Retrospectively, he saw the experience as useful, a time when he gained his 'first elementary knowledge of office organization'. He also continued with his study and gained Third Class Honours in Chemistry at the end of 1929.

Law's life changed little from when he had been a student. Money, generally, was scarce and few people could afford the luxuries of attending dances and other popular forms of recreation. Even the advent of 'talkies' could not keep the attendance up at the local picture shows. But this had little effect on the Law family which, with six children, had always needed to be careful with its money.

At the end of the year Arthur was appointed Inspector of Schools in the Geelong district and the Law family moved to Geelong. Still too young to enter Teachers' College, Phil was transferred to a position as Junior Teacher at Geelong High School. This meant another year of office duties, but he was also allowed to assist with the training of the various school sports teams and the daily gymnastics classes. Apart from studying, and passing, Honours Mathematics, his year at Geelong High School was 'one of the most active periods of my life in terms of physical exertion.' He gained the Royal Life Saving Society's top award, the Award of Merit, and continued with shooting and bike riding. He added a new sport to his already long list, cross-country running.

By the middle of 1930 the downturn in the economy began to take an even heavier toll on the Education Department as politicians and newspapers united to call for economies within education.[4] This action culminated, during 1931, in a Board of Inquiry being set up to investigate the Education Department budget. The recommendations that flowed from this Inquiry were later thought to have effectively demolished much of the recent progress made in teacher education.[5] The queue of applicants for teacher training grew longer as the teachers' colleges were forced to reduce their enrolments.

In 1931 Law was eligible to enter Melbourne Teachers' College, but the worst effects of the depression were evident and the three Victorian teachers' colleges, Melbourne, Ballarat and Bendigo, had suffered retrenchments. In December 1930 Cabinet reduced the intake into teachers' colleges from 320 to 230 and cut studentship allowances by amounts varying from 14 to 33 per cent.[6] Secondary studentships had also been cut back and, as Law's marks had not been exceptionally high, there seemed little chance of his gaining one of the coveted scholarships. His fears were confirmed and he was offered a Primary Teachers' Studentship at the Ballarat Teachers' College. This 'relegation', as he called it, to a primary teaching college was 'disastrous as far as my academic scientific career was concerned' and he was bitterly disappointed. There were no alternatives available and he had to accept the situation.

There was still one small chance for him to pursue a science career. The Education Department granted the two top students each year from the Ballarat and Bendigo Teachers' Colleges a 'second year' studentship 'to proceed to Melbourne Teachers' College to begin a University course. Law set out to win one.

Enthusiastically he threw himself into making the most of his year at Ballarat Teachers' College. He recalls particularly his first formal education in education and psychology, and developing a love for English under an excellent lecturer who introduced him to contemporary novels, plays and short stories and to writers like Shaw, Faulkner and Hemingway. Always on the look out for more effective ways of using his time, Law found that short stories and three-act plays were 'one of the best ways of having a survey of modern literature if you don't have time to read the novels'. He believed that his enjoyment of the study of English literature enabled him to 'soak up the technique', which in later years helped him to write 'concise hard hitting submissions to Ministers and government departments in order to develop policy or to get finance'. At the time, his work in literature was also favourably commented upon in his official report from the College:

A very fine type of student with a frank, pleasing personality. Has done very good work in literary subjects. Should develop into a very efficient rural school teacher. Has entered into many College activities. Confidently recommended.[7]

These activities included playing cricket and football for the College and winning the men's swimming championship, which he regarded as 'no great achievement because the swimming standard was not terribly high'.

Music also featured prominently in his life at Ballarat. He 'started to fiddle around on the piano' at the boarding house where he stayed, 'gradually teaching myself a bit'. At Geelong in the previous year, he had bought himself a second-hand soprano saxophone. Arthur had earlier forbidden him to buy one because he considered it a waste of money. 'You've already got a clarinet', he declared, 'what would you want a saxophone for?' Law thought explanations would have been useless since Arthur 'knew nothing of music' and was both insensitive and uninterested in his sons' music-making activities:

So I bought the sax from my spare, personal money and I hid it in the house. The whole year I used to practise and if dad walked into the room I would quickly switch to clarinet. He wasn't interested enough to take notice of the difference in the tone, so he didn't ever find out that I'd bought myself one.

After surreptitiously practising the saxophone for a year Law was now ready to play it publicly and started a jazz band. That year the College Newsletter, *Extra Muros*, recorded 'Phil Law, moderation in all things, except in saxophony.'

By the end of the year he had achieved the second year studentship he had set his sights on. This scholarship, he believed, 'retrieved to some extent the loss I had suffered by not obtaining a secondary studentship to Melbourne [Teachers' College].'

Law was part of the last group of students to go through the Ballarat Teachers' College. The Board of Inquiry into the Education Department had decided that the existence of three teacher training establishments in Victoria was wasteful and recommended that both the Ballarat and the Bendigo Colleges be closed.[8] All teacher training was to be conducted at the Melbourne Teachers' College.

At the beginning of 1932 Law moved to a boarding house in Drummond Street, Carlton. Although enrolled at Melbourne Teachers' College he was studying physics, chemistry, pure mathematics and mixed mathematics at the University of Melbourne and attending tutorials at the College:

I found the academic year a hard one. I had not done any physics or chemistry for two years and had forgotten quite a lot. I found that the quality of instruction I had had in the country in science and mathematics did not compare with the preparation given to students in the large Melbourne secondary schools.

Despite the difficult academic year, he continued to divide his time between scholastic and sporting activities, becoming a member of the College football club and taking up boxing. Boxing suited him well and he particularly liked the fairness of the weight limits that were built into the competition 'because I was small in build, and in boxing you were always put up against people of your own size.'

Law, who loved nothing better than to pit himself against others with higher intellectual or physical abilities, was now spurred on by the 'supreme athletes' at the University. These were groups of ex-public school boys and, in boxing, it was the Old Melbourne Grammar clique which reigned. Law began attending boxing classes, at both College and University, in the late afternoons two or three times a week. Boxing was the only sport in which he ever received professional coaching. In the middle of that year he entered for three competitions, the Novice Championships and the Open Championships in the Light-Weight Class at the University and the Light-Weight championship at the College. He won all three.

But the competitions took their toll. Law always became nervous before any test or competition, whether it was sporting or scholastic, but with boxing the nervousness had an extra dimension. Not only was there his usual fear of not acquitting himself as well as he hoped he might, but in boxing he knew he was likely to 'get a hiding as well ... you are facing a person whose main object in life is to beat hell out of you.' His nervousness was such that he fought the 'first round in a sort of daze with very little concentration at all; just going through the motions automatically as I had done in the training gymnasium.' It was not until the second round that he began to have some mental control over what he was doing.

Law set his heart on winning a University Blue in boxing. This meant he had to win the Intervarsity championship that was to be held in Sydney later in the year. Sydney University had a strong boxing team and approached the sport in a professional way. They had hired the Rushcutters Bay Stadium, Sydney's main stadium for professional boxing. Law's normal nervousness before a bout turned to almost paralysing terror when he was led to the ring through the huge stadium with its large seating capacity and blaze of strong lights. By the third round Law was beaten in a technical knock-out. He was disappointed with his performance because he had not acquitted himself to the best of his ability:

I had certain natural talents, quick reflex action and speed generally, but I had no conception of really hard training or what real fitness meant. This was a very amateurish attempt on my part.

So 1932 went by without him achieving his goal of a blue in boxing.

Nevertheless, he had passed his four academic subjects. This brought little joy, as his scholarship was for one year only and all avenues for the pursuit of a scientific career were now closed to him. As a second best, he hoped to begin teaching and continue with part-time studies at the University. But even this hope was dashed when he was appointed to a small country school, the Clunes Higher Elementary School, 24 miles north of Ballarat.

Clunes was to be his home for the next two years and, although its distance from Melbourne meant he could not attend University, he remembers his time there as 'two of the happiest years of my life', crammed as they were with sporting activities, cricket, football, tennis, swimming and shooting.

Despite the fact that his autobiographical notes pay scant regard to his new teaching career, he was in fact teaching science and mathematics and assisting students who were taking Leaving examinations by correspondence.[9] He was also, according to his first Inspector's report in April 1933, showing 'promise' as a teacher:

A very keen and enthusiastic young teacher of pleasing personality. Prepares with great thoroughness, shows a sound grasp of his subjects and secures excellent co-operation. Very promising. C+.[10]

Law also began instructing some of the local boys in boxing in a room in an old deserted hotel building in the town. Word got around that Law was a good boxer, and this helped protect him on the football field because 'it was not so likely that anyone would take a swing at me.'

It was at this time that Law's music making changed from amateur to professional standing and he was able to augment his meagre salary with fees earned from band playing. He teamed up with a pianist, a drummer and a trumpet player and, with himself on saxophone and clarinet, they played most Saturday nights at Clunes and received other professional engagements during the week all around the district. Later he was able to boast that he 'became a very expert sight reader [and] could put a highly complex bit of jazz music on a stand and play at sight with any orchestra.'

Music, sport and teaching were progressing well. But he was self-conscious about the fact that he was still a virgin, and that sex was still a 'damned nuisance'. Summoning up courage, he invited a teacher, whom he had met at Melbourne Teachers' College, to attend a Ball in Maryborough. This meant spending a night at the hotel. The weekend was enjoyable, but sexually proved to be a flop. His anxiety that his friend might become pregnant had not overcome the actual embarrassment of fronting up to the pharmacist to buy 'French letters'. So he went away without contraceptives. In any event it hardly mattered, for each of them booked themselves into separate rooms. 'Had she given me the slightest encouragement to go to her room I would have done so, [he later explained] but she didn't and I didn't suggest anything.'

Virginity intact, Law abandoned sexual exploits and instead spent his weekends 'shooting just about anything that moved'. He had bought himself a 22 calibre, Browning semi-automatic rifle and he and another teacher, Roy Crean, would go shooting a few miles out of town.

These were the years before myxomatosis, and rabbits had reached plague proportions, 'The whole mountainside ... was a grey moving mass of rabbits. We'd rush up the hillside shooting ... but it was silly, dangerous, but very exciting shooting.' His best shooting record, he recalls, was when he shot seven running hares and two rabbits with eleven shots.

During his time at Clunes he took stock of his life and faced another important decision:

> Should I be content with the happy life I was leading and settle down to the life of a country school teacher? Or should I apply myself to further study and attempt to complete my science degree?

With Law's need to prove himself to be as good as, or better than, others in everything he tackled, it comes as little surprise to know that his decision was to continue his science degree. But he was up against enormous odds. The only science subject that he could study away from the University was mathematics, and even then there were no provisions made for external studies students. He enrolled for Mixed Mathematics II and Pure Mathematics II. That done, he contacted a friend at the University and asked him to write his lecture notes in duplicate and to send a copy to Clunes, plus a copy of the problems set in the practice classes.

These duplicate notes proved only partly successful, because they were difficult to decipher and sometimes contained errors, which took Law hours to discover and to rectify. In addition, he had no one to assist him with problems that he could not solve. Then he heard that Allan Searle, the Head Teacher at Tourello, a small rural school about five miles from Clunes, was also enrolled in Part II Mathematics. They decided to study together. Each Friday night for the following two years Law would tramp five miles across the paddocks to Searle's home. After dinner, the two men would work until midnight and the following morning Allan would drive Law back to Clunes. Supplemented with books he could borrow by mail from the Melbourne Public Library, this arrangement worked quite well, except for the difficulty of studying in a boarding house with a dozen young teachers and bank clerks. 'Study meant separating myself from them for four nights a week to return to my small room after dinner to work. There was no electric light and I studied by the light of a kerosine lamp,' wrapped in a rug in a tiny unheated bedroom. Toward the end of the year Law felt his chances of passing were slim, but Allan persuaded him to present for the examination. To Law's delight he found that he was able to answer the required number of questions.

During this time Law had fallen in love for the first time. The girl, he thought, was both beautiful and charming and he felt they were sexually compatible. However, 'her education was elementary and she was not an intellectual sort of person.' After some months, he told her that he would not be prepared to marry her. She asked him his reasons and he, to his everlasting regret, told her that he could not see her fitting into the type of life that he anticipated leading.

Although unsure where his future career path would lead him, he knew now that it would not be the comfortable life of a country school teacher. And his future plans, hazy as they were, did not include a woman of limited intellectual background as a wife, no matter how compatible they may have been in other ways.

By the end of 1934 he had passed Pure Mathematics II and III, but had failed Mixed Mathematics II. He had also applied, and been accepted, for a teaching appointment in Melbourne, which meant that he could pursue the qualifications he knew he needed to gain promotion.

2.

At the beginning of 1935 Law spent short periods at Westgarth Higher Elementary School and Coburg High School, before being permanently appointed to the Elwood Central School. Although only at Coburg High School for a few weeks, one of the students, Richard Thompson, who would later work closely with Law in the Antarctic Division, recalls Law's teaching of that class of fifty-two students:

> I remember him as a most enthusiastic teacher. He certainly lived in my memory as one of the outstanding teachers. ... He had a gift of imparting the knowledge and telling you what it meant and he added a note of adventure and excitement to science. He wore glasses. He was pretty thin on top, even in those days.[11]

At Elwood Central School Law taught mathematics and science and was appointed Sports Master and also Form Master of the infamous Form E4 boys. E Form was the top class at the school, equivalent to Year 8 and the E4 group were the lowest of the E forms. 'They herded into E4 all the boys who showed the least academic talent', Law later explained. These students presented him with a challenge and he loved it:

> This form had a reputation for being extremely difficult because the boys were not terribly interested in school or work and they were pretty rough some of them. They gave the teachers a hell of a time generally. I had one great advantage, I was the Sports Master and I

used to take the kids out after school each night to train them in football or cricket or swimming, and they really responded wonderfully. They never played up with me and they would do what I asked; even made efforts to cope with algebra.

His enthusiasm for these particular boys paid dividends and the rating of his teaching moved up to B plus, with the comment that Law 'is clear, definite and stimulating in presentation. Uses sound, interesting methods and by encouraging class management, receives willing and spontaneous response. Lessons are successful in result.'[12]

To gain promotion under the Education Department regulations, Law needed to complete part-time education qualifications which were awarded by the Education Department for teachers who could not attend university:

So in 1935 I did Second Honours Education and in 1936 I did First Honours Education. In Ballarat Teachers' College we had a pretty good grounding in psychology, and in these Honours Education courses we had more psychology ... so I had a good fundamental grounding in psychology and its language and practices. I think that was useful later.

It certainly appeared so, particularly in relation to leadership and selection of staff for Antarctic work. This was highlighted when he was requested, in 1959, to deliver a paper on 'Personality Problems in Antarctica' as the 26th Sir Richard Stawell Oration to the Victorian Branch of the British Medical Association. This paper was highly acclaimed with many requests for copies coming from around the world.

During the mid 1930s Law became close to one of his sisters, Marjorie, although it is she who recalls their time together, not he. In May 1934 Arthur had been appointed Vice–Principal (Primary) of the Melbourne Teachers' College, to take charge of residential supervision and day-to-day administration.[13] Arthur, Lillie and the four other children all moved into the residence at Carlton. Law and Marjorie, although similar in age, had never been close. Now, for the first time, they both shared a common problem; they were new in Melbourne and had few friends. Marjorie recalls that:

He and I went around together for 2 years, like lovers. We'd go to films together and we'd go back to the Milky Way in Little Collins Street, with its big Cow outside the front. There we would always have Hot Chocolate. And we'd drink that and get really tizzy on it. And we'd probably have toasted raisin loaf and we would laugh immoderately all through. Stagger out as if we were drunk. We got on famously.[14]

Upon his return to Melbourne, Law's ambition to win a Blue at boxing resurfaced and he joined the University Boxing Club. In 1935 he fought in the University championships but was beaten. Again he had not achieved the coveted Blue, but he had achieved something else that he had always wanted. Arthur had begun to show an interest in his sporting activities, even later accepting the position of President of the University Boxing Club, with Law as Secretary. Arthur attended all the bouts that Law was involved in, showed concern for his physical well-being and even expressed pride in Law's achievements.

1936 proved a most successful year in many ways. Law resumed his study for a Bachelor of Science at the University. He wanted to continue with chemistry but found there were no Part II Chemistry classes available for part-time students. However, he was able to enrol in physics because lectures were offered between 12–1 p.m. on three days of the week and practical classes on two evenings and Saturday mornings. By arranging a free period at school just before lunch on the three days, Law was able to attend the lectures. But to get to the University from Elwood by public transport in the time available was impossible, so Law bought his first car, an A Model Ford roadster. At 11.30 a.m. he would drive from Elwood to the University in order to be there by 12 o'clock. At the finish of the session he would drive back along St Kilda Road, munching sandwiches so he would be ready to begin his own teaching at 1.30 p.m.

He continued with his boxing, and was now more determined than ever to get a University Blue. His friend, Athol Pike from the University Boxing Club, persuaded Law to go with him to a professional gymnasium in the city so they could get better practice with more highly qualified boxers. The experience terrified Law and for hours before, sometimes the whole night before, he would be full of apprehension about attending the gymnasium. Nevertheless, each Tuesday evening he faced these professionals and, at the end of the year, he again won the University of Melbourne Championship.

The Intervarsity Contests were held in Brisbane that year and the team travelled by train for two days to arrive there on the morning of the contest. Law won his first fight fairly easily, leading on points at each round. The next fighter was a Brisbane boxer who, Law had heard, had wanted to play hockey the following day and was determined to get the fight over as quickly as possible to conserve his energy for the hockey match. Athol and Law decided that the Brisbane boxer's tactics would be a 'rush job' and Law should take the same approach.

I had to move fast, when the bell went, and charge him and keep charging and try and make my charges and rushes more effective than his. As it turned out he came charging out of his corner straight for me. I charged straight out with my right hand covering my face and with a good left lead and that stopped his rush. Then I just threw punches in every direction and it was a very tough first round. The audience were highly delighted. When I got back to my corner, Athol Pike, as my second, was delighted too. He said 'Do exactly the same thing, go in and kill him this time.' So I moved in and just kept throwing punches and I finally landed a heavy one and dropped him back over the ropes on the other side of the ring. He didn't go down to the canvas, but hung on the ropes. Realising the referee would stop the fight if I moved, I moved straight over towards him as though I was going to hit him on the ropes. The referee stepped in between us and declared me the winner and stopped the fight.

At last he had won his Blue. That night, the abstemious Law, 'because it was a party and I had to drink something', slowly sipped a bottle of Johnny Walker whisky, neat. He was tossed head first over a balcony and crashed through the canvas hood of a parked car below. At the end of the evening he had the temerity to insist that all the others go to bed quietly so as not to get thrown out of the hotel. Then he passed out.

3.

During 1936 Law fell in love again with a student he met at the Saturday dance held at the Melbourne Teachers' College. These dances, or 'Palais' as they were called, were an important aspect of College life and were held in the upstairs Art Room, which was cleared of desks for the occasions. Law played in the band that was provided on an ad hoc basis by student volunteers. Whilst playing, Law noticed a very attractive female student, Nellie Isabel Allan. Nel was the daughter of a Gippsland farmer and, before becoming a student at the College, had spent the previous five years as a junior teacher in various country towns. Taking time off from the band Law asked her to dance and she accepted. The scene can be easily imagined. Law was older, more mature and assured than most of the students at the dance. He was a member of the band, a University champion boxer and, to cap it all, the son of the Vice-Principal of the College. One assumes that Law, with his heightened sense of self, would have expected a new student to be impressed. But Nel was not a lady to be influenced, or at least not to show she was, by such trifles. She spent their first few dances together trying to deflate his ego. Her repartee was sharp and Law's first opinion was that she was 'trying to be much too clever'.

Nevertheless, he thought she was the most beautiful girl who attended the Palais at the time. She also danced well and, when she wasn't hurling barbs at him, he considered her a good conversationalist. Law persisted and, after a few Saturday night dances, he asked to 'see her home'. This entailed walking her 100 yards around from the back of the main building of the College to the front door of the women's quarters.

Soon they were going on longer walks around the city, huddling cosily under an umbrella on wet evenings, or attending musical evenings and going to the cinema together.

> Nel was not only beautiful [Law later recorded]—she was <u>fun</u>. Vivacious, elegant, witty, highly original, daring (for those days) a very good ballroom dancer, and a woman with 'style' and great taste in dress.

In addition, she was 'educated and intellectual'. Nel Allan had everything that Law desired in a woman for both the present and the future. By the end of the year Law had passed Physics II, Nel had been awarded the Gladman Prize as the top student in primary teaching and the two of them were 'deeply in love'.

Just as Law had won a second year scholarship from the Ballarat Teachers' College to attend the University, so Nel was awarded a second year studentship from Melbourne Teachers' College to study for the first year of an Arts degree at Melbourne University. It was a busy time for both of them. Law's A Model Ford offered them a retreat where they could be alone although, with both of them studying at the University, they had little time to enjoy the private time together. They planned their 'trysting time' each day at a 'quarter to seven.'

> We decided we could concentrate better on our studies if we met briefly before studying; so, on most week nights, I would pick Nel up at the college at 6.40pm then drive to a dead-end street running off College Crescent behind the Melbourne Cemetery. No cars, no people, ever seemed to go there at that time. We would 'park' from 6.45 till 7.25 and I would deliver her back at the 7.30pm deadline at College.

There were strict controls in the College, particularly over women students' movements at night. The women's front door was locked at 10.30 p.m. and a Duty Girl would admit late-comers and take their names. If the student did not possess a late permit she was reported. Most students found these rules frustrating and Nel was no exception. But she was also daring. She and Law circumvented the rules:

> I reckoned that if I were locked <u>in</u> I could easily find a way of getting <u>out</u>. So on several occasions, notably wet miserable evenings, I would return Nel to College just on 10.30pm and sneak in with her, hiding behind settees in the women's lounge until the doors were locked and everyone had gone upstairs. Then Nel and I would 'park' on a couch drawn up before the Common Room fire. I found I could let myself out of the front door quite easily, with Nel locking it behind me.

Whilst Law recalls Nel's beauty, her vivaciousness and their passionate
love for each other, the members of the Law family, likewise, remember
her elegance, wit and outspokenness, but also her lack of care for other
people's feelings and her enjoyment of humiliating Law. The younger of
the Law children, who were adolescents when Law and Nel were courting, recall the stories heard about Nel's treatment of their admired Phil.
All the Law siblings can regale a version of a story when Nel and Law
were travelling on a tram along St Kilda Road and Law discovered he
had no money. He asked Nel would she mind paying and she refused,
presumably causing Law embarrassment in a crowded tram.[15]

Other stories include things Nel did which were 'just not done at that
time', such as painting her toe nails red, taking off her bra' and rolling
bare breasted in the sand, and other 'shocking' things she did, one
example being:

> When Phil was courting Nel they would go out to some paddock and
> on this occasion they had a rug and he was apparently making over-
> tures and she had a packet of matches and set fire to all the grass
> around the rug. Phil spent an hour, boiling with resentment,
> putting out this grass fire and she just laughed and laughed.[16]

Lillie was a jealous mother, particularly so in regard to Phil's girlfriends, and it was she who told the younger family members of instances
that she regarded as Nel's cruelty to Phil. Even discounting a mother's
jealousy, the Law family now agree that 'Nel was the all time deflater'[17]
and 'loved tormenting the hell out of Phil.'[18]

But Law was used to being tormented, having lived with Geof's version of it for years. Nel's particular form often embarrassed him, such as
when she demanded on one occasion that he kiss her in public;[19] or
when she riled him by arriving late for an appointment with him and
retorting to friends, 'Pooh, I'm not going to apologise to <u>him</u> I never
do!'[20] But, to Law, the good times with Nel more than made up for these
occasions. Torment was part of his fascination with her. It had also been
part of the excitement of being with Geof; and Law was always a lover of
excitement.

Meanwhile his studies continued, but the University timetable for
1937 classes was even more difficult to arrange than the previous year:

> In Part III Physics there was no evening practical work as there had
> been in Part II. There was a Saturday morning practical class, but
> that only gave me three hours a week of the eight hours a week prac-
> tical work we were supposed to do. I gave up being Sportsmaster and
> went in and managed to get a couple of hours in on Wednesday
> afternoons when sport was on.

The Headmaster again allowed him to organise his classes so he could attend three 12.00–1.00 p.m. lectures. Despite these added time constraints, neither the quality of his teaching nor the time he gave to extra school activities was apparently adversely affected. Alfred White, Head Teacher of the Elwood Central School later remarked on Law's 'vigorous and incisive manner of teaching ... his ability to control and his tactfulness on the handling of his classes,' and also noted that he 'gave ungrudgingly of his time—ready at all times to organize and take part in extra school activities.' White concluded that Law 'is destined by his ability to reach a position in the teaching, or other service, to which few may aspire.'[21]

Ability Law may have had, but at the University, rules were rules, and the stipulated hours of attendance at practical classes had to be adhered to. During the second term Law was informed that he would not be allowed to present for the Part III Physics exam at the end of the year because his hours of practical work did not add up to the required total:

> This appalled me because my practical work was good. I had done as many experiments as anyone else, my marks were as good as anyone else's and it just seemed absurd that I would be delayed another whole year because of some statute that demanded so many hours a week, regardless of how well you did them.

Almost immediately an Infantile Paralysis epidemic broke out and the Elwood Central School was closed for five weeks. Tragic as this epidemic proved for many Victorians, Law regarded the closing of the school as a 'stroke of remarkable luck':

> During that time I went into the University ... There were no more experiments for me to do, I'd finished the year's work, all I had to do was to get my hours up. So I'd go and sign on in the book and then sign off later and spend the time studying either in the laboratory or around in the University library. [22]

One of his lecturers had told him he had done so well in Physics II he should consider doing honours in Physics III. With the extra study time he now had, he took the advice and enrolled for Honours, which, at that time, entailed sitting for an extra examination paper at the end of the year. He was successful and gained first class honours in Physics III. He had now completed all the major subjects, but was still required to complete the reading courses in French A and B and German A and B. Nel had completed her own year at University but she was unable, as Law had been, to pay for another year. Instead, she had been appointed to a teaching position in the country township of Beaufort. So, with Nel away and there being few other distractions, Law decided to attempt the four subjects in one year.

4.

During the 1930s Geof and Law saw little of each other throughout the teaching period but often spent their school holidays together. Perhaps partly because of this limited contact, they now enjoyed one another's company, although Geof was often irritated by what he regarded as 'Phil's finicky ways'.[23] The stories of their holidays in their beloved mountains are crammed with tales of hazards, usually from the weather conditions or dangerous terrain, but often from blow-outs in car tyres, flat batteries, or other car related mishaps on narrow mountain tracks.

In 1932 Law had his first introduction to the Australian Alps. He and a university friend planned to take a pack-horse across the Bogong High Plains, but when they arrived at Harrietville they found there were no horses available. They decided to carry the supplies themselves: 'We tied our blankets in rolls with rope and we strung all our gear around our shoulder.' That day they walked from Harrietville via Mt St Bernard to the Mt Hotham Chalet and then on to the cattlemen's hut, Dibbins Hut, 32 miles in all. From there they pushed on, over several days, across the Bogong High Plains to Glen Wills.

A few years later, probably 1935 or 1936, Law and Geof decided to try the latest craze, skiing. The only place they knew to ski was at Mt Buffalo. Once on the mountain, Geof recalls, Law had 'his first (and last) snow-ball fight'. Then, tired of this frivolity, he 'fronted up to some girl' and asked 'Do you mind if I have a loan of your skis?' She obliged, and Law and Geof made their 'first attempts at skiing on a gentle slope at Buffalo'. Geof, who maintains that he never had the physical courage of Law, recalls 'I was terrified and inclined to throw myself off if the pace got too quick.'[23] Despite this, the skiing at Buffalo seemed fairly tame. Hearing that Mt Hotham was more exciting, they drove across to Mt St Bernard where the road was blocked by snow. They found a cattlemen's hut where they set up camp for a couple of days, almost freezing in their inadequate clothes. They went to the Hospice at Mt St Bernard and asked to hire skis. 'Can you ski?' they were asked 'Oh yes,' they said 'we've just come from Mt Buffalo where we've been skiing.' Their story was believed and they set off for Mt Hotham, about 7 miles away. Their skis were primitive and badly worn and, combined with their lack of skiing ability, they got into difficulties when trying to climb up to the summit of Mt Hotham. Law recalls:

> It was about 4 o'clock in the afternoon and the snow had iced up
> and even for good skiers this would have been difficult, but for a
> couple of young beginners it was pretty terrifying, because the ski
> edges wouldn't grip properly. We were in danger of sliding right
> back to our starting point again, or sliding over the edge to the drop

down into the valley. When we got three quarters of the way up Geof froze in sheer terror. He wasn't game to put one foot forward or one back in case he slipped. We had a five minute rest and sort of got together our mental resources and our courage and we finally made it to the top of Hotham.

Stretching out in front of them was a beautiful run down to a saddle leading to the Hotham Chalet. So they 'went hell for leather' towards the saddle. Unfortunately at the bottom of the run was a churned-up snow area where people had been playing. Law hit a mound at a great speed, catapulted into the air and landed on his face. With a tooth through his lip, blood all over his face, skis on his back, he and Geof headed to the Chalet and treated themselves to a comfortable, warm night.

Despite this inauspicious ending, they were spurred on by the success of their Mt Buffalo and Mt Hotham trip. Geof's next plan was to climb Mt Kosciusko, part of the Snowy Mountains and Australia's highest mountain. Although there already was a road from the north-east almost to the top of Mt Kosciusko, Geof's plan was to climb up the western side of the range which consists of precipitous slopes, deep gorges and rocky spurs. Mt Kosciusko is not a high mountain in world terms, but is more than double the height of the highest mountain in the Grampians.

During the summer Geof and Law made themselves skis, stocks and rucksacks. They bought army boots, strengthened the soles and rubbed in Dubbin to waterproof them. Geof had made enquiries from the Corryong Police about access into the area and was advised that there was 'little to be gained in wandering around the gullies of Kosciusko' and bluntly told to 'stay home'.[24] Geof disregarded the advice and during the May 1936 school holidays they set out to Khancoban. They hired a pack horse and arrived safely at Geehi Hut. Geof's plan was to walk up Hannels Spur from Geehi along a track that had been cleared a few years earlier by two stockmen, Hannel and Pierce. The stockmen had planned to run their cattle during the summer in the lush pastures in the Alps, but the plan had failed because of the difficulty of getting the cattle up the steep track out of Geehi. Consequently, the track had hardly ever been used.[25] Geof and Law spent the next two days searching for it. Finally, with help from some passing drovers, they found it. The following morning, their rucksacks crammed with food for a week and their skis on their backs, they set out again and, as Geof recalls in a note to Law:

[We] forded icy water (feet numb) and about 3 miles down track forded river again and started the Spur. This is approximately 6000 ft., the biggest drop in Australia. I was exhausted all the way, you drove me on up. Eventually snow-gum, then boulders, then the Abbott Range, where we had our first sight of the Seaman Hut.[26]

They were pushing themselves hard to arrive at Seaman's Hut before dark and before they collapsed. They were both so exhausted they discarded their skis and some of their equipment and stumbled on without them to Seaman's Hut, returning the next day to retrieve them.

The area they climbed that day from Geehi River at 1 640 ft, to Abbott Peak at 7 200 ft contains the entire range of vegetation that grows on the western side of the Main Ridge. They had passed through graceful, white trunked, eucalyptus that gave way to the sub–alpine snow gums and finally to the alpine snow grasses, herbs and colonies of wild-flowers.[27] Almost fifty years later, with the Hannels Spur track having been recleared, the Geehi Club advises walkers to do this trip by descending from Mt. Kosciusko to Geehi. Even this descent is classed as a full day's strenuous walk and a warning is given that it should be attempted only by experienced walkers carrying a compass and maps of the area.[28] The Law brothers had completed the ascent, a total of seven miles, in one day, without maps or compass, and with skis and rucksacks strapped to their backs.

They camped at Seaman's Hut and a day or so later, when light snow was falling, they were able to practise their skiing. 'So we had this glorious time on our own,' Law later recorded, 'stuck on the top of this mountain, knowing no one would ever be anywhere near us.' The alpine area had won their hearts, and Seaman's Hut became the retreat of these two young men, just as Jimmy's Hut in the Grampians had been when they were adolescents. 'Several summers we stayed three weeks there,' said Geof, 'no expenses! Went in the T Model Ford and bought three weeks' food at Cooma. There were miles of continuous drifts in December and January each year so we practised skiing; took walks around glacial lakes and studied alpine flora, magnificent snow flowers.'[29]

Letters written to Nel from Law during these summers contain some of the few written descriptions of the beauty of an area and its effect on him. Later in his life he would always be involved with something more practical than writing about nature. In the summer of 1937 he wrote to Nel:

Another perfect night! I've never known it so mild up here—it must have been scorching hot down on the plains. The stars up here don't wink—they blaze down with a sort of brazen stare. (I won't burden you with the scientific explanation!) And it is so still, Nell, and one is so alone, except for the stars. I spent half an hour watching one and feeling very happy.

And then to cap it, old ma Nature turned on an Aurora Australis! Down in the south, to the right of the Southern Cross, there suddenly appeared half a dozen cold, ice–white slender shafts of light reaching up from the horizon—like searchlight beams only narrower—moving gradually from right to left and alternating in intensity so that they appeared to reach up and then sink back down

again. All the while, at the limit of the beams, was the warmest soft-
est crimson glow! It lasted half an hour.[30]

The drifts they skied on doubled as their ice chest in which they would
store their supplies of food that stayed fresh and firm, unlike, Law disparagingly remarked, 'beach camping' with its 'flies and sand, and oily
butter and bad meat!'[31] The thousands of wild-flowers that bloomed, Law
imagined, compared with 'Switzerland in spring'.[32]

At Christmas time Seaman's Hut became a drop-in centre for other
walkers who stayed one or two evenings in the hut, or day trippers passing through on the road up to Mt Kosciusko, who called in to see the hut
and have a chat. 'The two biggest curses in this place,' Law wrote to Nel,
'are blowflies and tourists. Give me the blowflies!'[33] But campers were different and the stories of the brothers' time at Seaman's Hut are tales of
fascinating characters they met; of delicious five-course meals concocted
by Geof from the various campers' meagre cooking rations, followed by
music and song, and occasional moonlight skiing.

During the day the two young men explored the area, their particular
love being the beautiful glacial moraine lake, Lake Albina, nestling
between Mount Townsend and Muellers Peak. Even in summer there
was ice often floating on the surface and Geof would skylark around
swimming in the lake. Law's loathing of being cold kept him out most of
the time, but it didn't stop him suggesting they 'revert to nature' and
experience the freedom of walking nude across the range. They only
tried it once, for it proved less exhilarating than they had anticipated,
plagued as they were with troublesome March flies and the worry that
they might encounter other walkers.[34]

Summer in the Australian Alps taught them much about the fickle-
ness of the weather patterns in high regions. They learnt to take heed of
certain signs before an approaching storm, the 'absence of the usual
hordes of blowflies' for example, or a biting wind combined with 'the
sight of an ancient drover herding sheep down the road', would set them
chopping and stacking wood, covering and tying down the car and
preparing for a storm.[35] Storms were frequent in the summer, but Law
revelled in their power and spectacle and described them in detail in a
letter to Nel:

> Black clouds seemed to have banked up from no-where and there
> was a still, warm oppressive hush, while half the horizon blazed with
> sheet lightning. I've never seen such a display. For no complete
> second did it remain light, nor did it for a second stay black, but the
> two alternated so rapidly that one's eyes ached with the rapid alter-
> nation.

But, as usual, he had 'no time to stand and admire it' and he was off to
collect some friends' gear from their car:

We hadn't gone 100 yards when it hit us—a sudden deafening blast of wind that struck us like a wave, and immediately after rain and hail. And snow clothes are no protection against rain! Inside a minute we were soaked to the skin, and the hail grew so big that it bruised us through our caps.[36]

Unbeknown to him then, throughout these experiences Law was accumulating knowledge that he would later draw on to design clothing suitable for sub–Antarctic and Antarctic conditions.

The Kosciusko Plateau had been explored in 1901 and 1907 by a party which included the well respected Australian scientist, Professor Edgeworth David, who established clear evidence of former glacier ice on the Main Range.[37] In 1909 Professor David played an important role in Australia's activity in the Antarctic when he went as Chief Scientific Officer, with Dr Douglas Mawson as Physicist, on Ernest Shackleton's voyage to Antarctica on the *Nimrod*.[38]

Law was unaware of this particular Australian connection between the scientific research in both the Mt Kosciusko area and the Antarctic, but his interest in both skiing and adventure in cold conditions had been aroused by his experiences in the Australian Alps. As a consequence he began to read the then popular books on Antarctica, the writings of Amundsen, Shackleton, Scott and Mawson, and recalls that Appsley Cherry-Garrard's book on Antarctic exploration, *The Worst Journey in the World*, was still 'probably the greatest Antarctic book'.

The stimulation of these writings may have been the trigger that led him into an escapade that he was later to regard as 'about as hare–brained as anything I've ever done'. In 1938 he was transferred to the prestigious Melbourne Boys' High School, where he taught Matriculation Maths and Physics. There he met another teacher, Bruce Osborne, who was a fitness fanatic, a long-distance runner and an enthusiastic novice skier. With these attributes, it is easy to imagine the excitement each would generate in the other, culminating in a plan to climb Hannels Spur to Mt Kosciusko. This was the climb that Law and Geof had done a couple of years previously, but Law and Osborne planned their trip for winter. To their knowledge this had not been done and they hoped to be the first to do it.

During the week before they departed, Melbourne received torrential rain and continuous snow fell on the Alps. When the two men arrived at Scammel's Waterfall Farm to pick up the pack-horse, Scammel told them they could not use the track Geof and Law had taken on their previous climb because the recent heavy rains had caused the river to flood. Scammel offered to take them, by horseback, along a different route. They agreed and Scammel, with a pack-horse loaded with their gear, led the way. This route took them along spurs which dropped sharply away, hundreds of feet, down to the river. The mountain ponies were skilled in this terrain and picked their way competently over fallen trees and branches and traversed steep slopes and boulders. Nevertheless Law, unused to horse-riding and not trusting the ponies' ability, was terrified. With great relief, at least on his part, they finally arrived at Geehi Hut. Scammel returned to Khancoban, taking the horses with him.

The next day Law and Osborne rose about 4 a.m. and, laden with rucksacks, skis and stocks, set off for the beginning of Hannels Spur. Within a short while they were almost struck by tragedy. Part way across the second river crossing, in thigh deep, bitterly cold water, Osborne was knocked off his feet and washed downstream. Law rushed along the bank, waded in, grabbed Osborne's arm and the two struggled out. On their second attempt at the crossing Law stripped, tied one of the climbing ropes around himself and, half wading and half swimming, managed to get across to the other side. Using the ropes, they were able to ferry Osborne and all their equipment safely across. They lit a fire in an effort to get some warmth back into their bodies and then continued on.

They had expected the snow line to begin at approximately three thousand feet, but found snow, one to two feet deep, right down to the river level. This not only made it difficult to find the Hannels Spur track but, when they did find it, the low-hanging branches of the snow-laden trees often obscured the track. All the way to the tree line, some 4 000 ft up, the two of them had to beat the snow off the branches with their ski-stocks to uncover the track. Their feet became entangled in the thick undergrowth beneath the snow, the skis on their shoulders snagged in the branches above and they became saturated and even more exhausted.

Once out of the tree line, however, they were able to put on their skis, but the snow was deep powder snow, a texture they had never experienced before. With each step forward, their skis slipped back. In desperation they improvised by cutting lengths of rope and winding them around their skis. This allowed them to push forward but it was hard going. Each time they put their skis down they would sink up to their knees in fine, light powder snow. Nervousness at the conditions and the effort needed to pull the skis out to drag themselves upwards, began to sap their energy.

Within a couple of hundred feet of the summit of Mt Townsend the weather, which had been threatening, took an abrupt turn for the worse, and a blizzard developed with strong cutting winds and heavy snow. Visibility was zero, their drenched clothing had frozen solid like a sheath of ice armour and they knew their chances of ever finding Seaman's Hut in those conditions were almost nil. They decided to abandon the project and return. After sheltering behind a rock, changing into fresh woollen clothing and preparing a much needed snack of thick cocoa and biscuits, they headed back down.

But the descent was even more difficult than the climb up. They had removed the ropes off their skis, and their lack of control, combined with the speed of the skis on the dry powder snow, was frightening. They planned another, less hazardous, method: a series of long traverses, crisscrossing their way down the slope. At the end of each long traverse they had to make a 180-degree turn. Their inexperience as skiers made this manoeuvre impossible. The only way they could manage the turn was to throw themselves over, struggle up out of the snow, face their skis in the opposite direction and begin another long traverse.

Always nagging at Law's mind was the possibility of one of them breaking an ankle, or pulling a muscle, and he tried to plan what they would do in such an eventuality. The uninjured man, he reasoned, would be faced with a dilemma. He could either leave his injured companion and walk for two days to get help and walk back in again, by which time his friend would certainly have frozen to death. Or he could stay with him, in which case both would be likely to freeze to death. No alternative gave him peace of mind and his anxiety made him take extra care, and he continued to traverse in this awkward, exhausting, but relatively careful, fashion.

When they finally arrived at the tree line, they thankfully removed their skis and were able to stumble back, down the track they had originally beaten, to Geehi Flat. They stripped and forded the freezing water of the river crossing in the dark and heavy rain. In a later recollection of the event, Law commented that they had been 'lucky to get away with it' and made special mention of their 'courageous decision'[39] to abandon the project and return. Law saw courage, not so much in attempting an adventure but, in admitting defeat.

This trip became one of the earliest experiences that formed the basis of Law's self-perpetuating legend known as 'Law Luck'. It had other consequences as well. Later, when he was the Leader of Antarctic expeditions, he enforced a regulation that three men were the minimum number allowed to venture out for any field work.

One other significant formative experience occurred at about this time. This one caused him to abandon competitive boxing. He had entered State Amateur Championships in the featherweight class and had won the first fight. During the first two rounds each fighter knocked the other down three times. By the third round 'each of us had very little left. So we threw everything at each other that we could. But each of us was too tired to knock the other down any more. We retired to our corners at the end of the third round to await the verdict.' To his dismay, the referee's verdict was that the points were even and he ordered an extra round. Law was completely exhausted and reasoned that his opponent would be as well.

> I hadn't a punch left and knew that if I just pushed each arm forward, time after time towards his face and body it didn't matter whether they hurt him or not, so long as they touched him and registered points.

Geof and Phil at Mt Buffalo (1936).

Phil and Nel (1940s).

Law, Senior Scientific Officer, Albert Park Barracks (1947).

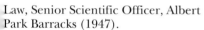

Law in cosmic ray laboratory on *Wyatt Earp* (1948).

Group Captain Stuart Campbell. (Courtesy
Mr A. Campbell-Drury)

G. Compton,
A. Campbell-Drury,
L. Macey and
F. Jacka, Heard
Island (1948).
(Courtesy Mr A.
Campbell-Drury)

HMALST 3501,
later renamed
HMAS Labuan.
(Courtesy Mr A.
Campbell-Drury)

Law used these tactics for the whole of the round and won the fight on points. But when he went back to his corner, he felt so sick he couldn't stand up. He was helped out of the ring, undressed and put under a shower, where he was violently ill. The following morning he awoke with a splitting headache and his balance was upset. He did not know what was wrong, nor did he go to a doctor for a diagnosis. Whenever he attempted to stoop he would fall down. During the next three weeks he had searing pain in the back of his head and his eyesight was distorted. He tried to train for the finals that were approaching, but every time he punched the bag his head 'nearly lifted off'. In the end he had to withdraw from the tournament. The major symptoms disappeared after three weeks, but for almost six months he had dizzy spells and experienced strange effects on his eyesight. 'I realised that for someone with an academic aspiration it would be ridiculous for me to go on with competitive boxing because I only needed another fight of that nature to suffer permanent damage.'

From then on he confined himself to gymnasium work, training with other university men, and coaching the University Boxing Team for Intervarsity competitions. Nevertheless, he always believed that boxing was a valuable skill, in that he was never afraid, physically, of any person:

> That meant that in the rough and tumble of leadership in Antarctica, where on occasion men might be drunk or aggressive or very angry, at no time did I have to condition my behaviour because of any aspect of fear of the other person or fear of getting hurt.

5.

Whilst Law could tolerate physical hurt, he found the strain of his stormy relationship with Nel psychologically debilitating. His frustrations, joys and hurts during the two years she was in Beaufort were poured out in his letters to her. Often he felt embarrassed after openly expressing his feelings and asked her, at the end of some of the letters, to destroy them. Luckily for the reconstruction of his life story, Nel ignored his requests. But, unfortunately these provide only a lop-sided view of their relationship, for she kept most of his letters and he kept none of hers.

The couple were seldom able to see one another now that Nel was in Beaufort. They were hampered by lack of money, and frustrated with letters that crossed, or didn't arrive or, when they did, didn't say what each wanted to hear. Alternatively, Law was elated by other letters that left him in a state where 'all is confusion of happiness and ecstatic tender joy.'[40]

Added to this was their constant worry about Nel's health. Nel had always been classed, by herself and her family, as 'delicate' and would become abnormally exhausted after a game of tennis. She suffered badly from colds and hay fever. This delicacy had been recently confirmed when the Education Department Medical Officers refused to allow Nel to be a contributor to the superannuation scheme because of a murmur they detected in her heart. Little was known about her particular heart problem at that time, and her condition was not diagnosed any further. But Nel's ill-health shaped much of their later relationship and her physical frailty is strikingly at odds both with her bright, strong character and Law's physical vigour.

Further exacerbating the situation between them was Nel's involvement with two other men. One was a New Zealander, to whom she had given, before she met Law, what she called a 'Gypsy promise'. Even as late as 1938 she could not decide whether she wanted this promise to be binding or not. The second man lived at Beaufort and he too claimed to be in love with her. After two years Law finally wrote to Nel and listed some solutions, coupled with ultimatums, about either finishing off the affair with the New Zealander or with him. He added a final rejoinder 'Do you think He would consider the promise kept if He saw you in my arms? You pride yourself on your common sense—let's have some of it!' Law's authoritative tone was diluted somewhat by a reminder, at the end of the letter, for Nel to 'take some Cod Liver Oil and look after yourself.'[41] In another letter he told her, with obvious exasperation, that he thought the Beaufort man-friend could do with a bit of the 'bitingly truthful words you have lashed me back to sanity with at times' and suggested some more tactics to put a finish to that particular relationship as well.[42]

Law and Nel loaned one another books and one which particularly impressed them was *We the Living* by a new novelist, Ayn Rand. It is not surprising that an author, whose later writings would spell out more clearly her philosophy of Objectivism—'founded on the supremacy of reason, with individualism, self-interest, science, technology and progress as its consequences'[43]—would appeal to Law.

Running through the letters to Nel is Law's love and his constant concern for, and advice about, her health. He admonished her for working or playing too hard. He begged her to 'get better and stronger—please no flu, no heart, no giddy fits! Write and tell me you are resting and eating, and that the "frailty" has vanished.'[44] He goaded her, or tried to, into eating more, 'Stuff it down, somehow!'[45] It is not clear whether she took his advice. He certainly didn't take hers when she, obviously concerned for his health, advised him to take 'long walks'. He could not do this, he explained, because he did not have enough time, instead he would 'try the strenuous exercise recipe again—dashing round the block morning and night.'[46]

They had pet names for one another, 'Nelw' and 'Philw', the origin of which neither can remember. As with most love letters, they were often moody, with swings of mood sometimes occurring in the same letter. In one he told her, 'I'm sick and tired of thinking and worrying, fighting and hating. I'm just so damn miserable and tired I could lie down and not get up again' and finished off with 'O skip it all Nelw-love. I'm going to bed. Write me a nice loving letter.'[47] Sometimes he even noted the change of mood himself and commented, 'I started out being sorry and sentimental and I've talked myself as hard and practical as a crowbar.'[48] Or, on another occasion 'I started out to write a love-letter and it's developed into a self-righteous sort of lecture.'[49] Overall, their letters were simply love letters, and his fascination with her particular blend of elusiveness and ridicule is plain to see:

> You are not of this world, Nelw, and never have been—I can never think of you as a real human being! Mixed up with you are all kinds of elusive, fairy-like, hovering things which never alight on this everyday world long enough for me to catch up with. So more and more am I constrained to flit away in pursuit of you, leaving more and more frequently the mundane things of this life behind me. Then you chide me and call me a mad ass![50]

But 'flitting' and 'leaving the mundane things of this life behind' belonged to affairs of the heart and were not Law's way of approaching life. By the end of 1938, having successfully completed his Bachelor of Science degree and receiving an Inspector's report that described him as a 'A young teacher of outstanding ability,'[51] he again took stock of how and where he was heading:

> Here I was, having been in the Education Department for ten years, still in the lowest Fifth Class on the Primary Schools Roll, with an 'A' teaching mark and a first class honours degree, yet number three hundred and something on a 'promotions list' from which some thirty or forty a year were being upgraded. I decided that, if I had to mark time for years, before gaining promotion, I might as well spend the time profitably. So I ... applied for two years' leave from the Education Department and enrolled for M.Sc. at the Physics Department of Melbourne University.

To stretch his slender finances he sold his car and, at the age of 26, after living away from home for eight years, he returned to live with his family in the Principal's residence at the Melbourne Teachers' College.

Notes

1. Russel Ward, *A Nation for a Continent, the history of Australia 1901–1975*, Heinemann Educational Australia, Victoria, 1977, p. 190.
2. EDR, ADM.
3. Victoria Year Book, 1933–34, p. 273, cited in Don Garden, *The Melbourne Teacher Training Colleges*, Heinemann Educational Australia, 1982, p. 139
4. L. J. Blake (ed.), *Vision and Realisation*, vol.1, Education Department of Victoria, 1973, p. 498.
5. Blake (ed.), p. 895.

58   A MAN FOR ANTARCTICA

6. Don Garden, *The Melbourne Teacher Training Colleges, From Training Institution to Melbourne State College, 1870–1982*, Heinemann Educational Australia, 1982, p. 140.
7. EDR, no. 27998.
8. Blake, p. 895.
9. Blake, vol.2, p. 776.
10. EDR, no. 27998.
11. Richard Thompson to author, July 1990.
12. EDR, no. 27998.
13. Garden, p. 146.
14. Law's sisters to author, 6 May 1988.
15. Ibid.
16. Ibid.
17. Ibid.
18. Geoffrey Law to author, 27 July 1988.
19. Law to Nel Allan, Monday 8.30, 1938, LP.
20. Ibid.
21. Alfred White, Head Teacher, Elwood Central School, Letter of reference, 1939.
22. Geoffrey Law to author, 27 July 1988.
23. Geoffrey Law, 'Recollections', 1989, LP.
24. Ibid.
25. Geehi Bushwalking Club, *Snowy Mountain Walks*, 1983, p. 35.
26. Geoffrey Law, 'Recollections', 1989, LP.
27. Geehi Bushwalking Club, 1983, p. 37.
28. Geehi Bushwalking Club, p. 33.
29. Geoffrey Law to author, 27 July 1988.
30. Law to Nel Allan, 26 December 1937, LP.
31. Ibid.
32. Ibid.
33. Law to Nel Allan, 2 January 1938, LP.
34. Geoffrey Law, 'Recollections', 1989, LP.
35. Law to Nel Allan, 2 January 1938, LP.
36. Law to Nel Allan, 26 December 1937, LP.
37. Geehi Bushwalking Club, 1983, p. 31.
38. R. A. Swan, *Australia in the Antarctic*, Melbourne University Press, Victoria, 1961, p. 116.
39. Law, Draft for 'You've Got to be Lucky', 1989.
40. Law to Nel Allan, Tuesday morning, 9 a.m., 1938, LP.
41. Law to Nel Allan, Sunday night, undated, LP.
42. Law to Nel Allan, 3.30 Thursday, 1938, LP.
43. Ayn Rand, *The New Left: The Anti–Industrial Revolution*, Signet, N.Y., 1971.
44. Law to Nel Allan, Wednesday 7 p.m., 1938, LP.
45. Law to Nel Allan, Sunday 3.30 p.m. 1938, LP.
46. Ibid.
47. Law to Nel Allan, after phone 9.30 p.m., 1938, LP.
48. Law to Nel Allan, 3.30 Thursday, 1938/9, LP.
49. Law to Nel Allan, Monday, 8.30, 1938/9, LP.
50. Law to Nel Allan, Thursday morning 9 a.m. 1938, LP.
51. EDR, no. 27998.

4. A University Man, 1939–1947

1.

DURING 1938 AND 1939 AUSTRALIANS WATCHED THE TENSE SITUATION in Europe and waited apprehensively as Hitler invaded one country after another. Friday, 13 January 1939, took their minds off thoughts of war to a more immediate danger. After five consecutive days of searing heat and wind, half of Victoria was ablaze with bushfires and seventy Victorians lost their lives.[1] Law, safe and walking down Lygon Street, Carlton, felt the effects from the fires with 'the sun and the sky ... obscured by smoke. Red–hot cinders were falling in the street.' The day would come to be known as 'Black Friday'.

By April of the same year the Prime Minister, Robert Menzies, warned the Australian people of the situation in Europe. 'Let no one imagine that we can stand neutral, or ... be treated as neutral in a war in which Great Britain is engaged.'[2] He urged them to remain calm and 'behave normally' in the face of increasing international uncertainty.[3]

At this time of mounting crisis, Law's own future too was far from settled. Although he was enrolled for a MSc degree, he was more excited about the prospects of a scientific position overseas with the Council for Scientific and Industrial Research. He knew his chances were slender, but he felt optimistic. 'You know,' he wrote to Nel, 'I have a sort of hunch I may fluke this job! The Law Luck is just aching to show what it can do!'[4] He had arranged numerous references, including one from G. S. Browne, Professor of Education, who wrote that Law 'stands out amongst his fellows as a natural leader.'[5] The alleged Law Luck did not come up to scratch in this case, however, and Law was not appointed.

Living with his parents and the younger Law children at the College Residence had both advantages and disadvantages and brought about various changes in their relationships. Having lived independently for eight years, he now found it difficult to cope with his mother's attempts to control his life and their relationship deteriorated. 'She wanted to know where Phil was going of a night,' Geof recalled, 'and he'd say "out". Or she would go through his stuff. She was a good mother ... but she interfered.'[6]

Lillie was seen by the students at the College as 'forbidding and stern' as she walked around in her dressing–gown to make sure the doors were locked at the allocated time in the female residence.[7] Neither she nor

Arthur knew that on many occasions students who arrived back late threw gravel on Law's window to alert him and he would go down and open the door into the Law residence. 'We would tip–toe stealthily upstairs, past my parents' bedroom and I would let them through a door from our upstairs passage into the women's quarters.'

The students at the College nicknamed Arthur, 'Tufty', the reason for which remains unclear, but from most accounts it was not meant affectionately, for Arthur did little to endear himself to his students. 'His owl–like look and his readiness to admonish, to warn and to repress' one of his staff members reasoned, 'turned attention away from his very real worth.'[8]

Somewhat surprisingly, Law's relationship with Arthur improved during this time, nourished perhaps by their mutual interest in boxing. He now had sufficient stature in Arthur's eyes to be able to influence Arthur's decisions about the younger Law children. Law had never forgiven Arthur for not buying him sporting equipment, or paying for sporting lessons or for university fees, and he was determined that the others would not be similarly deprived. At that time Wendy was showing an interest in the piano and Geof recalls that 'Phil got stuck into dad and dad said "Geof learnt to play on his own, she can do the same".' But Law insisted and Wendy was given piano lessons from one of the best teachers in Melbourne and became a fine jazz pianist, later studying with the famous jazz pianist, Graham Bell. Law also taught Wendy how to swim, correcting her stroke and coaching her on the finer points.[9] He gave Peter a clarinet, which Peter at first ignored but later took up and taught himself, finally becoming an excellent jazz clarinetist. A few years later Law demanded that Arthur pay for Peter to enrol for an Engineering degree, making Peter the only Law child to receive financial assistance from Arthur for tertiary education.

Geof too recalls the help Law gave him when he decided to study for his Diploma of Education: 'Phil wrote out all the lessons that I had to give in front of people. He was very clever at it. And when I did science, I got all his notes and all his books.'[10]

Geof and Law were now passionate about skiing and the younger Law children watched and admired their exploits. Wendy recalls that at that time there were two classes of skiers: 'the wealthy and the intrepid; the intrepid were those who made their own skis and went off and stayed in the huts dotted over the mountains.'[11] The Law brothers were most definitely in the intrepid class:

I grew up with absolute hero worship of Phil and Geof [recalls Wendy], because for weeks they would be planing wood and steaming it to bend the ends up, and waxing. And then this fascinating word 'Dubbin'. Then there would be the bindings to be screwed on and then they would make the stocks, pretty little things laced with leather. I just thought it was fantastic. None of my girl friends' brothers, nobody, did anything like this. So off they would go in a ramshackle car with the skis strapped on top and they would just disappear and we wouldn't hear anything. And then weeks later, you'd hear a car door and you would leap up and run to the front door and look out 'The boys are home. The boys are home'. And their skins would have that strange yellow colour that you get from snow and sun, yellowy brown, and they'd be peeling, ... oh so intrepid.[12]

The one relationship that did not change during those years was his and Nel's; it remained as turbulent as ever. Although he was eager to marry her, it was out of the question, for two reasons. Firstly, neither Law nor Nel could afford it and, secondly, Nel had refused Law's proposals of marriage anyway. She believed that with her particular heart problem she would not live much beyond thirty years of age and she considered it unfair on Law to get married. Thirty years later Nel's heart condition was diagnosed as a 'a hole in the heart' and she underwent extensive surgery to have it repaired. At the time the Law family did not believe the 'bad heart' story. In fact the Law sisters, rather shamefaced, now recall that they scoffed when they heard stories that Nel could not exert herself. 'Everyone used to say "what a lot of rot"'[13] whenever Nel's bad heart was mentioned. Despite her refusal to marry Law, Nel did agree to become engaged. 'I couldn't afford a diamond ring' recalled Law, 'but found a lovely little square-cut zircon.'

The two of them were in financial difficulties. Law no longer drew his teaching salary, although playing in a band on most Saturday nights and some week nights helped his finances. Nel was never good with money and she had difficulty covering her expenses whilst living at an hotel. She was still teaching in Beaufort and, now that Law had sold his car, they met less often than previously. Most of their letters during 1939 were taken up with financial matters; anticipated meetings that were thwarted because they could not afford the necessary fares or the hotel fee, 'I can't possibly go to Beaufort Nell!' Law complained in one letter, 'I'm living on less than 10/– week as it is.'

To supplement his finances whilst studying full-time, Law accepted the University's offer to take two demonstrating classes in practical Physics and began to coach several students privately.

2.

His supervisor for his MSc was the Chairman of the Physics Department, Professor Thomas Laby. To Law, Laby was 'the first mind of world class that I had known', but he found him difficult to work with. Law had proposed to Laby that his topic for his MSc would be research on direction finders and radio beams for aeroplanes. The topic appealed to Law, not only because he believed that the worsening situation in Europe would make such research valuable, but also because he thought it would be fun and he would be able to spend a lot of time at Essendon aerodrome.

Laby rejected the proposed research topic and did not suggest another one. Law fiddled round for two to three months with little to do, chafing at not working and railing against Laby's waste of his time. Then one day, Law jubilantly told Nel, 'Prof. Laby pulled me up as I was leaving at 5pm and gave me a job to do. Thank G. I have something to do!'[14] His job consisted of two preliminary short term projects, both to be completed before deciding what was to be his major research topic.

One project was the construction of a direct current amplifier and ionization chamber to measure the dose rate of x–rays being emitted from the new Van der Graf electrostatic generator that had just been completed in the Physics Department. The second project was construction of two condenser plates (made of silvered glass, for incorporation in equipment designed by Victor Hopper for the measurement of the charge on the electron) and the accurate measurement by an interferometer method of the distance between the plates.

He was now so busy that he set up a working routine, spending the full day at the University, without a break for lunch. 'I find I get on far better without it', he told Nel, 'feel better, eat better, don't get so sleepy during afternoons, and have an extra hour to work.'[15] At 5 p.m. he returned to the College residence for his evening meal, and then conducted private coaching lessons between 7–8 p.m. after which he spent time at the library delving into scientific journals. The work was interesting and challenging and he loved it:

I've only got 3 weeks to finish the job [he explained to Nel]. I'll be working harder than I have ever worked in my life I guess. The funny part is I don't mind—I'm enjoying it in fact! Though God only knows what I'll do when it comes to actually putting the thing together. Anyway in my present mood I'd willingly work all day and all night, I'm so keen.[16]

For Law, time and productivity were closely linked with personal worth; indeed he exemplifies the assertion that 'to achieve is to be'.

Although Britain and France had declared war on Germany on 3 September 1939, there had been virtually no fighting during the following northern hemisphere winter, and the period, until May 1940, would later be known as the 'Phoney War'. Numbers volunteering for the Second Australian Imperial Force were lower than expected, only 19 654 during October to December 1939. Those who did enlist were called 'the Thirtyniners' and even branded as 'economic conscripts' by people who were critical of Australians going to the war.[17]

Before the invasion of France, considerable frustration existed amongst the students and staff of the University, as they felt that the Government and the University's policy of 'business as usual' was unacceptable.[18] Many complained that full use was not being made of the technical facilities available at the University. This frustration culminated in many enlisting in the armed forces.

At the beginning of 1940 Law was officially appointed as a Senior Demonstrator in the Physics Department and Professor Laby suggested he also apply for a Tutorship at Newman College. Law was successful but found it 'hard work existing and studying'. Financially he was now better off and he enjoyed teaching at Newman. This rubbed off on the students, who remember the enthusiasm he brought to the classroom:

> Phil, in a word, was excellent. He was most enthusiastic, universally liked, had an incredible memory, blinking eyes, always blinking, knew you all, most enthusiastic about teaching. I think we medical students were not seen as 'real' students because we were only doing a year of Physics, but Phil seemed to be able to make the subject relevant to us. It was his enthusiasm.[19]

Another student also remembers that from Law's tutorials 'You learned a lot. He was encouraging but not demanding. You wanted to strive to be better.'[20] Fifty years later, this same student could even remember Law's appearance at that time: 'He was a very neat and tidy dresser, dapper, in light blue sports trousers, blue sports coat and soft rubber-soled shoes.'[21]

Law had just completed the second of his two short Masters projects when, in April 1940, Germany invaded western Europe and World War II began in earnest. By now the attitude to Australians joining the forces had changed and more people began to speak about it being their 'duty' to help the Empire. The numbers of volunteers into the services escalated.

In 1940 Professor Laby was appointed Chairman of the newly formed Optical Munitions Panel which had been set up to advise the Ordnance Production Directorate of the Ministry of Munitions on matters relating to the production of optical instruments for the three Armed Services. Laby immediately issued a directive that all research work conducted by graduates in the Natural Philosophy Department be directed toward the solution of the numerous scientific and technical problems that arose in relation to optical munitions. The topics selected for Law's MSc thesis were 'the metrology of optical components' and 'the protection of optical instruments from deterioration due to fungus and condensation in tropical climates'.

Although Law was not prepared to join the Services until he had completed his degree, he resolved to do something constructive towards the war effort. He and another staff member, Alf Butcher, called a meeting of all students who were prepared to assist the national effort. The meeting was held in the Union Theatre and, to Law's and Alf's astonishment and delight, over 300 students attended. Law was a good speaker, enjoyed a public performance and knew what he wanted to achieve. This meeting gave him the opportunity to bring these skills together. 'It was an exciting and exhilarating experience,' Law recalled, 'having all those people in the palm of your hand, able to persuade them to do something you thought was important.' From this meeting 30–40 groups formed, each to work on its own area of interest, each with its own elected leader who reported to the executive body of what was to be known as the 'University National Service' (UNS).

During the next two years the UNS launched an ambulance appeal, established War Savings Groups and a scheme by which Savings Certificates could be purchased by weekly instalments paid to the Union Office. Students assisted tutors in marking RAAF Correspondence Course papers.[22] During the summer vacations the students harvested fruit in the Shepparton district where a manpower shortage threatened the loss of the valuable and urgently needed crop. Students conducted social service work and set up a Waste Products Depot with materials gathered from all university departments, sorted and sold for recycling. Paper collection was sometimes carried out with a little too much enthusiasm. One student later reported that the Australian Medical Association's collection of early colonial medical journals was barely retrieved from a van before it left for the pulp mill.[23] A Physical Fitness campaign, which brought together the expertise of the Physical Education School and the Faculty of Medicine, was established and included a free medical examination, exercises, gymnastics, medicine ball work, and free movement exercises. Track and field athletics, boxing and wrestling, swimming and cross country running were also part of the scheme.[24]

Nel was proud of Law's UNS effort although, characteristically, she described it in indulgent and mocking tones to her brother-in-law, then in the RAAF:

Oh! Phil is a Patriot too! All on his little own, he addressed the Uni. and organized and buggered about and telephoned and worried for weeks n' weeks n' weeks and then suddenly posters and papers and Everything announced that Philw—my Philw—our Philw—was President and everything of the University National Service and now is he sorry because he has to werk and werke and wirk—all for Red, White and Blue! Oh, well, I'm pretty glad meself because it keeps him out of Other Things.[25]

Law was always miffed that *Farrago*, the University paper, paid scant attention to the work of the UNS, but then, as a student later pointed out, *Farrago* had failed even to mention the outbreak of war.[26]

By the end of 1940 Law had completed his Master of Science. Life should have looked more promising for him and Nel in 1941, for Nel had been transferred to a school in the Melbourne suburb of

Williamstown and they were able to be together more often, but the war had taken a turn for the worse. Germany had taken Bulgaria, and Yugoslavia was soon to fall. With his Masters degree completed, Law now decided to join the RAAF and become more actively involved in the war effort. Nel was displeased with his decision to go into the services, but did not actively oppose it. Nor did Professor Laby when Law told him of his decision. Laby responded, 'Law, it is not the policy of this department to stand in the way of any man who wishes to serve his country in a more active capacity.' So Law applied and on 19 March 1941 received advice of his acceptance with the rank of 'Pilot Officer' and an order to report to RAAF Station, Laverton at 10 a.m. on 25 March 1941, in readiness to commence a Navigation Instructors' Course.[27]

He resigned from the University, was given farewell parties from friends and colleagues and presented himself at Laverton on the morning of March 25. After listening to an introductory talk and then collecting his uniform and equipment he was called to the office of the Commanding Officer who said to him:

> I'm very sorry Law, but you will have to go back ... Your professor has complained that he is losing staff that he needs for the war effort that the Physics Department is carrying out and he has invoked manpower regulations to have us release you and allow you to go back.

Law had to return to the Physics Department and endure the embarrassment of friends, who had so recently farewelled him, showing surprise when they saw him and commenting 'Hello, what are you doing back here?' or, 'Didn't you go to the war?'

Law never found out why Laby blocked him from joining up for he felt he was neither sufficiently senior nor experienced enough to be indispensable to the Department. He always suspected Laby disliked him.

The day after his return from Laverton he appeased some of his anger by writing a report on the undertakings of the UNS during 1940. After listing all the activities, he criticised the repeated attempts by various people 'ignorant of the whole idea', to belittle and discredit the Physical Fitness scheme by referring slightingly to them as 'Physical jerks'. He sniped at the lamentably low participation rate of students in university sport and physical fitness programs, and concluded with the statement that 'to be really successful and worthwhile it should be compulsory for all students to take part, unless physically unfit.'[28] Law found writing an invaluable outlet with which to relieve his frustrations and he would use it as a palliative throughout his life. Later on the act of writing would often be sufficient to curtail his anger and the draft letter or report would frequently not be sent.

Changes were now occurring in the academic side of the University where, in general, students were encouraged to finish their courses as quickly as possible and move into activities associated with the war. In many departments special courses were introduced, or existing courses modified to conform with specific war-time needs. Facilities at the university began to be used more extensively for investigative and developmental purposes and the Ministry of Munitions frequently made use of the University's many workshops to manufacture goods needed urgently for the war effort.[29]

On Law's return from Laverton, Professor Laby put him to work with his optical munitions team for the Department of Munitions under the auspices of the Optical Munitions Panel. Law was responsible for the design, construction and testing of an instrument for measuring the radii of curvature of lenses. He also had to work on the tropic proofing of optical instruments as well as assisting Dr Jim Rogers, Secretary of the Panel, with administrative work for the Panel.

Working with Professor Laby became increasingly more difficult. Students were frustrated with him as well. One of them, John Fyfield, recalls Laby proudly telling the students that the yellow dog-eared lecture notes from which he was reading were the very same notes he had taken at lectures when he was eighteen. His lectures were abysmal, Fyfield recalls, completely out of date and the students quietly rebelled with almost constant murmuring throughout them. Laby frequently stopped a lecture in an effort to gain attention but with little success. By the third term Laby was no longer lecturing and the students were given a crash course in Natural Philosophy by the other members of the Department.[30]

By now Law was himself giving lectures and recalls:

I enjoyed seeing students learn. I loved the performance, the acting of being a lecturer. I enjoyed getting them in the grasp of my hand, the feeling of involving them. Never ever wanted to spend time with them [after lectures] sitting round chatting.

Both the intensity of his involvement and his control of sociability would stay with him. Whilst leading later Antarctic expeditions, he would, on many occasions, entertain the men by playing the accordion and initiating 'sing-alongs', but when he had finished he would retire to his room.

From all accounts Law was an excellent lecturer. He enjoyed it and took pains to make his lectures as interesting as possible:

As a Physics Lecturer I could set up the laboratory like a stage, with all the paraphernalia, and I could wander round doing quick experiments, making things go whizz and bang and hearing the gasps of admiration from the students.

Wendy recalls him returning to the Residence on many evenings after lectures 'bubbling and giggling with joy' over some aspect of the class. On one occasion, when he had demonstrated the properties of Liquid Air, he told her:

> I thought I might make it interesting instead of just going on about gases and things. I took in two eggs, pieces of bacon and some slices of toast on a toaster and put the eggs and bacon into the liquid air and they cooked.[31]

Marjorie was not as pleased as Wendy to hear Law's constant stories of his lecturing. She had become involved with a young man, John Liddelow, whom she later married, and she and John would be 'furious' at Law's lack of sensitivity in taking up the short time they had together.

> Phil would come in fresh and excited from his University lectures and would not GO. And John would be mumbling 'What's up with him, the egotistical so and so.' Next thing John would say 'well I have to run' and he would have missed the last tram. Phil did that sort of thing. Quite inconsiderate. He would come and talk about what had happened. Talk all the time.[32]

3.

Nel was now teaching at a Higher Elementary School in Upwey. Reports of her teaching continued to be positive, one stating that she had a 'bright encouraging teaching manner',[33] but Nel disliked both the school and the travelling. With Law earning two salaries, their joint financial situation was easier, but the war was escalating and 'the future looked grim', Law recalled. Nel changed her mind about marrying and they decided that if the war was going to kill them they at least should have some life together beforehand. They planned their wedding for what proved to be a 'black month for Australians', December 1941.

Nel resigned from teaching on 30 October 1941 and, by December, the war situation was far more grim than they had ever imagined. On 7 December the Japanese bombed the American fleet at Pearl Harbor and conducted simultaneous raids on Malaya, Singapore, the Philippines, Guam, Hong Kong, Wake, Midway and Ocean Islands. The following day Australia declared war on Japan and the news was announced to the people of Australia as they went to work on Monday morning. The Prime Minister, John Curtin, in a broadcast speech, announced 'This is the gravest hour in our history.' On 10 December Japanese aircraft destroyed two British battle cruisers off the east coast of Malaya, leaving no major Allied ships to dispute Japanese domination of east Asian waters.[34]

Suddenly there was a greater feeling of urgency about civil defence and blackout conditions were enforced. In Melbourne, windows were curtained or screened, no street lights were lit, car lights were shielded with louvered masks or painted blue and buses were camouflaged. The casual approach to air-raid precautions was laid to rest, drills became more regular and both civilians and those in the Services were rostered for duty on searchlights and anti-aircraft guns.[35]

Amidst the gloom, Nel and Law were married on 20 December 1941 in Scots Church, Collins Street, Melbourne. It was an afternoon wedding, with a wedding breakfast at the Wentworth Hotel:

> Nel's parents and mine were teetotallers, so the breakfast was to be 'dry'. We told all our young friends that we would meet them after the 'breakfast' at the Cafe Latin (our favourite restaurant) for dinner.
>
> Meanwhile Nel and I went to our room in the Australia Hotel, Collins Street, and changed clothes. I filled the bath with ice and grog.
>
> We duly had a wonderful evening at the Latin with 12–15 young friends. In those days the Latin was in Exhibition Street next door to Mario's Restaurant. In the dining-room there was a kind of balcony attached to one wall and on it was a piano. After the main course I played the piano and everyone in the restaurant sang. At about 11pm we all walked down to the Australia Hotel and continued the party in our room until, about 2am, the management intervened to close it down.

Next morning they had a three-course breakfast, beginning with oysters, and then packed their bags for their brief honeymoon. Law had only been allowed a week's holiday from the University and, because of the restrictions on interstate travel, they had decided to spend their honeymoon at the comparatively close seaside resort of Cowes on Phillip Island. They had salvaged four bottles of wine from the party of the previous evening and Law packed three in his suitcase, but the fourth, 'a bottle of Tokay, thick, brown and sweet,' wouldn't fit and he put it in Nel's suitcase.

> At the hotel I was horrified to see the truck driver just throwing suitcases from the pile on the truck down onto the pavement. When I picked up Nel's case there was an ominous trickle of brown fluid from one corner and my heart sank. Nel's carefully chosen trousseau garments and delicate fabric underclothing were dripping with Tokay.
>
> I have never admired her more. She set her lips and said nothing for a minute or two as she unpacked. Then she said—'You can wash these and hang them out.'
>
> I washed them in the hand-basin, wrung them out, carried them

downstairs and hung them on the lines in the backyard of the hotel. I was highly embarrassed as I stood there, pegging out the frilly vests and panties, while guests gathered at their windows and on the balcony and shouted encouragement.

It was the beginning of a long and happy, although, in Law's words, 'a very fiery marriage ... we were always arguing.' It would be almost twenty-five years before Law would remark to Geof that he and Nel had 'only lately got adjusted'.[36]

Once married to Nel, Geof's influence in Law's life receded. But the similarities between Geof and Nel are so striking it is difficult not to see Nel as, in many ways, a replacement for Geof. Geof and Nel were both creative individuals, each having a strong sense of personal pride and were frequently disdainful of other people's feelings, neither would attend social engagements if it did not suit them and both delighted in tormenting Law.

The family felt that Law deserved many of the cutting remarks that Nel threw his way, for they thought he had become self-centred and opinionated and, in the sisters' minds at least, chauvinistic.[37] Nel would not tolerate any of it, and cut him down whenever she could. She was, as the Law family recalled, anti-social. She seldom entertained and was not friendly with any of her in-laws. But, as Law pointed out, 'she was not very friendly with anyone. She hated socializing.' She was also often late for appointments and for Law, who abhorred lateness, this became a bone of contention. He tried to 'cure' her of her lateness by only waiting twenty minutes for her before leaving home for the appointment. But overall this had little effect. During the first years of their marriage he made up all sorts of reasons or excuses and apologised for Nel's absences. In later years, he would simply say that 'Nel did not want to come.' But when she did socialise, Law explained, 'she always looked magnificent because she said she didn't want to feel inferior.'

Although the Education Department had amended its regulation which had prevented the employment of married women, Nel had resigned and for her particular 'war effort' she worked as a 'draughtsman' with the State Rivers and Water Supply Commission. Law hoped that they would have a child, but Nel refused because she thought that a pregnancy would be dangerous for her heart.

Their one bedroom flat was in a 1930s block in South Yarra, a few minutes walk from the Yarra River and the beautiful Botanical Gardens. 'When they were married,' one of the Law sisters recalls, 'they had THE most unusual furniture ... and a huge circular mirror, which was very revolutionary then ... a glass dining room table, common now but you didn't see it then ... and an interesting unit-type lounge suite consisting of cushions.'[38]

The Commonwealth Government's 'austerity' program was introduced in 1942 and Australians were encouraged to accept sacrifices and to 'do without'. Restrictions were placed on drinking hours, restaurant meals, shopping and clothing. Nevertheless Nel, like Law, always dressed with style and managed to look elegant by designing and making her own clothes. Many suggestions were given in newspapers and journals on ways to save and Curtin asked the Australian people not to buy cotton and silk because 'we want silk to make parachutes, not to make your legs beautiful.'[39] It was suggested that women paint their legs with a cosmetic paint, including a darker 'seam' line down the back of their legs. Law's sisters recall that Nel was the first woman they saw who ever painted her legs.

Once married, Law and Nel began to move in a very different social circle and the rest of the family noticed the fact. 'Always knocking about with the intelligentsia,'[40] was Geof's summation. Law had joined the University Ski Club that had been set up for university graduates and had also become involved with two other couples who were excellent skiers, Willie and Malcolm McColl and Shirley and Mick Hull. Both couples, along with a small group of other ski enthusiasts, had recently set up the Alpine Club of Victoria and built the first private ski lodge at Mt Hotham. Soon Law had become a member of the Alpine Club of Victoria and had moved out of the 'intrepid' class of skier into the more refined class of those who stayed at lodges. At this time he was introduced to 'real skiing ... the "Arlberg Style",' which was the opposite of what he and Geof had taught themselves. With his need for mastery in whatever he tackled, Law now practised for hours, until he was too exhausted to do any more, to be competent in the new style. Ironically, years later skiing styles changed again, to what was called 'the reverse swing' which was exactly the style that Law had originally taught himself. Again he worked as diligently to change his skiing style back to what it had been twenty years earlier.

By the summer of 1941/42, the Federal Government had imposed daylight-saving to conserve fuel and soon the manufacture of non-essential items would be prohibited. On 15 February 1942 the alleged 'impregnable' British fortress of Singapore had fallen and Japan had occupied Singapore and had captured British and Australian troops. A few days later, on 19 February, the Japanese bombed Darwin. The town was ravaged and 243 people were killed, although the extent of the damage and lives lost was deliberately withheld from people in the southern States. By March, the Japanese had landed in New Guinea and had begun to advance on Port Moresby. An Australian invasion seemed imminent.

Australians now had to face the prospect of defending their country against invasion and more serious precautions were taken. 'Black-out' safeguards were instigated and the eerie sound of air-raid sirens often pierced the dark nights. Trenches were dug in public parks. The University moved quickly with its own precautionary measures. Air-raid drill was conducted in every class in every subject in the first week of term in 1942. University buildings were protected with mounds of sandbags; any windows difficult to curtain or screen were painted black and thousands of yards of slit trenches were dug all around the grounds. These trenches eventually became a hazard as they slowly filled with water, harbouring a myriad of mosquitoes. One University student thought they 'threatened anyone foolish enough to enter them with death by drowning or pneumonia.'[41]

4.

In November 1942 Professor Laby retired as Chairman of the Department and the Associate-Professor, E. O. Hercus became acting Professor. By March 1943 Law's position had been upgraded to Acting Lecturer and his salary adjusted accordingly.[42] Australians were exhorted to 'spend and consume less, work harder and to give all to the war effort'.[43] It was all too easy to comply with this at the University where the release of staff for active service or special duties placed heavy burdens on those who remained. Law again was appointed as Tutor at Newman College as well as Acting Lecturer in the Physics Department. Then in July 1943 an extra workload was handed to him when Jim Rogers, Secretary of the Optical Munitions Panel, was sent to the USA for six months to obtain information on instrument manufacturing processes. With one month's warning, Law was appointed Acting-Secretary of the Panel during Rogers' absence.

Apart from the usual duties associated with any large administrative position of this kind, the work entailed the drafting of accurate specifications for the mass–production of complicated instruments, the writing of reports on a wide variety of topics, the direction of laboratory tests and investigations, the supervision of production from the specification stage to the testing of the final instrument, and the maintenance of close liaison between the armed forces, the Ministry of Munitions and the various commercial firms and factories.

The meetings of the Panel usually extended over two or three days but, despite the added load, Law later saw the work as a 'wonderful administrative experience'. The experience also put him in close touch with industry, an opportunity he had not previously had. In fact, one of the great values of the Panel, a historian of the Panel later claimed, was the closer understanding that developed, during the war, between manufacturers and scientists.[44]

When Rogers returned from the USA, Law was retained on the Panel, now called the Scientific Instruments and Optical Panel, as Assistant Secretary.

During 1943, a subcommittee of the Panel was formed to look at the problems of the deterioration of binoculars, range-finders and gunsights being experienced in the Pacific, due to the effect of tropical fungoid growth. Law was appointed its Secretary and, at a meeting of the

Panel in December, Law suggested that a physicist should be sent to New Guinea to 'report on conditions under which the instruments were used and to carry out field tests.'[45] The members agreed and suggested Law should be the person to go. The project, under the control of the Army, was approved, with Law retaining his status as a civilian.

Law was granted leave of absence from the University and, on 17 February 1944, he began a protracted flight, via Sydney, Brisbane, Coolangatta, Gladstone and Townsville to Port Moresby. Law spent the following five weeks in New Guinea inspecting instruments and workshops at various bases, setting up experiments in the jungle, explaining experimental procedures to Army personnel, searching for mites, writing reports on tests and suggesting better ways to look after the instruments. He travelled extensively, visiting Milne Bay, Goodenough Island, Buna, Lae, Finschhafen and Nadzab. His diaries of the mission are written, mostly in pencil, in his tiny script, one way for half of the diary, turned upside down and written the other way for the second half. Although difficult to follow, they clearly show his interests. They contain notes on experiments, weather conditions, the Army personnel he contacted, the food he ate, the condition of the workshops, the names of the films he saw in the evening and even his sleeping conditions. There are no entries describing his impressions of the country or the fighting situation, nor any mention of the indigenous people of New Guinea.

Part of his brief was to ascertain the practicability of methods, suggested by the Panel, of tropic proofing of the instruments and to impress upon Army personnel the necessity for them to do their own tropic proofing. These suggestions were not always appreciated. At one base which he found in 'a bit of a mess', he suggested to the Captain various ways to ensure better care for the instruments. The Captain was clearly not pleased with this civilian, dressed in Army uniform with no badges of rank other than an 'SIOP Scientist' shoulder tab, telling him how to run his affairs. He insisted that Law's suggestions 'couldn't be done' and gave his reasons. Law was not to be put off and continued to give him the advice he thought appropriate. Later that day he recorded in his diary, 'Generally seem to have got off on the wrong foot.' That night he slept badly, probably only partly due to the poor sleeping conditions in a native mud hut, for diaries of his later Antarctic work show that he seldom slept well after a personal disagreement.

The following day things improved. An Air-Commodore loaned Law his jeep and driver. This pleased Law but caused some consternation amongst the two squadrons he visited because they thought the Air-Commodore had arrived for an inspection. 'Mixed relief and resentment when they found only me in the jeep,' Law recorded.

At no time did Law encounter any actual fighting on the trip. Huts and bedding reeking of mould, execrable roads, oppressive heat, poor food and risky air flights were the most discomforting conditions he had to endure. But the excitement of the flight from Port Moresby to

Queensland proved sufficient for the whole trip. The flight left Moresby, at 7.30 a.m. The aeroplane, a Lockheed Lode Star, was, Law recorded,

> a clapped out old plane that the crew had little faith in. Flew as high as possible over Coral Sea to allow maximum glide path in case of engine trouble. Made Townsville O.K. at 10.30am, left at 11.30 am. Shortly after, one engine cut out and we went on a long glide to try to reach Bundaberg. Just made it. Came in signalling with radio and lamp to clear runway of small training planes doing 'circuits and bumps'. Could not gain attention of air traffic control tower so landed at 2.30 pm in long grass on outer edge of airport, O.K.

The final leg of the trip, from Sydney to Melbourne, was in a DC3 'not lined—very noisy—uncomfortable steel bucket seats—typical Army lay-out'. They flew over his beloved Alps and he nearly froze from the cold in his light jungle clothing.

In some ways the New Guinea trip had given Law the satisfaction of foiling both fate and Laby's personal machinations to keep him out of active service, but it had done nothing to settle him happily in the cloistered environment of the researcher/lecturer role at the university. He felt as if life was passing him by and he attempted, unsuccessfully, to gain several other positions. In one application he stated that he was 'in excellent health',[46] but in fact very soon that would not be true.

In 1945, Dr Leslie Martin, who had previously been an Associate-Professor in the Department of Natural Philosophy at the University of Melbourne, but whose war work in radiophysics had been carried out in Sydney, was appointed as Professor and Head of the Physics Department at the University of Melbourne. Law was delighted at Martin's appointment, for he had always admired Martin whom he had first met when he attended his lectures during his undergraduate studies. He was not to know, at that time, just what an important role Martin would play in his future career.

Martin immediately arranged for Law's Acting Lecturer position to be confirmed as a three-year appointment as a Lecturer. Although the salary, at £450, was no more than he had been paid during the past two years, he now had the prestige of the Lecturer title. At last, too, he felt confident enough in his position at the University to resign from the Education Department, after 'leave of absence' of seven years. Again his Tutorship at Newman College was renewed. 'It was an anomalous situation,' he later stated, 'that a Lecturer in Physics was also a Tutor. It has never happened before or after. Today it would be severely frowned on.'

As the war was now drawing to an end, the Physics Department resumed its normal research roles. Martin asked Law to collaborate with an elderly physicist in the Department, Dr W. G. Kannuluik, on a project to measure the thermal conductivity of gases at low temperatures. Although Law found Kannuluik a fascinating character, with an extensive knowledge of ancient history, and a good classical physicist, he felt frustrated because 'Kanna' would not agree to various suggestions he made for more modern methods.

Exhausted after the punishing work-load of the war years, including no holidays, his double teaching load and the frustrations associated with this research, Law became ill. He had no energy and even a short walk would leave him exhausted. Finally, he was forced to seek medical attention. The doctor diagnosed it as 'Neurasthenia', a nervous debility. He told Law 'You are run down, go away for three weeks holiday. Here are some pills.' Law knew he had to relieve himself of some of his work-load and chose to resign from his position as Assistant-Secretary on the Panel. He tendered his resignation from the Committee, convalesced in Portland for three weeks and was then well again. He returned to find several 'thank you' letters from various members of the Panel who expressed their opinion that Law had 'shouldered the burden with great success' and had given 'an outstandingly credible performance and a contribution to our war effort which will not be underestimated.'[47]

Three months later, in August 1945, the atom bomb was dropped on Hiroshima. Law had much earlier been interested in nuclear fission, which he had heard about from Professor Kerr Grant of Adelaide University. One of Law's Physics students later wrote to Law, recalling the morning of the announcement of the dropping of the atom bomb:

I was a student in your Physics IIA class at the University of Melbourne, when the Atom Bomb was announced. The same morning we were amazed and spellbound to hear a somewhat excited Dr.[sic] Law give an exceedingly accurate description of how it worked, complete with blackboard diagrams. ... I later spoke to you and asked you how you knew so much about the bomb. You said you picked it from the scientific literature because it was obvious what was going on! That also was an astonishing statement.[48]

There is no hint that Law was disturbed by the dropping of the atomic bomb, or even distressed by the destruction it caused. It was the excitement of the workings of the bomb itself which was obviously uppermost in his mind and the pleasure he always derived from passing on information. Law seldom confused sentimentality with pragmatism and the bombing spelled the ending of the war in the Pacific. On 15 August 1945 World War II was over.

Professor Martin, possibly detecting Law's frustrations at academic life and his need to be constantly challenged, extended Law's teaching, his research and his administrative responsibilities. He asked Law to concentrate on specialised courses in Part I Physics, including physics for engineers, medical students, music students and physical optics for students for the Diploma of Ophthalmology. Martin also gave Law the responsibility of purchasing all the apparatus and equipment required by the teaching and research laboratories, for cataloguing all stock and for supervising the accounting associated with the general administration of the Physics Department. The knowledge gained here would hold Law in good stead when he began organising supplies for one-year-long scientific expeditions into Antarctica.

This administrative work brought Law into close association with Professor Martin, who Law believed 'was an ideal boss—the best I ever worked under', and a friendship developed between them that was to extend until Martin's death.

> He [Martin] was dignified but not pompous, paternal but not patronizing, considerate, sympathetic and encouraging. He created around him an atmosphere of intelligent efficiency while providing maximum freedom of operation for his subordinates. I never once saw him lose his temper or express impatience. I learned a lot about management from working under him.

Martin's leadership was a model that Law himself would later try and emulate.

5.

Law had now been with the university for seven years. He had thrown himself into university work because he had initially thought that university life was what he wanted. He had become what one student of the time referred to as a 'University man', identifying with and participating in university life.[49] He was Vice-President of the Melbourne University Ski Club and the Athletic Club and President of the Boxing Club. He was successful in his work as a lecturer, he was a competent researcher and a good administrator. But promotion at the University was slow, 'you waited years till a Senior Lecturer died' and, by the end of the war, he had decided that the life of an academic and researcher was not really his 'cup of tea':

> I had buried myself for some years into back-room work at Melbourne University, working in the lab. on my own or just with one other person. Day and night and on weekends. I always had that feeling, bred from the richness of my other activities, that I was missing out on such a hell of a lot of life.

But it was more than just 'missing out'. Law had measured himself against other men, and had found himself wanting in those areas in which he had previously hoped to excel:

> All my life I found tremendous value in being made aware of excellence by being placed alongside and having to compete with people who were excellent. In sport it was people like the Stewarts, or skiing

companions in the Alpine Club. I worked under Professor Laby who was a brilliant physicist. In the Physics department I ran into various other people of first-class intellect and learnt to realise what a really first class mind is and what it is capable of doing. It makes one very humble when one realises one's position on the pecking order of excellence.

He believed too, that there is an 'artistic creativity that is essential in all the best scientists' and he did not have it.

Real artistic talent is an incredible thing and its just not teachable. You either have it or you haven't. I'm very fast at latching onto an idea. I can pick a half formed idea out of the air and develop it and it looks original, but I know it's not.

Without these skills he believed he would never be a great physicist, only a 'competent, well organised, routine scientist.' Being anything that was routine, with a smell of mediocrity about it, was not something he could tolerate. He needed a wider sphere than the Physics Department at the University in which to work and he had decided to pursue a career in administration, as he realised that this was an area in which he could excel. His task was to find himself an organisation which would offer him the opportunity to grow, to expand and to push ahead.

He began applying for other positions, all of which were in administration. 'I have always been interested in administration,' he wrote in one job application, 'and possess strong ideas on the subject of successful organisation.'[50] He applied for jobs in other Australian States, including the Secretary to the Universities Commission in Sydney, and Registrar of the Australian National University in Canberra. Despite excellent references from various Professors and Directors of university departments, who described Law as 'highly competent', as one displaying 'great efficiency in making contact and in handling people', and as a man who 'stands head and shoulders above the general level', none of his many applications was successful.

Toward the end of 1946 Professor Martin suggested that Law should further his career by enrolling in the University of Melbourne's recently introduced PhD degree. Unfortunately Law's research could not be made retrospective, so his published papers on thermal conductivity[51] could not be considered as part of his thesis. Professor Martin proposed that Law join the Cosmic Ray Research Group that he was setting up at the University. Law agreed and was accepted as a part-time PhD student.

About this time Law heard vague rumours that an Australian Antarctic expedition was being organised but had not been able to find out anything about it. He wondered how he might apply and considered writing to Sir Douglas Mawson to enquire. He was unaware then that Professor Martin was being consulted by an executive committee which had been set up by the Commonwealth Government to develop plans for such an expedition during the summer of 1947–48. At early meetings of this committee decisions were made to appoint an Executive Officer for the Expedition and a Scientific Officer to organise the scientific programs.

On 12 May 1947, Group Captain Stuart Campbell, RAAF (Ret'd), was appointed as Chief Executive Officer of the expedition,[52] but no appointment had been made of a Scientific Officer. According to Law's oft-told story, about this time he and Martin were walking along the passage of the Physics Department at the University of Melbourne and Martin turned to Law and said:

> 'We have been talking about this coming Antarctic Expedition, Law, and we're having trouble finding a chief scientist.'
> Law stopped in his tracks and said, 'Did you mention my name?'
> Martin said, 'Oh, you wouldn't be interested in that Law, would you?'
> Law replied, 'I'd give my right arm to go on that.'
> Martin said 'Good gracious me, I'll go and ring up.'[53]

Events moved quickly. Martin made the necessary telephone call and Law was interviewed for the position. Of this interview, which was to prove a turning point in his life, he remembers little. Nevertheless, on 7 July 1947, he was offered a one year position as Senior Scientific Officer to co-ordinate the scientific programs and to carry out cosmic ray observations during the *Wyatt Earp*'s proposed voyage to the Antarctic. His annual salary was £900 and he was to be 'fully kitted and maintained at public expense whilst away from Australia'.[54]

Law was granted leave for one year without pay from the University of Melbourne and he advised Campbell that he would take up the position on 1 August 1947.[55] Campbell invited Law to attend the Executive Planning Committee meeting on 9 July 1947, and there it was decided that the official title of the expedition should be the 'Australian National Antarctic Research Expedition 1947 (ANARE)'.[56]

Law and Nel were both 'tremendously excited ... out of this world' at the news of his appointment. Some of his friends told him he was foolish to interrupt his career as a Physicist at the University for such a whim. But his enthusiasm could not be dampened, and he felt sure that somehow there would be a career ahead of him in Antarctic work.

Notes

1. *Argus*, Melbourne, 16 January 1939.
2. *The Age*, Melbourne, 27 April 1939.
3. R. G. Menzies in radio broadcast on 25 August 1939, reported in Frank Crowley, *Modern Australia 1901–1939*, Wren Publishing Pty Ltd, 1973, pp. 603–4.
4. Letter to Nel Allan, 4.45 p.m., Monday, 1938/9, LP.

5. Testimonials, Professor G. S. Browne, Professor of Education, Dean of the Faculty of Education, 2 January 1939, LP.
6. Geoffrey Law to author, 27 July 1988.
7. John Fyfield to author, 2 June 1990.
8. G. Wainwright, 'A Life filled with People', *Melbourne Studies in Education*, Melbourne University Press, Carlton, 1977, pp. 227–51.
9. Law's sisters to author, 6 May 1988.
10. Geoffrey Law to author, 27 July 1988.
11. Law's sisters to author, 6 May 1988.
12. Ibid.
13. Ibid.
14. Law to Nel Allan, Wednesday 1939, LP.
15. Law to Nel Allan, 9 a.m. Thursday 1939, LP.
16. Ibid.
17. Garry Disher, *Total War, The Home Front 1939–45*, Oxford University Press, Melbourne, 1983, p. 5.
18. The University of Melbourne, *Annual Reports 1939–1946*, Melbourne University Press, 1948, p. 135.
19. Desmond Hurley to author, 29 May 1990.
20. Bernard McC. O'Brien to author, 12 June 1990.
21. Ibid.
22. The University of Melbourne, *Annual Reports 1939–1946*, p. 154.
23. Diana Dyason, cited in *Memories of Melbourne University, Undergraduate Life in the Years Since 1917*, ed. Hume Dow, Hutchinson of Australia, Richmond, 1983, p. 107.
24. Law to Sam Cohen, SRC re Activities of UNS during 1940, 26 March 1941, LP.
25. Nel Allan to F. Pearse, 1940, LP.
26. Dyason, op.cit., p. 105.
27. Letter from Department of Air, Commonwealth of Australia, Melbourne, 19 March 1941, LP.
28. Law to Sam Cohen, re Activities of UNS during 1940, SRC, 26 March 1941.
29. The University of Melbourne, *Annual Reports 1939–1946*, pp. 135–6.
30. John Fyfield to author, 2 June 1990.
31. Law's sisters to author, 6 May 1988.
32. Ibid.
33. EDR 29813.
34. Michael McKernan, *All in! Australia During the Second World War*, Thomas Nelson Australia, 1983, pp. 96–9.
35. Disher, pp. 62–3.
36. Geoffrey Law to author, 27 July 1988.
37. Law's sisters to author, 6 May 1988 and Geoffrey Law to author, 27 July 1988.
38. Law's sisters to author, 6 May 1988.
39. McKernan, p. 170.
40. Geoffrey Law to author, 27 July 1988.
41. Dyason, op.cit., p. 108.
42. Official University of Melbourne Staff Record, LP.
43. Don Garden, *Victoria, a History*, Thomas Nelson Australia, 1984, p. 387.
44. J. S. Rogers, *The History of the Scientific Instruments and Optical Panel*, July 1940–December 1946, Commonwealth of Australia, Ministry of Munitions, Ordnance Production Directorate. p. 5.
45. Minutes of 22nd Meeting of Optical Munitions Panel Held 30 November, 1st and 2nd December 1943, AA, Brighton.
46. Law to Scientific Liaison Bureau, 15 July 1944, LR.
47. Mr Frank F. Davey, Director Ordnance Production Directorate, Ministry of Munitions, to Law, 20 June 1945, LR.
48. Ralph F. Jones, Chairman—Program Committee, Rotary Club of Chadstone/East Malvern, to Law, 26 June 1989, LP.

49. Mr Bernard McC. O'Brien, CMG, Director, Microsurgery Research Centre, St Vincent's Hospital, to author 12 June 1990.
50. Law, Letter of Application to Commonwealth Office of Education, for position as Secretary to the Universities Commission, Sydney, 24 January 1946, LR.
51. W. G. Kannuluik and P. G. Law, 'Thermal Conductivity of Carbon Dioxide over a Range of Temperatures', *Proc. Roy. Soc. Vict.*, December 1945 and 'Note on the Carbon Dioxide Point in Thermometry', *J. Sci. Inst.*, 25, no. 7, 1946.
52. R. A. Swan, *Australia in the Antarctic, Interest, Activity and Endeavour*, Melbourne University Press, Melbourne, 1961, p. 242.
53. Law to Tim Bowden, 30 November 1987.
54. Letter from Stuart Campbell, Department of External Affairs, 7 July 1948, LR.
55. Law to S. Campbell, 17 July 1947, LR.
56. Minutes of the Meeting of Antarctic Planning Committee, 9 July 1947, ADH.

5. Scientific Officer, ANARE, 1948

1.

THE COMBINED EFFORTS OF TWO MEMBERS ON THE EXECUTIVE PLANNING Committee helped lay the foundations of Australia's prominent role in the Antarctic and led directly to the setting up of ANARE. The main impetus came from Sir Douglas Mawson, the geologist and explorer, with support from Captain John King Davis, a ship's captain and veteran of seven Antarctic voyages. They were men with vastly different characters.

Their involvement in Antarctica began in 1908 when Mawson accompanied Ernest Shackleton's voyage to Antarctica. The First Officer on the *Nimrod* was John King Davis. In 1910 Mawson decided to mount his own expedition and embarked on fund raising activities both within Australia and in England. Whilst in London he appointed Davis second-in-command of his expedition. After months of arduous work, Mawson gained sufficient financial support from both private and Government sources to set up the Australasian Antarctic Expedition (AAE). The AAE achieved their three main objectives which were to establish a meteorological station at Macquarie Island; to establish an Antarctic scientific base near the Adelie Land coast and to explore the surrounding territory and to finally explore the coastline west of that base and establish a second station as far west as possible.[1]

Despite public acclaim and a knighthood in 1914, Mawson was left with a large debt of £5 000 which he had to repay over a period of years. Neither the Australian Government nor the public came to his assistance.[2]

Over the following years, Mawson and Davis continued their efforts to promote Antarctic activity. On 4 February 1929 Mawson accepted the leadership of the British–Australian–New Zealand Antarctic Research Expedition (BANZARE). Davis was appointed to command the *Discovery* and to be second-in-command of the expedition.[3]

The expedition consisted of two voyages in the summers of 1929–30 and 1930–31. Valuable oceanographical and hydrographical work was carried out and three landings were made, at Proclamation Island (Enderby Land), at Cape Bruce (Kemp Land) and at Scullin Monolith (MacRobertson Land).[4] At each of these landings 'good views of the terrain were obtained, backed up by further views from aeroplane flights.'[5]

Combined with the AAE expedition, the BANZARE 1929–31 expeditions 'laid a solid base for what was later to be proclaimed as Australian Antarctic Territory.'[6]

On 7 February 1933 a British–order–in–Council proclaimed British sovereignty over all Antarctic territory, with the exception of Adelie Land, and placed it under the control of the Commonwealth of Australia.[7] The Australian Antarctic Territory Acceptance Act was passed later that year and came into operation in August 1936.[8]

The legal grounds on which Antarctic territorial claims are based are many and varied,[9] nevertheless it had generally been believed that 'presence' was of prime importance. At the end of the Second World War seven countries which had carried out exploratory, scientific and commercial expeditions in the Antarctic, (the United Kingdom, New Zealand, France, Norway, Chile, Argentina and Australia), had made formal territorial claims to parts of Antarctica.[10]

After the Second World War, Mawson, then 64 years of age, doggedly returned to his campaign to persuade the Commonwealth Government to establish a permanent base in Antarctica. His main argumentative thrust was the political need to have a presence in the area so as to consolidate the Australian territorial claim. Finally, in 1946, Mawson managed to persuade the Minister for External Affairs, Dr H. V. Evatt, of the importance of establishing a base on the Antarctic continent, and on 2 December 1945 Mawson met with representatives from the Government. A recommendation was made at this meeting that plans should be developed for an expedition to the Australian Antarctic Territory to find an ice-free area on the continent upon which to set up a permanent base.

On 20 December 1946, Cabinet accepted this recommendation and proposed that an executive committee be formed to develop expedition plans, with Mawson as adviser. It was as a result of these meetings that Stuart Campbell had been appointed Executive Officer and Law, Senior Scientific Officer.

Campbell had been seconded from the Department of Civil Aviation, where he held the position of Director of Air Navigation and Safety.[11] He came with a combination of skills well suited for the task because, as Law explained, 'He was a good administrator and ... he had been the pilot with Mawson's 1929–31 expedition, flying a little Moth aeroplane. He was one of the only men in Australia who'd been to Antarctica and was available.'[12]

Campbell set up the ANARE Office in a suite of rooms, in the Victoria Barracks, St Kilda Road, Melbourne. He gathered a small staff comprising a secretary, Trevor Heath, a storeman, George Smith, and several typists. All were at the St Kilda Road Office, except Smith who was stationed at Tottenham, a suburb eight miles west of Melbourne, where the RAAF had provided a building in their No. 1 Stores Depot as a packaging and storage area for the use of the Antarctic Expedition.

Arrangements moved swiftly. The Government approved the Executive Planning Committee's recommendations for three expeditions; two to establish scientific stations at Heard and Macquarie Islands and another to conduct reconnaissance of the coast of the Australian Antarctic Territory with a view to establishing a permanent scientific station on the Antarctic continent.

The administrative arrangements to support the three expeditions were complex and ultimately proved cumbersome. The office of the ANARE was loosely attached to the Department of External Affairs (DEA); CSIR accepted responsibility for administrative finances for the ANARE and the Royal Australian Air Force acted as purchasing agents, except for victualing which was carried out by the Royal Australian Navy. Rates of pay and conditions for the civilian members of the Expedition were established with an allowance of 12/6d per day for single men and 17/6d per day for married men, with six weeks' annual leave. Each man was to be fully kitted and maintained from the date of departure until return and would receive a free issue of liquor and tobacco.

The proposed plan for the *HMALST 3501*, the naval ship that was to be used for the two island voyages, was for it to leave during November, set up a station at Heard Island; establish a fuel base at Kerguelen Island and arrive in Melbourne in mid January; remain in Melbourne for a week then proceed to Macquarie Island. The personnel to go to each of the islands were three meteorologists, three radio operator/mechanics, two physicists, a geologist, a medical officer, a surveyor, a cook and a diesel mechanic.

The *Wyatt Earp* was to be used for the Antarctic Continent expedition, and the proposed itinerary was to proceed direct to Commonwealth Bay and spend five or six days there taking anchorage soundings and carrying out magnetic observations; then proceed to Princess Elizabeth Land with the object of searching for a suitable spot for future landing parties and then to refuel at either Heard or Kerguelen Islands on the return journey.[13] The proposed personnel for this expedition, were to be the Chief Executive Officer (Campbell), a physicist (Law), a meteorologist, a pilot and a mechanic.[14]

So far so good. The plans sounded well thought through and efficient but the practicalities of the situation were different, as George Smith, the storeman at Tottenham recalls:

> God Almighty, it was like Brown's Cows ... Nobody seemed to know what was going on ... by September 1947 I don't think we knew if there was a boat or even a suitcase ... From the word 'go' the green light was there ... they were going, IF they could get a boat.

George Smith's responsibility was to procure supplies to outfit the proposed twenty–four expeditioners for the two Island stations with clothing and all supplies for twelve months, and to outfit the men who were going on the *Wyatt Earp* trip. George Smith further recalls:

> The parameters of the job were this: ... the two of us [Smith and Norm Jones, a Clerk] were to set up this Division to cope with the inwards supply of goods to go south. We were told virtually nothing, we were given nothing, and we had nothing.
>
> We had a shed that was 120 ft. long and about 30 ft. wide and about 15 ft. high. And there was absolutely nothing in it. So it was a case of scrounging ... Across the road from us we had an old building that was full of tent pegs and mallets and mallet handles and so forth and I reckon between Stuart Campbell and Jones and myself, we ended up with more tent pegs, more mallets and so forth than what the RAAF had in the end, because we worked on the basis that 'Well if we can't use the mallets,' we can burn them. There is nothing down there, so take what we can get ... it was just a matter of take everything you could lay your hands on.[15]

Smith and Jones, together with Trevor Heath, the Administrative Officer, consulted the RAAF supply catalogues and selected all the equipment they thought would be needed, 'We picked everything' Smith recalled, 'nothing was spared.' But when it came to packing the thousands of items, they found that there were no cases. They solved that problem too, by stealing them from the nearby RAAF store.

2.

Campbell invited Law to attend the Executive Planning Committee meetings and it was there that Law met Sir Douglas Mawson and Captain Davis. Law, of course, was well aware of the reputations Mawson and Davis had gained through their Antarctic work. He knew that Mawson had been described as 'the Australian Nansen', afer the famous Norwegian polar explorer, Fridtjof Nansen, who made the first crossing of Greenland in 1888, and that Davis was referred to as 'Gloomy'. His expectations of both were confirmed:

> Mawson ... to the end of his days was young at heart and young in mind. He was always ready to pick up the new idea, he was never reactionary.
>
> J. K. Davis was the ultra-conservative, the dour, head-shaking man to whom nothing modern is any good, you know 'It's not like it was in the old days.' Whereas Doug was always looking forward. 'Why don't we do this?' And if you'd suggest anything new to him his eyes would sparkle and he'd get all enthusiastic about it ... He was always looked up to as the father of our Antarctic work by everybody. There was no doubt about his supreme status.[16]

Law's first meeting with Mawson was particularly memorable, and was to be the beginning of a friendship that lasted until Mawson's death in 1958:

> I was introduced to a tall man with pale, ice-blue eyes who bent over me with a genial smile and spoke a few words of welcome in his gentle voice. My first impression of Mawson did not alter over later years. I have never heard the term 'raw-boned' defined, but that is the description that came to my mind when I saw him. His bones seemed large and he gave an impression of great physical strength.[17]

Law officially began work as the Senior Scientific Officer on 1 August 1947 but had little time to spend at either the office or the Tottenham store, for he was working on testing cosmic ray equipment at Mt Hotham. Professor Martin had earlier seized the opportunity to give a focus to the University's Cosmic Ray Research Group, headed by Dr Henry Rathgeber. Martin suggested to the Executive Planning Committee that Rathgeber's group prepare cosmic ray equipment to accompany the proposed Antarctic expedition and test the equipment in the snow during the winter before sending it south. Martin placed Law in charge of the logistics to set up a hut suitable for both testing the equipment and for training Antarctic personnel. Rathgeber and Law had, earlier in the year, selected a site at Mt Hotham. Knowing that the winter would soon close in and snow would make the roads impassable, they had authorised builders to immediately go ahead with the construction, without having obtained the necessary building permit from the Forestry Department. Law applied for permission to build, purchased the hut materials in Melbourne and had them sent up to Mt Hotham. The builders promptly set about constructing the hut and when the Inspector from the Forestry Department visited Mt Hotham he was most annoyed to find the hut already built. Law convinced him of the national importance of the whole expedition and the permit was granted for what was later called the 'Cosray Hut'.

The Cosmic Ray Group included six post-graduate students, David Caro, Ken Hines, Fred Jacka, John Jelbart, John Prescott and Charles Speedy. Despite working long hours to complete the equipment, it was not ready until mid August, by which time both access roads, one via Harrietville and the other via Omeo, were blocked by snow.

The group packed the equipment carefully in small wooden framed boxes, each weighing approximately 110 lbs. On Monday 18 August they left Melbourne in cars with the equipment and, next morning, met with Erik Jonson, a Norwegian skier who made his living during the winter packing stores and ski gear from Harrietville to Mt Hotham, and his twelve horses. They packed the cases onto the horses, one either side, and, walking beside them, set off up the snow-covered Ben Accord Spur.

It soon began to rain, the snow became slushy, and one horse slipped and rolled fifty feet down the steep slope, neighing shrilly and losing its load. The horse was not badly hurt but the men were very anxious about their equipment. It took another two hours to haul the equipment back up the snow slope and it was almost 6 p.m. before they arrived at Jonson's hut. The following morning Jonson harnessed a draught horse, clad with snow shoes, to each of two sleds of equipment and began the many trips to the top of Hotham (6 100 ft) and downhill for about a mile and a half, past the Mt Hotham Chalet to the Cosray Hut. Finally, by 4 p.m. the following day, all the equipment was at the Cosray Hut and they were able to unpack the cases, apprehensive about what they might find. To their relief they found that the damage to the equipment was quite repairable and, by Saturday 23 August, it was again working. 'Mechanical counters clicked intermittently and neon bulbs flashed as incoming mesons of the cosmic rays triggered off the Geiger counters.'

A few weeks later, Caro, Jelbart, Speedy and Waters transported an ionisation chamber, plus electrical and recording gear, weighing 450 lbs to the Cosray Hut. The equipment was too heavy for a pack-horse so they took it in a utility, via Omeo, to the bottom of Slippery Pinch, between Omeo and Hotham, where they were blocked by snow. Meanwhile Jacka, Prescott and Rathgeber, who were at the Cosray Hut, hauled a sledge from the hut down the snow-covered road to meet them. Together the seven men struggled for two days in soft snow, to haul it the remaining 11 miles.

So much of the group's time was spent at the Cosray Hut during the next few weeks that it was later referred to by a journalist as 'Mr. Law's Mount Hotham Head Quarters'.[18]

It was during these trips to and from Mt Hotham, often in dangerous conditions, that Law established a leadership style in field work that changed little over the years. Fred Jacka, the 22-year-old physicist, was impressed by Law's knowledge of the mountain conditions and his capacity to get things done, 'Phil was a small man but extremely energetic, fiery. His drive, his energy, his determination was very apparent, right at the beginning.'[19] Law, Jacka maintained, 'was very much the leader in the field exercises' and recalls that Law's style of leadership was 'very effective ... very sympathetic, but there was no letting up at all', and illustrates the style with a poignant story:

I had been skiing a couple of times earlier at [Mount] Buller but Phil was already quite experienced. He had to cope, to look after himself and the equipment and to offer sensible guidance on how to behave ... I remember Phil and me pulling one sledge and a couple of other people pulling the other sledge. We slogged away pulling sledges all day and it was getting late in the afternoon, but still light, and I was absolutely done in. I can remember Phil was a very, very sympathetic companion. Even though he was a much smaller man than me he didn't seem to be particularly worn whereas I was absolutely exhausted. I can recall ... we paused to have a bit of a rest and I just literally fell asleep standing up. I've no idea how long this lasted, but then Phil came and tapped me on the shoulder and said 'Come on, I think we will have to get moving.' He was very sympathetic, but he didn't let up. He said 'You have to keep going.' If I had been on my own, I might very well have ended my days there.

On one occasion six men were stranded at the Cosray Hut, constructed for only two, for several days. Law had come up with a driver in a Commonwealth car to collect some of the equipment, but heavy snowfalls buried the car and the men were unable to move from the hut. In another pertinent illustration of Law's leadership capacity, Jacka recalls that:

Phil again took charge in a very masterly way and entertained the gathering very well, with a clarinet I think. He played music and we sang songs and he told stories. He was very much the centre of the whole social scene at that time.

Finally, because of time considerations, the men had to make the attempt to get down to the snow line. Once started, a difficulty occurred with the driver of the Commonwealth car, as Jacka recalls:

He was a puny little fellow [the Commonwealth car driver] and his mug of beer was fairly important to him. He presented a major problem, because he simply couldn't make it. ... It was an emergency situation in that if he weren't forced he would have died, there is no question about that.
We tried to carry him but we were too exhausted ourselves ... Phil's handling of this Commonwealth car driver was firm, to the point of ruthlessness, but always sympathetic and always sympathetic to the rest of us ... Phil really handled all this very, very effectively ... particularly as he must have been very tired himself.[20]

By mid September the testing was completed, the equipment had been brought back to Melbourne and the Cosray Hut episode was over.
All the men concerned had received a tough introduction to the discomforts and difficulties of working in snow and blizzard. And they needed it, for the lure of the Antarctic had captured them. Jacka and Jelbart had been appointed to take one set of cosmic ray equipment to Heard Island, Hines and Speedy to take another set to Macquarie Island and Law to take a set on the *Wyatt Earp* to the Antarctic.
On 6 November 1947, the Prime Minister, the Rt Hon. J. B. Chifley, publicly announced that Australia had organised an Antarctic Expedi-

tion.[21] Overall, the proposed expeditions received good media coverage. One article entitled 'Southward Ho! To Chart Antarctic Weather', included romantic descriptions of the men as 'adventurous-minded', Group Captain Campbell as 'tailored to measure for the job' with 'iron determination' and 'great strength of character'. Lieut. Commander G. M. Dixon, skipper of the *LST 3501* was 'bluff' and 'grizzled'.[22]

By 17 November 1947, the *LST 3501* was ready to leave for Heard Island. Apart from Dixon and Campbell, the ship had a complement of 112 officers and men, 8 voyage support staff and 14 men for the Heard Island wintering party.

During the voyage, on December 6, a gale developed and huge seas battered the *LST 3501* for days. The vessel behaved 'like a caterpillar in motion' Captain Dixon reported, as 'it rippled from stem to stern.'[23] No serious damage was done, this time. They arrived safely at Heard Island on December 11 in good weather to see the ice clad peak of Big Ben looking, as one expeditioner described it, 'like a great big ice cream cone sticking up.'[24]

Campbell set up the base in the sandy, low-lying isthmus of Atlas Cove because of its advantage 'that supplies and personnel can be landed from any type of vessel at almost any time of the year without undue delay.'[25] His report of the unloading, however, made a mockery of this optimism and gave a vivid portrayal of the weather conditions during summer on Heard Island. An easterly gale blew on 15 December, forcing the ship to put to sea in a hurry, leaving a group of six men on the Island. Loading continued on the 17th with good weather but a south-westerly gale on the 18th, of force 8–9, again halted the unloading. On the 19th a high swell stopped the boats working in any degree of safety. A north-easterly gale blew on the 21st with 'surf rolling into Atlas Cove [that] had to be seen to be believed'. During this storm the lashings round the Walrus aircraft, which had been tied down ashore, gave way and the Walrus was blown over sideways and completely wrecked.

23 December began with favourable weather but by mid morning a north-westerly squall blew up, making it 'prudent to pull off and abandon the attempt for the day'. 24 December was a 'magnificent warm calm day' and the 'back of the work had been broken.' But by Christmas day there was a 'strong squally south-westerly gale blowing' and the ship was unable to pick up the shore party to share in the ship's Christmas Dinner of turkey and plum pudding. On Boxing Day, 'as there was now no longer any doubt about being able to establish a station satisfactorily,' the official flag raising ceremony was held and the last of the stores came ashore about 7 p.m., fifteen days after their arrival.

Over the New Year period the ship visited Iles de Kerguelen to depot fuel for the *Wyatt Earp*, called in again at Heard Island, to pick up Campbell, and arrived at Fremantle on 18 January 1948. Campbell laconically informed the Executive Planning Committee (EPC) on his return that 'the operation has at no time been hazardous', but did add that it had 'undoubtedly been more difficult than at first anticipated'.[26]

3.

Whilst the Heard Island expedition was underway, the refit of the *Wyatt Earp* was proceeding in Adelaide. The *Wyatt Earp* was a wooden ship that had begun life as a Norwegian herring trawler. She was later used by an American Antarctic explorer, Lincoln Ellsworth, whose childhood hero was Wyatt Earp and he named the ship after the legendary marshal of Dodge City and Tombstone.[27] Before the Second World War she was bought by the Australian Government and used as a tramp ship on the Australian coast; then, after the war, she was moored in the Torrens River and used as a Sea Scouts' headquarters. 'Mawson and Davis both knew it was there', Law explained to an interviewer 'and because it had stout wooden timbers and [was] therefore fitted for going through ice, they each recommended it for this [Antarctic Expedition] purpose.'[28]

During the latter half of 1947 the Navy had her refitted with new diesel engines; the upper decking was rebuilt and the bridge super-structure was moved forward to allow more cabin accommodation. Her sails were retained—a large main, a mizzen and two head sails. This, the First Lieutenant, W. F. Cook, later reported, 'was really a step backwards to the turn of the century, but nevertheless exciting.'[29] The sails increased the *Wyatt Earp*'s speed by up to two knots and also slowed down her rate of roll by at least two seconds, which, on a ship that was said would roll in heavy dew, was a distinct advantage. 'An echo sounder, gyro-compass and small radar set', Cook also reported 'were our con-cessions to modernity.' The refit had been beset with industrial troubles and, consequently took longer than expected, leaving little time for suit-able trials. Although doubts were expressed about the ship's suitability as an Antarctic ship she had, optimistically, been 'painted a brilliant orange and the hull sober black to ... stand out against the snow and ice of the Antarctic.'[30] She was nicknamed the 'Twerp' and captained by Commander Karl Oom, RAN, who had had experience in Antarctic waters when he had accompanied the BANZARE 1930/31 voyage as hydrographer.[31]

The *Wyatt Earp* expedition also received a wide media coverage with the *Wyatt Earp* described as a 'sturdy little wooden motor vessel'. Com-mander Oom reported that 'She is a fine ship, capable of travelling any-where and weathering anything. There's new life in her now.' Law and the team of young cosmic ray research men were reported as having 'already survived a baptism of blizzard' in the 'snow-garmented Mt. Hotham'.'[32] Nel was interviewed and described as 'Tall, slim and attrac-tive ... an enthusiastic and able painter of portraits and landscapes.' The text was accompanied by a photograph of her, impeccably groomed, holding painting brush and palette. She was reported as saying she had two concerns about the expedition: 'First, that her husband might return with a beard, and secondly, that he might not have hot water for showers on board the *Wyatt Earp.* To be on the safe side she has included an electric jug in his kit!'[33] Both of her fears were to be realised.

On 12 December 1947, David Caro, Nel and Law drove to Adelaide where Caro and Law installed one set of cosmic ray equipment in the laboratory that had been built on the boat deck of the ship. A reporter gave a graphic, if irreverent, description of the equipment as:

A 6 ft x 6 ft. contraption composed of tubes, batteries, plugs and what–not; a thing like a speedometer recording figures, and a camera which automatically took a shot of the figures every hour.[34]

Caro and Nel drove the truck back to Melbourne and Law stayed on to sail in the *Wyatt Earp* to Melbourne. The *Wyatt Earp* sailed from Adelaide on 13 December 1947, many weeks behind schedule, and as Cook, the First Lieutenant, later reported:

With head winds and rough seas all the way to Melbourne, it was a very wet trip. Water came in everywhere; into the mess decks forward and down into the gyro which it put out of action—into the cabins and wardroom aft; and all this necessitated bailing. A steering breakdown was thrown in for good luck (or bad luck)![35]

Law was unused to sailing. He was apprehensive, eager to prove himself but became violently ill; so ill in fact, that by the time they arrived at Melbourne on 17 December, Commander Oom decided that Law was unfit to be a passenger and suggested that he not make the final trip down south.[36] Law was appalled at the thought of this opportunity for excitement and adventure slipping away from him and, by the time repairs had been carried out on the *Wyatt Earp*, he had persuaded Oom to allow him to stay on.

The *Wyatt Earp* left Melbourne on Friday, December 17 but, half way down the bay, the engine starting-handle jammed and it took three hours to repair it. On the Saturday they ran into a force 10 easterly and they had to shelter in the lee of Flinders Island.

Law described the conditions in a letter to Nel:

You have absolutely no idea what can happen in a small ship in a heavy sea. Every 5 minutes there would be a series of extra large rolls, and you'd hear crash, crash, crash as moveable objects were hurled to the floor. Even things lashed down work loose and come adrift. All night long the crashing went on until the whole place was a shambles.

To add to the confusion the ship sprung leaks just above the water line, level with the cupboards under the bunks, and each time the ship rolled water would come in. Well, inside an hour every cabin (except mine!) had six inches of water swishing back and forth in it. Even the Captain didn't escape, because although his cabin was too high for that, it leaked rain water.

And Nell, you should have seen the galley at the height of the trouble! Pots full of stew and vegetables disgorged their contents onto the floor which became greasy and 2 inches deep in glutinous muck. You couldn't stand up in the slippery mess and every heavy roll you'd hear a new crash as all the plates or all the pots or all the cups or provisions would crash down.[37]

Law was not exaggerating. Cook's letter home on the same day painted a similar picture of events. Although an experienced seaman, Cook remarked that 'it was the worst weather I had ever met in Bass Strait.'[38]

By 20 December, the Captain's report, showing a wry sense of humour, read 'A strong gale from the East contradicted storm warnings that gales could be expected from the West!'[39] He also reported, what Cook was later to say was the 'understatement of the voyage,'[40] that 'the ship's movement was extremely violent and uncomfortable.'[41]

Despite the conditions, Law was undoubtedly in high spirits and he signed the letter to Nel, 'All my love darling, Nautically—Phil', then asked her to 'Show this around then preserve it.' For a man described later as one who had 'never been interested in history', and who could not get 'excited about what happened yesterday only about what might happen tomorrow',[42] this voyage was a turning-point in his life. Law had begun to see his work as important and worthy of recording. From now on letters, telegrams, diaries and lecture notes would all be carefully filed as he began to see his life and work with one eye on posterity.

On 22 December, with the weather deteriorating, they arrived at Hobart where the ship again underwent repairs. They did not want to spend Christmas alongside a wharf so, early on the morning of Christmas day, after 'Herculean efforts',[43] they were ready to leave. But first of all the ship moved out into the estuary to swing compasses and, upon returning, the engines refused to go astern and she crashed into the pier. Christmas day was, after all, spent tied up at the wharf. But it was pleasant enough with a 'grand Christmas Dinner ... Hock and Claret very fine.' They eventually departed on Friday 26 and Law immediately began to feel 'pretty miserable'. Seasickness tablets were having no effect 'except to churn me up' and, to make matters worse, he was, he recorded, 'constipated and livery, with a large pile as a result. What a b——! This will complicate the seasickness angle considerably.'

Law and Edward (Ted) McCarthy, the magnetician who had joined the expedition in Melbourne, had to spend hours, sometimes 15–18 hours, every day working on the cosmic ray equipment. In addition, Law and McCarthy, as men with officer status, were expected to do their share of the bridge watch. Law thought this added responsibility was unreasonable:

> A most depressing day—one of the most unpleasant of my life. Rose at 4am to take the morning watch. Found a rough sea, wind strength 6–7 from SSW, ship making practically no headway and pitching and rolling heavily ... Became very exhausted fighting sickness and trying to keep balance. Barely lasted it out. Seemed bl— senseless subjecting myself to such misery because I was completely superfluous on the bridge, No. 1 and 3 seamen being there also. However, we are expected to take watches, so there we are.

The next day Law spoke with Cook and told him it was impossible for McCarthy and him to do justice to their scientific work as well as taking watch duties. Cook agreed to relieve them both of the task.

New Year's Eve was spent in an atmosphere of foreboding as their chances of continuing the voyage receded but, as Cook recorded, we 'forced ourselves to a certain amount of merriment accompanied by Phil Law's accordion.'[44] New Year's Day, 1948, dawned and Law awoke to 'bright sunshine, sea not bad' but the ship had received 'lousy news'. The radio reports the Captain had been sending on the conditions of the ship had obviously worried the Naval Board and the ship had been ordered to return to Melbourne. 'We argued by signal,' Cook reported, 'hoping that the Board would change its mind but got back a terse "comply with my signal".'[45]

Law recorded in his diary: 'Everyone most depressed ... So now we are making our humiliating way homewards. And it would happen on a day when everything is beaut!'

The *Wyatt Earp* arrived back in Melbourne on Wednesday 7 January 1948, and went into dry dock at Williamstown for repairs.

4.

On 23 January Campbell, Law and members of the EPC flew, in the Prime Minister's plane, to Canberra, to make new arrangements for the *Wyatt Earp* voyage. Owing to the lateness of the season, the original plan for a 3 000 mile voyage could not be contemplated and it was proposed that the *Wyatt Earp* should proceed to that part of the Antarctic Continent closest to Australia, and should concentrate on a detailed examination of the King George V Land coast.[46]

Law raised the question of the magnetic work to be carried out at Commonwealth Bay and asked for an assurance that he and McCarthy would be put ashore. Prolonged discussion followed, but the general opinion was that, with the lateness of the season and the slow speed of the ship, it would be unlikely that a party could be put ashore. Campbell opposed the idea of leaving scientists ashore whilst the *Wyatt Earp* recon noitred, claiming that it might be impossible to pick them up in the time available. There was general agreement with this opinion, except for Mawson, who supported Law's idea and maintained that 'the party should be landed and given time to further the work that had been done at Commonwealth Bay'. Mawson believed, and was supported by Captain Davis, 'that there would be no difficulty in picking up the scientists in plenty of time.'[47]

The Committee finally resolved that reconnaissance of the Antarctic coastline in the vicinity of longitudes 140–150 E be carried out; that every effort be made to carry out reconnaissance work, preferably at Commonwealth Bay and, on the way home, the *Wyatt Earp* should approach the Balleny Islands to do whatever work appeared desirable.[48]

Law was concerned over several things. Although he agreed that the primary reason for the *Wyatt Earp* trip was exploratory, he was disappointed at the lack of interest shown in the scientific work and was 'convinced that no-one cares greatly if the scientific programme is carried out or not.' This is the first indication of Law's belief that the Australian Government and the key departments lacked any real commitment to scientific work in Antarctica. It was an issue that would plague him, and which he would contest, for the rest of his Antarctic career.

After three successful days of sea trials in and outside Port Phillip Bay, the ship was ready to sail again on 8 February. But by now the press had begun to raise doubts about the whole expedition, particularly the suitability of the ship for such a venture. One journalist, in an article, entitled 'Antarctic Folly?' implied that Australia's political need for a stake in Antarctica might be creating a dangerous situation for the men on the ship. He wrote:

> The voyage is as much inspired by political reasoning as it is by the quest for material knowledge. As a nation we are raising our voice loudly in the United Nations forum: as a nation we must indulge in pursuits commensurate with our international standing. No one would suggest that the grab for the Antarctic is going to parallel the partition of Africa in the late XIXth century, but quite obviously the powers that be in Australia are going to take no risks.

He went on to remark that although the *Wyatt Earp* had been proved seaworthy to the satisfaction of the Naval authorities, 'the question must still be asked "Is this trip justified, in view of the particular vessel allotted to the task, and in view of the date of departure?"'[49]

Campbell had decided to join this *Wyatt Earp* trip and, with accommodation scarce, he shared Law's and McCarthy's cabin. The men gloomily referred to the cabin as the 'black hole of Calcutta', which Law described as:

> 8 ft x 8 ft in the centre of the ship, with no portholes and no ventilation except, just above my pillow, an iron grating which opened

onto the boat deck above. As the deck was always wet, water dripped through onto my face until I nailed a piece of tin over the opening. Thereafter we had the choice of suffocating overnight with the door shut, or opening it and becoming asphyxiated by the oily diesel fumes ... which wafted in from the open engine-room casing next door![50]

The conditions were exacerbated by Campbell's inadequate personal hygiene, as Law later described:

Stuart liked to be tough for its own sake, I think ... all his life he'd been proving something about his own toughness. For example, on the *Wyatt Earp* I shared a cabin with him and, as part of this tough-ness business, he believed in not changing his clothing. He reck-oned he could put up with wearing the same garments, the same as the old explorers used to way out in the field. But being cooped up in a cabin that had no ventilation with a bloke who wore the same underclothes for a month was not a very pleasant situation.[51]

The 'old explorers' too had complained about Campbell's personal hygiene. When Campbell had been on Mawson's BANZARE voyages, Mawson had noted in his diary that 'We [Captain and Mawson] also had a long talk about the scientific staff and water. He rightly contends that Campbell is dirtier than he need be. I point out that there is no excuse for such dirt but stress the fact that Campbell is a hard worker and on dirty jobs.'[52]

For the first few days the trip was uneventful and the *Wyatt Earp* appeared quite stable, but by Thursday, 12 February Law reported 'the ship is right back to her old rolling form today. And leaks have started again on the starboard side.'

On Saturday 14 they were treated to a wonderful display of Aurora Australis. The sight is awesome, beautiful and said to be unforgettable. Although Law had already seen one some years earlier at Mt Kosciusko, that evening he described it in detail:

Went to bed and had started reading when McCarthy told me there was an aurora in the northern sky! I got up and dressed and went up onto bridge ... The night was perfectly clear and the aurora was bril-liant. Started with two parallel curtains stretching from W to E ... At their brightest they showed green, yellow and red colourations. As a grand finale the rays grew longer and reached right up to the zenith, forming a pointed canopy over our heads which stretched down to horizon over the whole northern half of the sky. Finished finally as a corona localized at the zenith like a great spiral nebula.

Law had stuck to his resolve to refuse to do watch-duty and a few days later, after a party, one of the men 'who had drunk enough to become loquacious' told Law that the others were resentful of his refusal to keep watch. 'I had sensed this for some time and so had McCarthy,' Law wrote, and then declared, 'It leaves me completely indifferent' but one gains the impression that it didn't.

On Wednesday 18 February they sighted their first iceberg. Law wrote:

> General air of excitement. Everyone very happy and dashing about
> with cameras ... The icebergs loomed up after 7am very suddenly
> and inside two hours half a dozen could be seen. We began passing
> them at distances of about 4 miles. They appeared 200–300 ft high,
> flat or slightly hump–topped ... By lunch time (12 noon) small
> pieces of ice were beginning to float past the ship, varying in size
> from 1 c.ft. to pieces bigger than a large room.

By Friday, 20 February they had reached the pack-ice, an area of sea ice, and were cruising back and forth, east and west, outside its limits, waiting for the wind to moderate:

> Later in the morning got in the lee of the pack and the sea
> smoothed right out like a lake. We were soon passing down a lane of
> pack [-ice] with the white parallel edges some miles apart. The pack
> grew thicker and the lane degenerated into something more like a
> canal, with lovely ice floes gliding past on both sides from 20 to 200
> yards distant. On some of these sat penguins, which waddled around
> or tobogganed on their chests if we shouted at them. Pretty cape
> pigeons flew about the ship and amongst the floes on one side four
> killer whales blew and 'porpoised'.

Law's excitement was tempered by the Captain who, apparently deciding the pack-ice was too thick, turned the ship about. Law was suspicious:

> Don't know what the Captain plans doing. If he turns east tonight I
> think it means he has given Commonwealth Bay away. If he turns
> west it means he'll have another go at it further along.

The following day Law jubilantly reported that they were headed south and attempting to get through the pack. But he soon recorded that they 'failed to find an easy open path through and gave up.' Law's frustrations were palpable:

> Apparently the Captain does not intend to do any floe–pushing or
> even navigating in closed lanes or restricted space in case the drift of
> the floes cuts off his retreat. Rumour has it that he was instructed by
> the Navy not to try to penetrate actual pack.

Despondently, he continued, 'In any case it is obvious that unless there is a wide easy lane of clear water leading through the pack, we shall not make land.' Later on the ship tried ramming one of the smaller floes but 'we cracked it and bounced off,' Law recorded and disparagingly concluded, 'as an icebreaker this ship is a gnat.' After lunch they headed out to open sea again.

The following day, Sunday 22, the *Wyatt Earp* steamed into the vicinity of the Mertz glacier, hoping to find clear water, but had 'no luck'. By Monday they passed the Mertz glacier:

> Magnificent scenic grandeur! Huge bergs by the dozen strewn in our path like mad. Apparently they break off the end of the Merz glacier and float out. ... Sailed quite close to some and took what I hope are magnificent photographs.

Although Law had dabbled in photography at Hamilton High School, he had never seriously taken it up as a hobby. For this voyage he had borrowed a cine camera and a Leica 35 mm camera from the office and he was eager to get a good record of his Antarctic adventure. He was also taking wire-recordings of sounds for the film. By the end of this trip he had become a keen photographer.

Later on Sunday morning the *Wyatt Earp* tied up to an ice floe and Law was able to get off the ship and onto the floe itself for a few minutes. The men filled buckets with ice for water for washing and Law took photographs of the emperor penguins.

Law's and McCarthy's long hours working with the cosmic ray equipment continued and they were seldom able to go to bed before midnight. The equipment laboratory, luckily, was in one of the few dry areas in the ship and they had lashed down everything so securely that seldom was anything broken or dislodged. When breakages did occur, they proved a nightmare to fix:

> If you want some idea of the trouble we had [Law later explained to a reporter] take one soldering iron and one very expensive wireless set. Put the wireless set on a deck which rocks through 35 deg. every five seconds, smash up the inside of the set, and then try to repair it.[53]

On Tuesday 24 the party was in the Ninnis Glacier Tongue: 'Afternoon—Magnificent scenery! Huge dome-shaped icebergs on either side—as far as the eye can see ... Indescribable,' he raved, before making a stab at depicting the effect of the moon on the scene:

> About 9pm moon rose—full, orange red, huge—and shone across this loose pack, showing up new ice-crystals forming on top of the

still water. I shall never forget the moonlight, the calm water, the pack and the background of domed bergs. Have never witnessed anything as perfect.

Unfortunately, the conditions were ideal for a 'freeze up' and the Captain was determined to get clear and not remain too deeply in the ice overnight.

By now Law was sure the possibility of a landing at Commonwealth Bay was slim. By Wednesday 25 he reported mournfully that they 'were well out to sea, off the [continental] shelf, headed east' and, finally, on Friday 27, his hopes were completely dashed as they were now 'headed definitely for Balleny Islands.'

On the morning of Saturday 28, with heavy snow, Law recorded: 'Balleny Islands about 30 miles ahead. With luck Mac and I should get ashore and do magnetic work.' And with his usual forethought, mentioned that he was 'just going to make up a list of what we require.' But by the evening they had cruised around all day and had found no likely landing spots.

On Sunday 29, however, he finally made it ashore and this diary entry shows his excitement:

What a day this has been! Mac and I slept in until 10am, and were awakened by one of the crew telling us they were preparing a boat to go ashore. We got dressed and went up on deck, I grabbed a camera and before there was time to think about wearing correct clothing, I found myself in the whaler tossing about in a choppy sea with an oar in my hand.

There were six other men in the boat including Campbell, Mac, and Cook. They rowed for approximately two miles to the shore of Borradaile Island, towards a small spit of land where there were rocks and lumps of ice five feet or six feet high with a steep shelving approach from the water:

We cast anchor 30 yards from shore and let the boat come in yard by yard by playing out rope. When within a few yards, noticed quite heavy swell breaking on the narrow strip. Wallace in front was supposed to jump with a rope and make a turn around an ice block or stone. Got within 3 yards of edge of water and he remained stationary in bow, apparently waiting for the water to recede before jumping ashore. In meantime waves were breaking over the stern of the boat, drenching the others, particularly Cook and Mac, so Campbell, who was next to Wallace, grabbed the rope from him, leapt into the surf up to his thighs and ran up to an ice block where he took a turn. However, he was unable to hold it on his own, and Wallace still did not go to his assistance, so I pushed past Wallace, jumped into sea (filling my flying boots with icy-cold water—Boy was it cold!) and went to lend a hand. Seeing us both ashore, Wallace suddenly clicked and came too.

While the men struggled with the rope, waves crashed over the whaler, slewing it broadside.

Cook yelled to us to get aboard again, so we scrambled back in through surf up to our waists. Campbell had the presence of mind to grab a stone from the beach! We then rowed like mad and got out.

Law was later to refer to this episode at Balleny Islands as 'an extremely brief landing'. In fact it was the second landing there, the previous one by a Captain Freeman who, over a 100 years before, had also made only 'a brief landing ... to secure a few pieces of rock'.[54]

The following day, March 1, they sailed along beside the Islands. Law wrote:

Still hoping to go ashore, but prospects are fading more and more. Have never seen anything less inviting than the Island coasts we passed today. Some of the cliffs must reach nearly 1000 ft.—black and topped with 40–50 ft. of snow ... glaciers end in ice–falls, sheer into the sea and up to 100 ft. high. No wonder so few have landed. ... One cliff face on the end of Young Island must be 600 ft. to 1000 ft. high and absolutely vertical [small sketch]. Most remarkable— seems even concave. Terrific!

He sent a telegram to Nel: 'Greetings from Balleny Islands Comfortable Happy Well Love, Phil.' By Thursday, still unable to land, they saw 'lots of whales—two schools of killers, each about 8 strong, three humpbacks and several blues.' On Saturday, 6 March his hopes for a landing at Commonwealth Bay were raised again:

We are out at sea again, headed west, away from Balleny Islands, going back towards Commonwealth Bay. Good. I was becoming restless sitting in the one spot. The Ballenys have nothing else to offer me now, so I'm glad to be moving off again.

By the following Thursday they had once more reached the pack-ice. There was a heavy swell, it was snowing and the great masses of floe-ice looked strange, 'heaving restlessly up and down' in the snow. Law disdainfully commented that 'snowballing continues to be the main amusement of the wardroom. I'm not interested—got it out of my system years ago.' He was also feeling pessimistic about a possible landing: 'We are headed east to have a look, en passant, at the region of the Mertz Glacier Tongue in the forlorn hope that we may get closer to shore there.'

By Friday 12 Law was pleased when they arrived back in the region of the dome-shaped bergs. On Saturday there was some excitement when they at last managed to have the right conditions to fly the aircraft, a Sikorsky Kingfisher, a single-engine, single float seaplane, after hours of struggling to first get it off the ship:

> Very amusing really—a helluva lot of time wasted and messing about. (I'd hate to have to launch the whaler in a hurry for a man overboard or a shipwreck!)

Finally they managed to get it airborne, but it 'did not go far and could not see land. Saw lots of new ice, some clear water some miles away, and little else' before it came in again.

Despite this diversion, Law was still angry about, what he regarded as, the lack of interest shown in scientific work.

> Throughout the trip there has been evident a lack of interest and understanding of scientific work by the non-scientific members ... The layman's attitude to pure science, 'What is the use, what good are those results, why do men want to know anything about an emperor penguin's egg ... what's the use of wasting time pulling up water samples, etc. etc.', has been thoroughly exemplified on board this ship. We scientists are regarded with amused tolerance (and in some cases resentful intolerance) as rather queer examples of a rather stupid species.

This attitude further fuelled his growing belief that few people, apart from scientists, were interested in the research possibilities of Antarctica.

By Monday, March 15 the *Wyatt Earp* was still sailing east between Ninnis Glacier and Cape Freshfield, where the men saw a huge iceberg, approximately 15 miles long. But by Tuesday the ship had turned and was heading north away from the continent and towards Macquarie Island. Law, who had obviously given up any hope of landing some days before, simply recorded that they had headed north and left the icebergs.

The trip to Macquarie Island was uneventful, except for grumbles about the restrictions on water and a note stating that 'It seems that the non-naval blokes have given up watch-keeping! After all the fuss they raised earlier in the piece! Well, well.'

Macquarie Island's vibrant green slopes offered them a sight that contrasted strangely with the Balleny Islands' stark blackness. The *LST 3501* was off-shore, having arrived on 7 March to set up the wintering party. Law was able to go ashore during the next two days and see how the station was progressing and to explore the area around it. Speedy took him up the cliffs to watch the rock-hopper penguins and to the back beach to see the sea elephants and giant petrels.

The *Wyatt Earp* left Macquarie Island on Wednesday 24. She had taken on 18 tons of fresh water from the *LST 3501*, which, Law happily recorded, 'should be ample with no restrictions', but made caustic remarks about the way the job was handled: 'The usual inefficient mucking about. Very poor seamen—young unskilled—on *LST.*' Although Law smarted at the lack of tolerance from the officers for his scientific work, he showed little tolerance for the work of the seamen.

Weather conditions were bad and Cook recorded,

We rolled like a log, pitched, tossed, yawed, rose to incredible heights on crests and plunged to abysmal depths in the troughs. She did everything but stand vertical although once or twice she tried her damndest.[55]

The next day was Good Friday 'Have never known Easter feel less Easter–like,' Law wrote on Friday 26. He had already spent Christmas day and New Year's day on the *Wyatt Earp* and he was thinking now of home. He dejectedly noted that he had not received a cable yet from Nel.

The ship passed through the Port Phillip Heads at 6 p.m. on Wednesday, 31 March and a party was held on board. Many of the men, including Campbell and Mac, but not Law, stayed up all night. Law awoke the following morning at 5.30 a.m. to a 'funny scene—the all-night drinkers as full as boots. Campbell fell in—ship turned about and picked him up.'

The *Wyatt Earp* finally tied up at Station Pier, Port Melbourne at 9 a.m. on 1 April 1948. Law was disappointed to note that there were 'very few onlookers', but Nel was there and it was 'great to be home'. Later that evening they had dinner with friends, with 'wild pig, champagne, imported liqueurs'.

Law had confirmed one of Nel's worst fears expressed to a reporter at the beginning of the trip. He had grown a short beard. The beard would become a distinctive Law feature, often ridiculed, frequently commented on by reporters, but he 'dug his heels in' and never shaved it off.

Although the *Wyatt Earp* mission had failed to achieve its purpose of locating a suitable base for future operations, and Law had been unable to go ashore on the Antarctic continent, he had accumulated a wealth of information about life on board ship and Antarctic conditions. His diary included notations on what had worked well and what was inefficient and this knowledge would be invaluable in the years to come.

5.

A month or so later, in May 1948, an Antarctic Division of the DEA was established and Campbell's title changed to 'Officer-in-Charge'. A new ANARE Planning Committee was formed consisting of representatives of the various departments and organisations that were involved with the expeditions' activities. Campbell was Chairman of this Committee and, at the first meeting on 18 May 1948, *Wyatt Earp*'s seaworthiness was again questioned. The Committee finally recommended that Campbell should go overseas immediately to find a suitable ice-breaker ship to replace it.

In the meantime, by courtesy of the Australian Army, Law had undertaken to join the *MV Duntroon*'s trip to Japan to extend cosmic ray latitude variation measurements across the equator and the tropics. He and Colin McKenzie, one of the post graduate students who had helped with the construction of the equipment, sailed from Sydney on 2 July 1948.

Compared to the *Wyatt Earp* voyage, the trip to Japan was a pleasure cruise. Day followed uneventful day with time for Law to play the piano, the accordion or deck tennis, take baths, consume crayfish, pork cutlets, jelly and fine wines and, in the evening, to watch films or consistently lose at 'Housie Housie'.

The *Duntroon* arrived in Japan on Sunday 18. Complications now set in. Although the DEA in Canberra had sent a telegram to the Australian Mission in Tokyo, asking it to arrange for Law and McKenzie to go ashore whilst the vessel was in port in Japan, no permit was available when they arrived. To compound the problem, the DEA representative from Tokyo, who was supposed to meet Law, was not there. Law explained his predicament to the US Major at the Customs Section and told him he would like to go to Tokyo. The officer assured Law that he would fix everything. He did, and his efforts triggered off a chain of events that gave Law 'the maddest day of his life'.

Unbeknown to Law, he had been mistaken for a member of an Australian Parliamentary Delegation which had come to Japan to see General McArthur, the Supreme Allied Commander. Law and three military personnel were taken by special train to Tokyo. They had the six-carriage train entirely to themselves: an observation lounge car, dining room, sleeper, excellent meals and service. Law was delighted. 'Scenery magnificent', he recorded, sounding surprised, 'Why didn't someone tell me that this country was so beautiful? I have never seen anything to equal it.'

When they arrived in Tokyo, Law was taken to the first-class Imperial Hotel reserved for top ranking US officers. He told the organisers that he thought he was to have gone to the Maranouchi Hotel, but they insisted that he was booked into the Imperial Hotel. There he was given a splendid room with private bathroom, replete with sunken bath.

The following day the US officials who were acting as hosts for the Parliamentary Delegation discovered that Law's name was not on their list. The American Colonel in charge of the Delegation was furious to find an Australian, as Law later explained, 'unauthorised to enter Japan, no permission to come to Tokyo, no right to be at Imperial Hotel etc.'.[56] The Colonel left a message at the hotel for Law to contact him. Unaware of the furore he had caused, Law spent the day at the Tokyo Meteorological Bureau and casually called into the Colonel's office late in the afternoon. The Colonel was not in, but Law was hit with a tirade of accusations from a Major who told him that the Colonel had written out a deportation order for Law to be returned to Kure:

> He [the Major] went for me, boots and all, taking the attitude that I was an impostor and had got to Tokyo by false pretences, fraud and Lord knows what. I couldn't get a word in at all for the first 20 minutes, but as he became exhausted I took over.
>
> The thing that finally wrecked him was when I asked him to explain how my name got into the book at the Imperial for a booking. Gradually it began to dawn on him that someone on his side had made the mistake of thinking I was with the Delegation. So he took me for a cup of tea and became quite friendly. However, he said I would have to wait till the Colonel returned so that he could revoke my deportation order.

That night Law was 'turfed out' of the Imperial Hotel, but not before he had attended a cocktail party, to which he had been invited by the Australian Mission, in honour of the Parliamentary Delegation. He later wrote to Nel and gleefully told her the story:

> Had a grand evening. The beard was worth its weight in gold thread. Everyone said 'Who is the man with the beard?' and I met all sorts of big wigs.
>
> I made a point of explaining that at any moment a military police detachment might arrive to arrest me and it became quite a joke. By the end of the evening I was sitting pretty and I don't think anyone smaller than McArthur himself could have sent me back to Kure! At 8pm nearly everyone went home but I was asked to stay on for dinner (buffet style) which we ate under Chinese lanterns strung between trees on the lawn.[57]

The following morning Law was advised that the Colonel now did not wish to see him, and that he could stay and finish his business in Tokyo as he had planned. 'It's a hard life,' Law told Nel in a letter written on

Imperial Hotel letter-head, 'but it's a helluva lot of fun.'[58] He returned to the ship, with no money, on July 23.

The *Duntroon* arrived in Auckland on Monday, 9 August where Law and the cosmic ray research received a good press. His equipment, it was reported, created some rumours initially about 'atom bombs and such like' and was referred to by the troops of the *Duntroon* as the 'infernal machine'. Much was made of his talents in scientific work, sport and music, with interest in his beard coming in second best behind his boxing ability. 'A non smoker', one article went on to say, 'he laughs off his fetish for physical fitness by claiming that a fast tilt with the gloves does as much good to a scientist as it does to anyone else.'[59] After a few uneventful days, 'rest of cruise devoid of incident', Law arrived in Sydney on Friday, 20 August 1948.

6.

When he arrived home there was a letter waiting for him from Colin Moodie, Counsellor-in-Charge of Antarctic Affairs, DEA, bringing to his notice an advertisement which had appeared in the Commonwealth *Gazette* while Law was away for the position of Assistant Officer-in-Charge (Scientific) for the Antarctic Division. The duties of the position were:

> Assist Officer-in-Charge in planning and organisation of scientific parties to be isolated for long periods in remote localities. Responsible in collaboration with Council for Scientific and Industrial Research for collation of all scientific knowledge gained; to act as Officer-in-Charge of the Division during his absence.[60]

A few days later Moodie told Law that Stuart Campbell contemplated leaving the Antarctic Division to return to his permanent position with the Commonwealth Department of Civil Aviation. Campbell's major interest in the Antarctic work had been to set up a base on the Antarctic Continent, but he had failed to find a suitable ship to replace the *Wyatt Earp*. Without a ship the Antarctic program would be limited to running the Heard and Macquarie Island stations. Moodie intimated to Law that the person to be appointed for the position of Officer-in-Charge (Scientific) would very likely be appointed as Acting Officer-in-Charge when Campbell left.

Law was delighted with the news. He now desperately wanted to work permanently in the Antarctic Division for he could see that this organisation offered him boundless opportunities to demonstrate his worth as an administrator. Besides that:

> I was fascinated, of course, like all adventurers are, with the exploration and discovery aspects of it, and my interest in mountaineering and snow and ice gave me a strong adventure motivation. But as

well as all that, I was fascinated by the research potential of the islands and Antarctica, so I was deeply interested as a scientist.

The one snag which had dampened his enthusiasm in applying for a position with the Antarctic Division was that he could not stomach working under Campbell:

> Campbell and I didn't actually clash because I was a good Public Servant. I certainly had arguments with him and I certainly had my opinions about him, but I was very restrained and careful in my dealings with him ... We were poles apart in temperament. He was cynical and negative, he used to put people down as a matter of course. He would always try and obstruct or oppose and contradict and you had to justify yourself tremendously strongly in order to get anything through. It was the antithesis of my optimistic approach of encouraging people to come up with ideas and do things. So I couldn't have worked under Campbell permanently.

There now seemed little likelihood of the two of them having to work together. By 30 August 1948, Law had applied for the position of Assistant Officer-in-Charge (Scientific).

Law's credentials for the position were hard to better. He was one of the few Australian scientists who had been to Antarctica, he had put together the scientific programs of ANARE for Heard and Macquarie Islands and for the *Wyatt Earp* voyage; he had successfully undertaken two cosmic ray investigations and had since written scientific papers and submitted them for publication with the *Australian Journal of Scientific Research*. Added to this, his previous work with the SIOP had given him a range of administrative skills and he had become familiar with much of the administration of the Antarctic Division headquarters.

Yet the path was not going to be smooth. At that stage Law was blissfully unaware that Campbell was taking steps to stop him from getting a job with the Antarctic Division. Before Law had left for Japan he had frequently asked Campbell to let him know of any position that came vacant with the re-organisation of the Division. Campbell always told him that nothing had been decided. In fact, three days after Law had left for Tokyo, Campbell had written to the DEA and advised that Law's appointment would terminate on 1 August and added further that, 'in view of the pending re-organization of this Division, it is not proposed to recommend an extension of Mr. Law's appointment.'[61]

Campbell's animosity towards Law is hard to account for, but his determination to block Law may well have succeeded had Law not had allies in the DEA. Colin Moodie, for example, admired him:

> I had met Phil Law earlier at an Executive Policy Committee Meeting. I liked him straight away. I thought he was a bit shy, didn't talk

too much, a very nice man ... Lively eye, a clear way of expressing his views.

Moodie, however, did not like Campbell. Added to this, John Burton, the Secretary of the DEA, was not keen to extend Campbell's involvement with the Antarctic Division.[62]

Behind–the–scenes manoeuvres began in earnest on 20 August. Following a suggestion from Moodie, Burton wrote to Campbell and recommended that a panel of three scientists should consider, with Campbell, the applications for the OIC (Scientific) position. The three scientists suggested, including Professor Martin from the Melbourne University, all knew Law well. Campbell objected to having scientists on the panel but Burton insisted, although he did agree with Campbell that perhaps Professor Martin should be replaced. Burton also insisted that Mawson, who lived in Adelaide, should be on the selection committee, and he wrote and invited him to serve on it.

On 12 October Campbell wrote to the Public Service Board Inspector and added the following new requirements for the position of OIC (Scientific):

[The person should be] of mature age and have a wide general experience, with particular emphasis on handling men and departmental organisation as well as technical or scientific qualifications.[63]

Subsequent events show that Campbell was supporting the application of a Wing Commander H. W. Berry, of the RAAF. Berry was older than Law, had no scientific qualifications, but had very good technical and administrative experience, making him well suited for the new requirements.

Campbell wrote to Mawson inviting him to attend the interview in Melbourne the following week, but added 'Personally, I very much doubt if it would be worth your while coming.' Not surprisingly, Mawson declined to attend the selection interviews, but arranged to see the documentation. Campbell also told Mawson that he would soon return to the Department of Civil Aviation and the new appointee would take over his job. This would mean, Campbell maintained, that wide general experience and organising ability was more important for the Assistant OIC (Scientific) position than academic or scientific qualifications.[64]

It is reasonable to assume that Campbell made similar statements to the other members of the selection panel for, when Law was interviewed he was asked if he were 'still anxious to proceed in view of the change in the nature of the job'. Law, completely unaware that the requirements for the job had been changed was 'staggered'.[65]

Now suddenly aware of the moves to thwart his objective, Law began to take action on his own behalf. Once he believed the boots were being put in, Law was not averse to using the same tactics. He contacted Trevor

Heath, Secretary of the Antarctic Division, and Heath kept him abreast of what was happening. Next, Law wrote a long letter to Moodie and told him that he suspected foul play by Campbell:

> That C.[Campbell] dislikes me I have always known, just as I dislike him. We are completely incompatible. Our ideas on everything are irreconcilable. That he is determined that I shall not get this job I have hesitated to believe, but I cannot delude myself any longer in spite of his recent ingratiating friendliness towards me.
>
> Why he is so concerned lest I get the job I cannot quite figure out. I have made various guesses.
>
> First he may honestly believe me to be incapable of doing the job, for if he is sure his methods are right he must be equally certain that mine are wrong, because they are certainly very different from his ... Secondly, I have many grounds for suspecting that he still cherishes the idea of returning to lead the Expedition when it finally goes south. If so, he knows that if I get the position I would oppose him as leader with all my strength.[66]

He then went on to list many of the political manoeuvres that Campbell had engaged in, including the fact that he had not formally assembled the selection committee to discuss their decision:

> The method [Campbell is using] is now obvious. He never at any time gathers together the whole committee. They write their opinions, which he then takes around personally to each of the committee in turn, coloring, distorting and twisting the facts to suit his plan.
>
> Trevor [Heath] tells me that Campbell returned from Adelaide [after seeing Mawson] very disappointed and talked of re-advertising the position to eliminate the bias on scientific knowledge. Did Mawson refuse to be talked around? I think, like myself, the old boy is very concerned at the short shrift being meted out to science, not only now but right through the history of this venture.

He concluded his long harangue to Moodie with the observation:

> Look, if they appoint a 'pure administrator' even the Island programmes will degenerate into routine, unimaginative exercises in 'logistics', ... and the Antarctic show itself will just never materialize ... Pick a good reputable scientific bloke for this job and I'll withdraw my application. But I'll fight 'pure administrators', particularly heavy-handed ex-service administrators who believe in handling a scientific expedition like a military exercise, as long as I have any breath left.[67]

Campbell continued to work against Law's appointment. On 3 November he advised the DEA that the selection committee agreed that neither Law nor Berry 'appear to possess all the necessary qualifications and experience to be considered as future Officer-in-Charge should this position be created in the future'. He suggested that the appointment of Assistant OIC (Scientific) be deferred and that a position of Assistant OIC (Technical Administration) be created.[68] Burton then asked Campbell to send him all the available reports from members of the selection panel.[69] At the same time, he wrote to Dr Woolley (ex SIOP member), asking him his opinion of Law's work whilst Law was Secretary of the SIOP.[70]

Campbell finally brought the selection committee together on 8 November. Whether or not this was under Burton's instructions is not clear. After the meeting, Campbell advised the Secretary DEA that the committee recommended 'the position of Assistant Officer-in-Charge (Scientific) be not filled at present' and suggested instead that another position of 'Principal Administrative Officer' be created. Then, perhaps foolishly, he overplayed his hand, by stating that:

Subject to such other applications as may be received for the position of Principal Administrative officer, I think all members of the Committee agree that W/Cdr Berry would be a very suitable appointee now that the stress on a strictly scientific qualification has been removed.[71]

About ten days later, after receiving a favourable report from Woolley on Law's work with the SIOP,[72] Burton wrote to the Public Service Board, advising it of the background to the interviews, part of which stated:

In considering the applications, members of the panel apparently had in mind that, once an Assistant Officer-in-Charge (Scientific) were appointed, it would be difficult at a later stage to appoint an Officer in Charge over his head. They, therefore, did not consider the applications purely in relation to the duties of the position as advertised. This approach is erroneous, as it was at no stage contemplated by me that the Assistant Officer-in-Charge (Scientific) would have special claims to being appointed Officer-in-Charge should such a position be later created in order to carry out a full Antarctic Programme.[73]

He then advised them that the appointment to the position of Assistant Officer-in-Charge (Scientific) should be proceeded with and that Law was the most suitable application for the position.[74] That same day, 18 November, Burton also wrote to all the scientific members on the selection committee with similar information.[75]

It was not until 8 December—and for some unknown reason the letter was not despatched until 13 December—that Burton finally advised Campbell of the decision to appoint Law. Campbell was obviously furious and continued the campaign against Law's appointment right up until 21 December, the day Law was advised that his application had been successful.

Law now had a permanent appointment to the Commonwealth Public Service as Assistant Officer-in-Charge (Scientific) 3rd Division, Antarctic Division, Department of External Affairs on a salary of £742 p.a.[76] On 29 and 30 December he visited Canberra for a briefing. By 31 December 1948 Campbell had returned to the Department of Civil Aviation and Law had resigned from Melbourne University.

On 1 January 1949 Law was appointed Acting Officer-in-Charge of the Antarctic Division, which included the responsibilities of Leader of the ANARE. He now had 21 days to prepare for his first voyage as Expedition Leader.

Notes

1. Law, 'The Mawson Story—No. 2, A Powerful, Stubborn and Gentle Man', *Royal History Society of Victoria Journal,* 1984, vol. 57, no. 1, p. 13.
2. R. A. Swan, *Australia in the Antarctic, Interest, Activity and Endeavour,* Melbourne University Press, 1961, p. 143.
3. Swan, op.cit., p. 187.
4. Law, *Antarctic Odyssey,* p. 5.
5. Law, unpublished review of *Mawson's Antarctic Diaries,* 1988, LP.
6. Law and John Bechervaise, *ANARE, Australia's Antarctic Outposts,* Oxford University Press, Melbourne, 1957, p. xiii.
7. Swan, op.cit., p. 347.
8. Law, *Antarctic Odyssey,* p. 5.
9. Rolph Trolle–Anderson, 'The Antarctic scene: legal and political facts', in Gilland D. Triggs (ed.), *The Antarctic Treaty regime—Law, Environment and Resources,* Cambridge University Press, Cambridge, 1987, p. 58.
10. Rolph Trolle–Anderson, op.cit., pp. 57–8.
11. Law, Obituary for Group Captain Stuart Campbell, 1903–1988, LR.
12. Law to Lennard Bickel, 19/20 April, 1975.
13. EPC Minutes, 23 July 1947, ADH.
14. Notes for Discussion at EPC Meeting, 26 May 1947, ADH.
15. Smith to Tim Bowden, ABC, 2 December 1987, ABC:SHU.
16. Law to Bickel, April 1975.
17. Law, 'The Mawson Story, A Powerful, Stubborn and Gentle Man', *Royal History Society of Vic. Journal,* 1984, p. 3.
18. Henry Erskine, 'No Atom Bombs in His Pocket', *New Zealand Observer,* 18 August 1948.
19. Jacka to author, 8 August 1990.
20. Ibid.
21. EPC Minutes, May 1950, ADH.
22. *The Australian Women's Weekly,* 22 November 1947.
23. Cited in Swan, op.cit., p. 244.
24. J. Abbotsmith to Tim Bowden, ABC, November 1987, ABC:SHU.
25. Preliminary Report by Chief Executive Officer, Mr S. A. C. Campbell, on the establishment of the Scientific Station of Heard Island presented to Antarctic Planning Committee, on Friday, 23 January 1948, ADH.
26. Campbell Report, 1948, ADH.

27. Captain W. F. Cook, 'HMAS Wyatt Earp, Australian National Antarctic Research Expedition 1947–1948', Naval Historical Review, December 1978.
28. Law to Lennard Bickel, 19/20 April 1975.
29. Cook, op.cit., p. 5.
30. Newspaper article, 'Last Minute Rush to Get Wyatt Earp Away', undated, LP.
31. Swan, op.cit., p. 200.
32. The Australian Women's Weekly, 22 November 1947.
33. The Sun, Saturday, 1 November 1947, p. 14.
34. Erskine, 18 August 1948.
35. Cook, op.cit., p. 9.
36. Law to Bowden, 1 December 1987.
37. Law to Nel Law, 22 December 1947, LP.
38. Cook, op.cit., p. 9.
39. Captain Karl Oom, Report of Proceedings, 20 December 1947, cited in Cook, op.cit., 1978, p. 7.
40. Cook, op.cit., p. 9.
41. Cited in Cook, op.cit., p. 9.
42. John Hetherington, 'Tomorrow is his Business' in Australians, Nine Profiles, F. W. Cheshire, Melbourne, 1960.
43. Cook, op.cit., p. 9.
44. Cook, op.cit., p. 11.
45. Ibid.
46. Appendix II, Proposed Revised Programme for Wyatt Earp and L.S.T. 3501, presented at the Meeting of the Planning Committee at Canberra on 23 January 1948, ADH.
47. EPC Minutes, 23 January 1948, ADH.
48. Ibid.
49. 'Antarctic Folly?' The Argus, Saturday, 14 February 1947.
50. Law, 'Tribulations at Sea', Talk given to Shiplovers' Society of Victoria, 11 May 1966, LR.
51. Law to Bowden, 30 November 1987.
52. Fred Jacka and Eleanor Jacka, Mawson's Antarctic Diaries, A Susan Haynes Book, Allen and Unwin, Sydney, 1988 p. 383
53. Erskine, 18 August 1948.
54. Swan, op.cit., p. 27.
55. Cook, op.cit., p. 17.
56. Law to Nel Law, 27 July 1948, LP.
57. Ibid.
58. Law to Nel Law, 19 July 1948, LP.
59. Erskine, 18 August 1948.
60. Commonwealth Gazette, no. 122, 12 August 1948.
61. Campbell to Burton, 5 July 1948, AA:CRS A1838/245, Item 1251/819 Pt. 1.
62. C. Moodie to author, 7 August 1990, LP.
63. 'Summary of Antarctic Division's File', Assistant OIC (Scientific), November 1948, AA:CRS A1838 T173, Item 1256/22.
64. Campbell to Sir Douglas Mawson, 13 October 1948, AA:CRS A1838 T173, Item 1256/22.
65. Law to C. Moodie, 27 October 1948, LP.
66. Ibid.
67. Ibid.
68. Campbell to Burton, 3 November 1948, AA:CRS A1838 T173, Item 1256/22.
69. Burton to Campbell, 5 November 1948, AA:CRS A1838 T173, Item 1256/22.
70. Burton to Dr R. Woolley, 5 November 1948, AA:CRS A1838 T173, Item 1256/22.
71. Campbell to Burton, 8 November 1948, AA:CRS A1838 T173, Item 1256/22.
72. Dr R. Woolley to J. W. Burton, 9 November 1948, AA:CRS A1838 T173, Item 1256/22.
73. Burton to PSB, 18 November 1948, AA:CRS A1838 T173, Item 1256/22.
74. Ibid.
75. Burton, Draft Letter to Scientific Members of Selection Committee, undated, AA:CRS A1838 T173, Item 1256/22.
76. Commonwealth of Australia, Public Service Inspector to Law, 21 December 1948, AA:CRS A1838 T173, Item 1256/22.

6. Acting Officer-in-Charge, Antarctic Division, 1949

1.

ALTHOUGH LAW'S POSITION WITH THE ANTARCTIC DIVISION WAS A PERmanent one, he was still only Officer-in-Charge in an acting capacity. He felt as if he were on trial and his first hurdle was to successfully lead the change-over voyage to Heard Island.

The *LST 3501* had survived its first trip to Heard Island and Stuart Campbell advised the EPC that its performance 'had proved beyond all doubt that these ungainly looking vessels are well found ships capable of taking anything the Southern Ocean has to offer.'[1] An LST (Landing Ship Tank) is a ship approximately 300 ft long with two-thirds of the front section forming a floating hull for carrying tanks. The bridge, the engine and accommodation are located at the back of the ship. It has blunt bows comprising doors that can be opened outwards and a ramp that can be let down to enable the tanks to drive straight out onto a beach. Some LSTs had broken in half whilst on duty in World War II, but it was generally believed that most of those which did break were welded ships and that the welding contributed to the failures. 'They had the good sense,' Law wryly commented about the 3501, 'to pick an LST that was mainly riveted rather than being welded.'[2]

Despite the Australian Naval Board's initial concerns about the suitability of an LST for sub-Antarctic work, the *LST 3501*'s first successful voyage to Heard Island had dulled their original fears and little more was said. Coupled with the fact that there was no alternative ship, the *LST 3501*, which had recently been renamed the *HMAS Labuan*, was again to be used for the Heard Island voyage.

Heard Island lies approximately half–way between Australia and South Africa and nine hundred miles north of the Antarctic Continent. Since it was first sighted in 1833 it was, until the 20th century, the haunt of sealers and whalers. During 1929 the BANZAR Expedition visited it briefly. The island is ice-ribbed and rock-bound. 'It sprawls like a gigantic sea monster in the long green swell of the South Ocean,' wrote one journalist, who proclaimed it as 'probably the most isolated speck of land on the face of the globe.'[3] Battered by incessant gale force winds its desolation is menacing. But its very desolation holds and fascinates, for many who have spent time there, return again and again.

A solitary mountain, 'Big Ben', dominates the island and from its

9 000 foot summit, permanently covered in ice and snow, glaciers sweep down forming ice cliffs 50–60 feet high where they reach the sea. As the island is seldom free of cloud, the first view from the ship is usually of the hostile glacier cliffs looming out of the mist. Occasionally the mist does clear and the traveller is rewarded with one of the most dramatic sights of the southern ocean, Big Ben's dome, seeming to float in the sky, above the surrounding mist.

The weather conditions that had plagued Campbell's expedition were not unusual for Heard Island. 'I have not had a ship's captain who has not been glad when he has been able to leave [Heard Island],' Law later wrote.[4] Even Captain Davis, with his years of experience in Antarctica, is said to have described it as 'the most god-forsaken place he had seen in all his life'.[5]

Lieutenant Commander George Dixon, who had been in charge of the ship on the previous Heard and Macquarie Islands expeditions, was to be in command again. The ANARE party consisted of Law as Expedition Leader, eleven men who would spend the following year at Heard Island, and six men, classed as 'supernumeraries', doing the round trip. These latter included David Eastman, a photographer who had been on the previous Heard Island round trip and J. Atkinson, a journalist, and three Royal Australian Army Service Corps personnel to handle the DUKWs. DUKWs are versatile amphibious vehicles which evolved during World War II. In the water, they are driven by a propeller, with pumps to keep the bilges free of water, whilst on shore their six-wheel drive and high clearance enable them to traverse rough terrain. They had been used successfully during the previous year's Macquarie Island voyage, streamlining the task of ferrying men, stores and equipment from the ship to the shore.

The *Labuan* left Melbourne on Friday, 21 January 1949, with 'the usual last-minute panic'. Law thought his cine camera had been stolen, but after rushing back to the office, he found it safely locked up in his filing cabinet. Three men were late and, when they arrived, Law found they had been drinking. One of the men resented having to present for the departure ceremony and it was not until Law had 'made an outright order of it that he came to heel'. By evening, with the sea fairly calm and a comfortable ship, Law was feeling tired but optimistic. 'A really pleasant evening,' he wrote, 'What a change from the "Earp"!'

The next day Law was feeling sick. He was very heavy-headed and wanted to sleep, but he forced himself to work. He organised bird log observations and meteorology observations, helped sort the mail and talked with the Captain about landing arrangements. He interspersed these activities with long periods of sleep, and even slept through a party some of the men held in his cabin.

On Heard Island, the wintering-over expeditioners had received the long awaited news that the relief party had left Melbourne. Alan Campbell-Drury, the Radio Operator on Heard Island, recorded his feelings:

Yesterday afternoon Radio Australia broadcast to us the heartening news which so many of us have been looking for. The relief ship, renamed *HMAS Labuan,* has sailed today with the relief party. Cheers went up as we were all grouped around the radio in the rec. room. We believe they will take about fourteen days to reach us, given fair weather.[6]

After 13 months of isolation, the news triggered off a flood of reflections as Campbell-Drury contemplated the coming reunion and the return home with a mixture of apprehension and excitement. The loneliness and isolation of Antarctic work is graphically evident from his diary:

I, like most of us, find it more and more difficult to conceive that the relief ship is already on its way. In another few weeks we will be headed homewards.

... Each night now the rec–room presents a scene of much activity as men talk and speculate over the relief. In the past you would walk into the rec–hut of any evening and find no one there. If not work-ing, they'd all gone to bed—but now it is different. If you do go to bed you can't sleep anyway as thoughts flash through your mind—exciting thoughts of reading mail, of things to be done, and of new and fresh faces to see.

You wonder if civilisation will be just like it was when you left it, and perhaps if you will be coming south again soon to the land which has become so much a part of you and you of it. You wonder what people will say to you as they bid the time of day, and in the general course of the conversation, you will have so much to talk about—experiences, fascinating experiences which you imagine will cast a spell over a listening audience.

First of all there is the voyage home and the thought of being entertained with movies—movies taken of the landing operations by Dave Eastman and which have since been screened throughout the whole world. Eastman is on board the *Labuan* so his life will be worthless if he does not bring those films with him.

At night you lie awake wondering who will be in the new party—if possibly you will know any of them. I have been awaking at 3 o'clock of a morning and eating candy waiting for it to come time to get up, then I find I have gone to sleep again and overslept breakfast. It is hard to describe just what the feeling of seeing a ship soon is like after all this time.[7]

Fortunately, with fine weather and a calm sea with little swell, the *Labuan* was making good time. However, even with these near-perfect conditions, Law was concerned about the antics of the ship:

When a large wave gets under this ship the bow and stern sag and then as the wave passes down along the whole length of the ship the structure flaps up and down like a spring-board with much groaning and clanging. Feels as though it would just shake apart.

The voyage soon settled down to a pattern for Law of breakfast, work on different aspects for the landing, sometimes a sleep during the day, more clerical work in the afternoon, before-dinner drinks, and dinner followed by films in the evening. Law's interest in films was evident. He usually noted in his diary the film's name, whether or not he bothered to watch it, and a short statement of his opinion of it. 'Naughty Marietta' had 'terrible dated acting,' he had already seen 'Boom Town' so didn't bother to watch it and 'a Canadian Mounted Police yarn' was 'not bad.' One film, 'Walkabout,' merited more comment: 'Very good—Central Australian Aborigines in natural (completely naked) state, with grand color shots of mountains. Nel would have loved it.'

The men, Law included, began to show an interest in bird observations. Law wrote, 'This bird watching becomes quite fascinating.' They had begun a log book recording sightings, which became the basis of valuable data for research workers that would be kept over the years. Law believed that having responsibility for a particular aspect of work could often spark off a new interest and, by giving these observational duties to the men, they became keen bird watchers as a result.

Before their arrival at Heard Island Law made detailed arrangements for the landing. He held discussions with Captain Dixon, selected the men required, read the previous year's instruction manual, checked supplies, made notes for himself regarding matters that were not up to the standard he desired, noted items he wanted to follow up when he returned to Melbourne and worked with the men in the hold to prepare the supplies to be taken ashore. 'Lads all worked well,' he reported.

The comment is interesting for this particular group of men had previously worried Law. He was not at all sure how they would work together, but he noted that 'They are shaking down well into a good group. Some of my earlier misgivings seem groundless.' His belief, too, in the power of hard, physical work to bring out the best, or the worst, in men was apparent when he recorded: 'By the end of the unloading period, they should be welded into a strong team.'

The fine weather continued for a week, but by late Friday, 28 January, the wind had changed and the ship again started its violent 'caterpillar' bending that Captain Dixon had remarked upon in the previous voyage to Heard Island. Law's description was that it 'feels as though you have struck a bad bump without shock-absorbers,' followed by a remark which hinted at his underlying concern about the ship, 'you would swear the ship had broken in half.' The following day he recorded that 'during the night some time the ship split her upper deck forward,' but he made no further comment.

At 4 a.m. on Sunday 30 he awoke to see the first icebergs of the trip:

Small iceberg—a remnant really, little more than a fragment ... A
larger one ahead. Changed course and went within 1 mile of it. Estimated it to be 400' long, 60' high. Tabular type, blue-white, consisting of two bits joined under-water.

Later on in the day he recorded that the seas were the biggest they
had yet seen on this trip, 'Huge "breakers" 30–40 ft. high, foam-flecked
surface, short steep swell.' He was obviously worried about the ship's
ability to survive the conditions, particularly with its split across the deck,
and the mountainous seas:

Ship 'bashing' again. It is an amazing effect. Imagine a ship
mounted on 6 pairs of wheels running along road and coming to
deep drain. No shock absorbers. As it runs over the drain the successive jolts jar hell out of everything and cause a banging of the bulk-
heads as though they were belted with huge hammers. After the last
jolt the whole ship vibrates with decreasing amplitude coming to
rest about 10 seconds later.

Despite his concerns with the conditions, that evening 'We had a sing-
song party.' Law played the piano accordion. 'Very enjoyable,' he pro-
nounced, 'the lads got through quite a bit of beer and everything was
very merry. Broke it up at 10.30 in wardroom, but others continued in
cabins till 12.' Law seldom attended the private parties in the cabins, and
on this occasion he was in bed by 10.45 p.m.

In the interests of the physical fitness of the men during the long sea
voyage, Law had arranged for the tank space at the front of the ship to
be set up with a punching-bag where the men held boxing, gymnasium
and volley-ball sessions. The springboard effect of the *Labuan*, produc-
ing successive ripples of four to six inches as they passed along the deck,
made volley-ball difficult:

It was quite fascinating trying to play because every now and again
you'd get thrown up in the air with one of these ripples, or alternatively you'd land down after jumping and go into the trough of one
of these ripples. Very disconcerting.

The voyage continued pleasantly with Law completing many clerical
tasks. 'The boys are playing bridge, writing letters, sleeping,' he
recorded, sounding contented, and the film that night 'Weekend at the
Waldorf' was 'very good'. The weather was improving and he wondered
if the Law Luck was going to hold for the unloading.

On Saturday, 5 February, in the early morning, the first penguins and cape pigeons were sighted, visual proof that they were nearing Heard Island:

> There is a general air of excitement—everyone hastening about making last minute arrangements. Men are packing kits for going ashore, DUKW's are being given final check, and being juggled into position on the tank deck in preparation for lowering the ramp and being driven up on deck.

The excitement of the men on the ship could hardly be compared to that of the 1948 expeditioners who were anxiously waiting on Heard Island to catch the first sight of the *Labuan*. Campbell-Drury described the events in his diary that evening:

> 5/2/49 Last night we all sat round and chatted in the rec-hut, on the prospect of seeing, and who would be the first to see, the relief ship today. It was indeed one of the merriest evenings we have yet spent together, for amid several tunes and songs around the piano there were many jokes and wise-cracks. It was truly a night of high spirits and goodwill amongst men if ever there was. Even long after going to bed we talked of reading and wading through the many bags of mail which the *Labuan* said they have for us.
>
> ... We expect the *Labuan* to arrive sometime this afternoon but this has not discouraged me from scaling the radio mast already several times this morning. Much haze has obscured the horizon and there is little hope of seeing any distance yet—otherwise the weather is fine.[8]

Meanwhile, on the *Labuan*, the men had sighted 'Big Ben'. Law later noted that they had 'caught some magnificent glimpses of Big Ben and glaciers. Crevassing is terrific!', but at the time he was far more concerned that their bearings were out. Finally, at 6.45 p.m., the *Labuan* anchored safely in Atlas Cove with the 'Law Luck' intact, 'calm water. Weather still holding.'

Campbell-Dury, on the island, recorded the first sight of the *Labuan*:

> As I stood watching out to sea, suddenly—almost magically, through the slight mist, the form of the *Labuan*, almost indistinguishable at first, grew as it were, and became a solid thing. It was all too difficult to realise—the first ship we had seen in fourteen long months. I flashed the words of welcome to her captain—Lt. Cmdr. Dixon— 'Welcome George, this is Heard Island, please don't miss us!'
>
> We had just time to get back to Atlas Cove to see the *Labuan* come peacefully to anchor in the still quiet waters of the cove. She fired rockets high into the air as some of the men ashore replied similarly.

For a time it was like Guy Fawkes' Day. Abbotsmith and Doc Gilchrist were speeding out towards the ship in the 'ANARE' and I learnt later, that the Doc's beard, draping almost like seaweed over the bows of the dinghy, presented an astounding sight to the sailors. In no time they had a DUKW over the side and speeding inshore with that valuable cargo—the precious mail.

It was just one of those moments when no-one spoke—this great DUKW crawled up out of the sea onto the beach as the first men ashore to greet us were Phil Law, Dave Eastman (cine camera-man), Jack Atkinson (news reporter who I met first of all in Perth) and some of the new party.

Jacka, also waiting on the island, recalls how impressed he was with both the new DUKWs and Law's handling of the landing:

It was just amazing to us to see them lower these things [DUKWs] over the side and people climbed into them and they just drove over and just landed on shore.

It was like the Messiah coming. He [Law] was in control of the situation ... He came there with a definite idea of what he wanted to get done and it was done expeditiously.[9]

Law was thrilled to see his friends again 'no time for instructions—everyone talking.' That night, the photographer, Eastman, showed the film he had made of the first landing, Law played his piano accordion, and the original expeditioners later sat quietly and read or reread their mail from home. 'Most of us were still reading our mail at 2am,' Campbell-Drury remarked.

Law was accommodated ashore in a hut the men had converted into a surgery. He slept on the operating table, but not for long. By 2.45 a.m. the following day, Sunday 6, Law had contacted the ship and by 4.30 a.m. the first DUKW had left to begin the hazardous task of unloading supplies. 'Stuff began to roll in. Weather very mild, little wind—barom. up to blazes! What phenomenal luck!'

During the morning Law and six men went by DUKW to Saddle Point, on the far side of Corinthian Bay, to collect three of the Heard Island expeditioners. Law, normally well prepared, was, this time, careless and berated himself for it:

I was very worried—forgot to take Walkie Talkie until half a mile from camp, then decided not worth returning for. Crazy! Had to cross 3 miles of rough water with ice cliffs for shore. If our motor had stopped! But it didn't.

They picked the men up safely, although the DUKW got bogged during the operation, and then he 'worked like a madman all day.

Panics every now and again, but things went amazingly smoothly! Stuff continued to pour ashore.' Later he triumphantly recorded 'all unloading had been finished by 7pm—15 hours!' It had been a successful unloading, probably the quickest that would ever be recorded.

The next tasks were to discuss the previous year's work with Gotley, the leader of the 1948 Expedition, to plan for the next day's work and to write up his diary. Law noted that Atkinson, the journalist, had 'been a tower of strength,' but that Eastman, the photographer, was a 'lazy b— — [who] spent most of afternoon wandering around distracting the blokes who were working!' Law finally got to bed at 12.20 a.m. after almost 22 hours of continuous work. Luck he had certainly had with the weather, but he had worked himself and his men relentlessly to take advantage of it. This feature was to become a Law trade-mark: 'Get in and get it done whilst the weather is good.'

He was up again at 3.45 a.m. the following morning and spent a strenuous day working with the men clearing rocks to make a uniform gradient for the motor boat slip; unpacking and sorting supplies; building a new hut for a biologists' laboratory, taking photographs 'brilliant (I hope)', of the camp and Big Ben. This manual labour was combined with preparing numerous administrative details such as lists of men who were to stay ashore, those who were to have meals ashore, and those who were to go to the ship. By 11.10 p.m., after more than 19 hours' non-stop work, he described himself as 'very tired—in a good healthy sort of way. What a difference to my energy now I'm off the ship.' The weather was still favouring them, with early fog but later a 'brilliant day—perfect! Law luck continues!!' He was looking forward to spending the next day on the ship and conducting a survey of the west coast. 'I am going aboard to take some photos and have time to think!'

On Tuesday he arose at 5.10 a.m. and was out at the ship two hours later. The weather was still 'absolutely perfect. The highest temperature the party has recorded in 14 months!' Whilst the coastal survey was being carried out, Law photographed continuously for four hours. Then the weather changed. The wind came up, cloud appeared and 'the whole thing blotted out,' but the survey had already been completed. The Gods were certainly looking kindly on him. That evening he spent the time 'planning and sounding out various men on their impressions, personal relations etc.' and cabled his 'dear wife'.

The men devoted the next two days to familiarising the new group with the work they were to do during the ensuing year; completing two new huts, dispersing drums, shoring up the boat, painting the roof of the mess hut and loading the penguins, birds and Kerguelen cabbage to be taken back to Melbourne. Law recorded the handing-over ceremony on Thursday 10, and later examined the camp in detail and took notes on the conditions of the buildings.

On Friday 11 February he was up at 5 a.m., walked two miles and then gave a skiing session to one of the incoming biologists. This particular man was from Penang, Malaya, and on the trip to Heard Island he had experienced some social difficulties and felt isolated from the rest of the group. After the skiing lesson, the biologist told Law that he did not think that he could usefully spend a year on Heard Island. Jacka remembers how well Law handled the matter:

> Phil was a bit disappointed, for he was keen to see worthwhile work done. At the same time, Phil had no qualms, no doubts at all that it was out of the question to leave the fellow there if there were doubts.[10]

Alan Campbell-Drury also recalled how 'beautifully handled' this episode had been. 'Rather than Phil being terribly put out about it I gather he more or less thanked the biologist for telling him.' Campbell-Drury also commented 'that is the sort of thing you would expect Phil to do.'[11] Law was later to say that the biologist, by refusing to stay, had shown 'great moral courage'.[12]

By the middle of the day they had said goodbye to the men on the Island and the ship set sail at 12.50 p.m. Law recorded:

> Then had my first meal for the day. Then washed socks and gloves, then had shower (getting out of my clothes for the first time since we arrived) then went to bed. Slept till 6 (2 hours) then had drinks with Captain in his cabin. Tonight there are pictures, but I'm going to bed.

His first changeover as leader had been a triumph, but he had only sufficient energy to heave a sigh of relief and record, 'Thank God the whole thing went off O.K.!' The party's next challenge was to visit the Iles de Kerguelen where Law hoped to spend some time relaxing—'take photos and shoot ducks.'

The Iles de Kerguelen lie far south in the Indian Ocean, in the latitudes of the Roaring Forties, and comprise a group of more than 300 islands and islets. Early this century there had been a whaling station at Port Jeanne d'Arc and during World War II the islands were used as a rendezvous and base for German raiders. In 1941 the cruiser, *HMAS Australia*, laid mines at four localities to prevent the use of the main harbour by raiders.

When the *Labuan* arrived there on Saturday, 12 February, these mines blocked the normal entrances into Port Jeanne d'Arc and the *Labuan* had to pass through a narrow gap, barely 120 feet wide, between two rocky islets. Law admired the masterly feat of seamanship needed to manoeuvre such an ungainly ship through a narrow passage in strong wind, and found the experience 'quite a thrill'.

Iles de Kerguelen, as Law later described it, is a 'fascinating place':

A main island about 60 miles across, surrounded by numerous small islands. Scenery is on the grand scale, with snow-clad glaciered mountains, great harbours, magnificent fjords and an abundance of grassy vegetation and wild life: seals, penguins and flying birds.[13]

Relics of the whalers' trade littered the ground, old harpoon heads, iron cooking pots and implements for flensing and boiling down blubber, and Law and some of the men 'had the extraordinary experience of tramping around the abandoned living quarters and the processing factory, all of them in a remarkably good state of preservation.'[14] Ever the opportunist, Law noted the 'sound order' of the buildings and recorded that it 'would be a good idea to call in on way to Heard next year and collect roofing iron and building timber.'

The weather at Kerguelen is normally abominable and, as Law remarked, 'accounts of it given by explorers and sealers differ only in the vehemence of their expletives.'[15] This time it was reasonable with only intermittent rain. On Sunday 13, Law announced that the men could, at last, have a day off. Captain Dixon, Law and two other men went shooting. A bet was wagered—two bottles of beer on highest average. Law returned to ship at 3 p.m., having 'covered a lot of country, mostly at the double. I had shot seven ducks and one rabbit with seven cartridges (one clear miss but three with one shot more than made up). So I won the beer.'

There was another side to this story that was not mentioned in Law's diary. Fred Jacka and John Jelbart had watched Law and the others go off 'in their hunting gear, guns and bags'. Jacka and Jelbart had none of these trappings, just their much used Heard Island winter clothing. After walking for a while they too decided to catch some of the game as the rabbits and ducks were so tame that they were able to snare them with their hands. They were so laden with their rabbits and birds when they returned to the ship, that they had to be helped up the rope ladder. Aboard they found Captain Dixon and Law admiring their catch on the foredeck and exchanging hunting tales. Jacka and Jelbart dumped their catch next to the others. 'We had twice as many as Phil and Dixon had— and we had no guns!' Jacka later delightedly recalled.

The *Labuan* left Kerguelen at 2 p.m. the following day and Law, 'aching all over from the exertions of the last two days,' immediately turned his attention to the administrative details of the voyage, sending cables, paying out money and writing the necessary reports. 'There is a lot to do,' he wrote, 'before I hit Melbourne.' The seas were rough and, all the while, the *Labuan* rolled unmercifully. 'Heavy rolling. One went 35 degrees this p.m.' Nevertheless, he continued to write reports and to send and reply to messages from the Antarctic Division. In the evenings he played chess with the Captain, talked, played the piano accordion, but could not sleep.

'It has not been a very good day' he recorded on Tuesday 22. Not only had he had to resolve a disagreement between the men about the destination of the penguins, he had also been involved in an altercation with Atkinson, the journalist:

> Atkinson came in in a rage and complained bitterly about all manner of things—got right off his bike. I'm sorry it happened— he's quite a good chap at heart. Fortunately I didn't feel the least bit wild, so it was a one-sided row. He'll feel better in a day or two. Main grievances are lack of recognition, Captain writing the articles, my refusal to send his personal telegrams as official, Scholes being paid for articles, the jobs he's done (particularly captioning photos) and Eastman [Photographer]. Quite a roll of pin pricks—no wonder he got fed up.

Sympathetic though Law may have been to Atkinson's plight, he made a resolution: 'By jove, I'm never going to permit any journalist or official photographer again on these shows.'

Whenever men came to him with a problem, Law believed that he should be able to remain detached, rational and decisive. In the conflict during the last two days he had handled himself and resolved the situation to his satisfaction, but he was, as yet, still unable to master the insomnia that was invariably an aftermath of personal altercations:

> Didn't sleep a wink last night. Watched the dawn break and finally drowsed off at 7 a.m.!! I do not remember in my life ever having been so wide awake. Couldn't even doze! Ship rolling, but that's not the trouble.

Not until two nights later was he able, finally, to get a decent night's sleep. On Friday 25 he recorded 'Slept in till 11 am. Much refreshed.'

The *Labuan* arrived at Dockyard Pier on Monday, 28 February 1949, after receiving a telegram from Burton, Secretary DEA: 'Minister and Department send warmest congratulations yourself Dixon on conclusion successful operation which fittingly continues first year's Antarctic work, Burton.'[16]

The changeover had been completed in excellent time and with few hitches; the *Labuan* had held together and all the members of the expedition had returned safely. Law had proved his worth as leader of an ANAR Expedition. Now he had to demonstrate his ability as the administrator of the Antarctic Division.

2.

When Law took over the Antarctic Division, its staff consisted of an administrative officer, two typists and a storeman. From this small band he had to create a permanent division of a Government department.

Law threw himself into the administrative tasks with the same enthusiasm, dedication and attention to detail that he had applied to leading the expedition. He took pride in his administrative ability as well as his leadership skills and, years later, complained that 'the thing you never get credit for is the administration.' Indeed, the establishment of the Antarctic Division is really the story of Law's ability to create an environment where staff remained as committed to the effective carrying out of the day-to-day administrative work as they were to the long term vision of setting up the first Australian base on the Antarctic continent.

With the promise of five-year funding from the Australian Government, Law now set about shaping the general public's image of the Antarctic Division. He wanted it to function as little like a public service department as possible and aimed to have it seen as both permanent and autonomous. To this end he gained permission from the DEA for the Antarctic Division to have its own letterhead. Nel designed an emblem, depicting a map of the Antarctic surrounded by a border of Antarctic flora and fauna which was later used on all stationery, official reports and publications.

Law then turned his attention to the Division's accommodation, which had been transferred from the Army's Headquarters in St Kilda Road to other temporary accommodation in a fibro-cement office building, owned by the Department of the Navy, at the Albert Park Barracks. First Law gained approval to have the accommodation made permanent. He then requested permission for the drab olive-green and brown interior to be repainted with white woodwork and pastel-coloured walls. The new colour scheme met with immediate opposition from the Department of Works. After a good deal of argument the offices were refurbished as Law had requested and he was amused to often see Department of Works officers proudly showing visitors the 'new look that they had introduced'. He was less amused to later receive instructions from the DEA to cease using the Antarctic Division stationery and return to using official DEA paper. Law ignored these requests and the Antarctic Division retained its own letterhead until he resigned in 1966.

His next concern was the ordering of supplies through the Department of Air for the island expeditions, which was a particularly cumbersome system and needed revamping. A simple spare part for a piece of equipment, for example, sometimes took from six to eight weeks to obtain. This delay was unacceptable, particularly when an urgent request for a part was received within a few weeks of the impending departure of a ship. As the welfare of the men in Antarctic conditions depended on both high quality supplies and an efficient speedy service, Law decided that the Division must have its own Supply Department.

Negotiations to achieve this brought Law up against the slow-moving machinery of Government departments. After much time and persuasive argument he obtained the necessary approval from DEA. He then needed authority from the Public Service Board to appoint the necessary staff. Next, submissions had to be prepared for Treasury to provide for the extra funds. Finally he had to convince the Departments of the Navy and Air to relinquish the supply work they had previously handled for the Antarctic Division. Eventually, when these administrative hurdles had been scaled, the Antarctic Division acquired its own Supply Department.

His attention to administrative detail extended a long way and, always interested in the finer points of food and drink, Law took personal control of victualing. He continued to have the Navy provide the food for 'if they said they'd packed certain things they were jolly well there ... I could rely on them absolutely.'[17]

Law could also depend absolutely on George Smith, the Storeman at the Tottenham Store:

> George was a remarkable person. Intelligent, independent, blunt and forthright, he played a most important role in the total ANARE scene. Blessed with a remarkable memory he could tell you the case number of the container in which any particular object out of many thousands was packed ... One could depend upon him in this regard absolutely, for he never made mistakes. In all my years in the Division I cannot recall any important article or piece of equipment being left behind because of his neglect when a ship sailed.[18]

Smith was vital to the success of Law's enterprise, for the Tottenham Store was more the centre of the Antarctic Division's activity than the official head-quarters at Albert Park. When expeditioners first arrived at the Antarctic Division they spent most of their time at Tottenham being fitted for clothing, packing supplies, improvising equipment and buildings needed for the expedition, as Smith describes:

> Everything was done as cheaply as possible. There was no money whatsoever. I can remember the days when we built our own huts; we estimated, including the carpenter's wages, we were building prefabricated huts for about £350 each. We were using the Doctor [Medical Officer] as chief assistant to the carpenter ... for weeks and weeks on end. See there wasn't a Public Service set-up ... to get anywhere you broke every rule in the book as far as getting on with job. You had to, you just couldn't run with that system, because you only had weeks to do a job, not months or years. Now the money wasn't there, so we learnt to live with the little we got.[19]

Everyone knew the Store was George Smith's domain, as Law recalls:

[George] used to run Tottenham Store with an iron hand ... make
the blokes work and stand over them ... belt them into action, he'd
sort out the weedy ones and stimulate the slow ones and annihilate
the lazy ones. He had a tremendous role out at Tottenham Store.

Smith's ability to 'sum up a man in about two minutes flat' became an
Antarctic Division legend, believed in by most, including Law. 'His
assessment of men was spot on, because he worked with them ... hand in
glove for weeks. If he said the bloke was no good, he knew.'[20]

One of the first tasks undertaken by the new expeditioners when they
arrived at Tottenham was to be fitted for clothing for the voyage south.
Often the clothes didn't fit, particularly when expeditioners arrived late
and some sizes were unavailable. One of the many ANARE catch-phrases
that developed from this was 'if the clothing doesn't fit, you're
deformed.' George Smith, always blunt and direct, had his own inim-
itable way of quelling complaints about ill-fitting clothing. If a man
grumbled that the trousers were too long George would take them and
enquire of the expeditioner: 'How much too long? Oh, 10 inches. Right!
Fixed!' and produce a machete from under the counter and threaten to
hack off the offending length.[21]

Money was scarce and, during that first year, Law was initiated into the
ritual of presenting a set of forward estimates to Treasury. The official
channel was for the figures to be sent to the DEA in Canberra which
would then present the case to the Treasury. However, Law never trusted
anyone in the DEA to put the Antarctic Division's case to Treasury
exactly as he wanted it. He believed that unless the person who put the
case was 'obsessed with the necessity' of what was being asked for, 'he
would just get bashed back.' Law asked to be present at the submission
and his request was granted.[22]

Although he knew it was necessary to wheel and deal to get what he
believed was needed for the Antarctic Division, Law had a high sense of
probity and disliked playing, what he called, 'public service games'.
Some rituals and practices, such as Government departments adding on
a certain percentage to their proposed budget on the understanding
that Treasury would cut a proportion back, he even thought blatantly
dishonest. He aimed to establish a reputation for honesty in his requests.
He met with reasonable success, as Evan Collings, Chairman of the
Public Service Board, later described:

I remember that Phil told me once or twice he would never ask for
anything he didn't need. And I think he would seriously and sin-
cerely believe that. ... The PSB could trust some and couldn't trust
others and Phil was certainly in the group that you could trust.[23]

Law had also succeeded in gaining approval from the many bodies, the EPC, the DEA, the Commonwealth Public Service Board and, finally, the Commonwealth Treasury, for an increased budget for staffing. By the end of 1949 the Antarctic Division had grown to 11 permanent staff members: Law as Acting Officer-in-Charge, a Secretary, a Supply Officer, a Storeman, four scientists and four typists. The scientists had all spent the previous year at either Heard or Macquarie Islands; Fred Jacka, the Cosmic Ray Physicist who had worked with Law at the Hotham Hut, Alan Martin, a Meteorologist, Ron Kenny, a Biologist and Gersh Major, an Ionospheric Physicist.[24]

Law also changed the Division's practices for employing expedition staff. He had always been resentful of the 'old boy' network that Campbell had used to gain staff for the first ANAR expeditions. He realised that had Professor Martin not mentioned to him the difficulty they were having gaining scientific staff he would probably never have had the opportunity to go on the *Wyatt Earp* voyage. 'I determined then that if ever I became leader I would advertise on the open market throughout Australia, to give everyone an equal chance.'[25] Accordingly, the Antarctic Division placed advertisements for expeditioners in the main newspapers throughout Australia and, once a year, Law travelled interstate to interview the applicants.

In the early years his interviewing techniques lacked their later polish and many of the early 1950s expeditioners attest to Law's questioning which clearly indicated those answers he wanted. There were such questions and answers as:

'Do you like the rough and tough?' ... 'Yes.'
'How do you think you will stand the cold weather?' ... 'Fine.';
     or
'Will you be able to take the cold weather week after week?'
'Yep.', etc.[26]

Law admits that at first he was taken in by what he thought was a 'wonderful sign of enthusiasm' when a man would say to him, 'I will do any job. I don't care what job it is, so long as you take me.'[27] He later realised that in an isolated environment like Antarctica, a man is judged by his companions largely on the basis of his efficiency in his job. So, Law concluded:

The most important thing, I think, in picking an Antarctic person is that he should love his job, because he's got to be at it fourteen or sixteen hours a day for a whole year. If he's good at it then he gets the respect of the other men regardless of his personality.[28]

Combined with a competence in, and commitment to, their particular fields of expertise, Law wanted men who were in first-class physical health and were psychologically suited to the isolated conditions of the Antarctic. Law defined the ideal temperament of an Antarctic expeditioner as a man who was 'easy-going, amenable, unselfish, loved his job and prepared to work sixteen hours a day seven days a week.'[29] Acquiring men with such a range of qualities was not an easy task, particularly when many of the highly technical positions attracted few applicants. He always double-checked referees' reports by telephoning the referee to discuss the applicant. Nevertheless, 'we continued to make mistakes in the first few years,' Law confessed, 'but every year our selection got better as we got more and more experience.'[30]

Communications between the Antarctic Division and the Islands also needed streamlining. The messages were transmitted through the Overseas Telecommunication Commission's beam radio stations at special financial rates. Each man was allowed free transmission of 175 words and any excess had to be paid for personally. During that first year, 1948, it became clear that radiogram charges for the men would be very costly. Trevor Heath suggested that they use the 'Bentley's International Code,' for all their cable and radio communications. A copy of the code was supplied to each station and to the family of each man, and a supplementary code was designed for the unique requirements of ANARE men, such as:

YASEL = We've just had a blizzard
YIOCH = Glad to hear you are happy and well
YARAJ = Have met with an accident.

'YIKLA' meaning 'Having a wonderful time,' became an ANARE catch-phrase. And, of course, there was a section for messages about beards, which ranged from the disgruntled: 'YIGUM = I have just grown a beard which is awful,' to the coy 'YIHKE = I have grown a beard which is generally admired.'[31] WYSSA, meaning 'All my love darling,' was an important inclusion in any message to the expeditioners because the receiver of a radiogram was often asked, 'Did you get a WYSSA?' This inquiry became so common that radiograms were ultimately called 'WHIZZERS'.[32]

When the cables became too numerous for the typists to handle, Law employed a Cables Officer. The person appointed, Mynwe McDonald, was, Law believed, one of the best appointments he ever made. 'Mrs Mac', as she was affectionately known by everybody, not only expanded the list of words in the supplementary code but also dealt with many personal problems and matters of morale between the expeditioners and their next of kin; reminded expeditioners of the birthdays of wives, mothers and girlfriends and smoothed out misunderstandings between the men and their loved ones.[33] Mrs Mac stayed with the Division for 19 years until her retirement.

Even though Law was excited by the possibilities of the scientific research at Heard and Macquarie Islands, he was now determined to gain a foothold on the Antarctic continent itself. This goal became a personal obsession and drove many of his actions. During the early part of 1949 he sensed that the Australian Government would not approve the funding for another base whilst there were two island bases operating. He believed that if he could relinquish one of the islands, he would have a better chance of gaining approval to set up an Antarctic base. The problem would be to convince the authorities that, without one of the stations, the requisite information would still be available. The different geographic locations of Heard and Macquarie Islands provided a broad base suitable for scientific observations. Macquarie Island experienced unique environmental conditions and Heard Island was a strategic meteorological centre. Law reasoned that if the French were to set up a meteorological station on Iles de Kerguelen, only 320 miles from Heard Island, he would be able to argue that the information from Heard could be just as easily obtained from Kerguelen. His first move, therefore, was to persuade the French to man Kerguelen.

During March 1949 Law went to Canberra where he had a personal interview with the Governor-General, Sir William Slim, which lasted one and a half hours instead of the expected twenty minutes. Amongst the many issues they discussed, were Iles de Kerguelen and the need for a suitable ship for the Antarctic Continent attempt. Whilst on the same Canberra visit, Law also attended a diplomatic cocktail party and enjoyed himself talking with the British High Commissioner about carrier pigeons, with the French Minister about Iles de Kerguelen and Macquarie Island, and with the Indian Minister about beards. Superficially, these conversations passed for social chit-chat, but Law later maintained that he had used the opportunity to plant the thought in the French Minister's mind that Australia had its eye on Kerguelen. To reinforce his efforts, he provided the French Government with a copy of a 16 mm colour film he had produced about Kerguelen. He hoped that his tactics would prompt the French to establish a station there.

The French Government, of course, would have had their own strategic reasons for going to Kerguelen and it is difficult to say whether or not Law's manoeuvres were in any way instrumental in their decision to send an expedition to Kerguelen. Nevertheless, by the summer of 1949 the French had installed a temporary meteorological and radio station there. Law, naturally enough, was delighted, for he was now in a position, if needs be, to negotiate the release of Heard Island for the funds to set up a permanent station on the Antarctic Continent whenever a suitable ship became available.

Meanwhile, in June, Law chaired his first EPC meeting where an issue arose that threatened the future of the whole ANARE endeavour. At the beginning of the meeting Mawson enquired whether the Government intended to pursue the current Antarctic research indefinitely. He expressed the opinion that there should be some limit to the activities of ANARE, unless it could be made to pay for itself. He then suggested that a critical analysis be made of the scientific programs to discover if the Government's money might be more usefully expended elsewhere.

Law side-stepped this suggestion by reminding the committee that the Government had already made commitments to the Island program for at least five years, and had set up a permanent Antarctic Division to carry on this program and to plan for the establishment of a base on the Antarctic Continent. Apparently not satisfied with this reply, Mawson persisted with his argument, pointing out that when he had first suggested an Antarctic expedition to the Government he had never contemplated the present large-scale expenditure. In fact, he had proposed that any Antarctic activity should be allied with a commercial venture, particularly whaling. He thought that if attention was not paid to the commercial side of the Antarctic work then maintaining the base camps indefinitely was far too expensive. Law parried this argument with the reply that 'in his view, recommendations to the Government regarding the set-up of a whaling industry lay outside the functions of this Committee.'

At this point, Dr White (CSIR), entered the discussion and reminded the committee that, at the last meeting, members had requested direction from the Government as to its future policy on the exploration and development of the Antarctic. He asked Law whether a reply had been received from the DEA. Law said that it had not, but advised the members that 'the Department had been given all possible information and must be presumed to realise the position.' He then closed the discussion with a statement that 'the question of the period of operation of ANARE was a matter for his Department and further consideration of this matter should be postponed until near the end of the five year period.'[34]

With this stance, Law had successfully blocked the discussion on the economic viability of the ANAR expeditions, a matter which, if pursued, may have proved disastrous for the Division. He had also demonstrated that he did not take kindly to interference and had given notice that the Antarctic Division was to be his show. The EPC's role, as Law later described it, was a valuable one, for 'it helped me generate long-term policy and short-term programs, and when these were decided, it played a powerful role in gaining government acceptance for them.'[35] But, at that first meeting which Law chaired, he had deftly established its parameters.

The minutes of this meeting also show how Law successfully used a skill he had learned from Jim Rogers, Secretary of the Optical Munitions Panel, in minute-taking:

I always believe that the Minutes should record the shades of opinion expressed by various people that form the atmosphere in which the final resolution is made [Law later explained] ... It is terribly important that the Minutes are written in such a way that they contribute constructively to the direction in which you want to go, and you can write Minutes that do influence things in one direction or the other. So I was always very careful to be the person who edited the Minutes before they were finally sent out ... I believe that if I was heading in a certain direction, vigorously attempting to achieve something, then the Minutes, properly written, could contribute to that. I didn't believe in falsifying Minutes, or 'rigging' them in any way, but I am sure that if you write the Minutes with an object in view, you can, over the years, influence the way a thing goes.

A reading of any minutes of meetings which Law chaired attests to his ability to achieve this intention. They resemble a well structured play with Law as both author, main character and editor. The plot is clear, the actors have their allotted roles and the story unfolds with few surprises.

Projecting the correct public image, of either himself or the Division, was paramount to Law, and he considered public relations on behalf of the Antarctic Division to be one of his most important tasks. The convention, in relation to publicity, was that DEA staff always wrote press releases which were then issued by the Minister. Law persuaded the DEA to allow the Antarctic Division to prepare its own press releases without these being vetted by the Department. Law later maintained that he thought he was the only civil servant in Australia who had this authority 'and I was very careful about it. I was very cautious that at no time did I release anything that wasn't purely factual.'[36] Nevertheless the issue of publicity continued to surface throughout Law's years with the Antarctic Division. On some occasions the DEA clearly thought that the publicity was directed at Law himself, rather than at the Division. A later Secretary of the DEA, Sir Arthur Tange, explains:

There is always a certain lack of sympathy on the part of public servants in departments against publicity attached to individuals ... There would be some public servants who would say 'Is this a matter of personal publicity to satisfy personal motivations rather than the general good?' If there was any thought that it was for personal aggrandizement ... as distinct from winning public support for the activities of the Antarctic Division ... well then he [Law] wouldn't get sympathy.[37]

Law believed that the Antarctic Division was on a very insecure footing and he wished to gain as much public support as possible in case it was needed to sway any future Cabinet decisions on Antarctic matters. Whenever the Division received requests to talk at different venues about Antarctica, Law accepted them all. For the next eighteen years, presenting talks, illustrated with slides or films, became an important and time-consuming part of Law's job. He also expected past expeditioners and most staff members of the Antarctic Division to be involved with these presentations.

Law not only had a vision for the Antarctic Division, but he had the ability to communicate it to others, and he never wasted an opportunity to do so. Unlike the Polar explorer, Roald Amundsen, who saw himself as 'just part of a lecture machine', and is said to have found the whole process a 'deadening exercise; raking over the embers of past triumphs',[38] Law revelled in the publicity. His public talks, sometimes two or three each week, were always illustrated with photographic slides, the equipment having been set up to Law's precise specifications well before-hand by Campbell-Drury, who was now the Photographer at the Antarctic Division. The photographs included 'icebergs and towering snow-capped mountains, deep impassable crevasses, inland lakes and harbours ... the layout of ... meteorological installations with comfortable housing quarters for the staff ... animal and bird life of the island'.[39] Law's lecturing skills were also apparent with one journalist commenting that Law's 'illustrated Lecture ... was of unusual and outstanding interest', and was made 'doubly attractive by an almost complete absence of technical terms when explaining scientific data.'[40]

Although Law took great care to align his topics to the interests of his audience, some underlying messages were always stressed: the necessity to occupy the area that was claimed as Australian Antarctic Territory, the importance of scientific work and the possibility of the mineral resources that might be found there.

On the first point he brought out the necessity of an Australian presence and warned his audience that 'no nation can hope to rope off a section of the earth as its property unless it sustains its claim by actively occupying portion of that area and carrying out useful work there.'[41] Ever the scientist, Law emphasised both the importance of the scientific work and, not to miss an opportunity for positive image-making, also the successes that were being achieved:

Regarding the Island Stations, I can state quite definitely that, scientifically, they are paying dividends ... The reports radioed back to Australia have proved more valuable than was even hoped when the Stations were first established. We are receiving more and more requests from scientists throughout the world for information gathered at our Stations, and in the next few years a mass of valuable data will be collected.[42]

And of his hope of finding mineral resources, he told an audience:

It was reasonable to assume that so vast an area of the world's surface must contain deposits of value, the present difficulty, however, being to discover payable means of extracting the wealth the continent may contain. The rapid changes of science would probably solve the problems and it behoved Australia to be prepared to avail itself of whatever opportunities offered in the future. [He warned them that] other nations were already directing their attention to Antarctic possibilities.[43]

These were messages he would deliver over and over again during the following two decades, only marginally altering his stance on the availability of some resources and on the difficulty of exploiting them.

Law's already high public profile was given another boost when, in November 1949, he was selected as 'Man of the Week' by *The Australasian Post*. The article was appropriately titled 'A Bearded Scientist with a Mission' and announced that Law planned to set up an Australian base on the Antarctic continent and was on the look-out for a suitable ship. Readers were also advised that 'as a preliminary canter, he will join a Norwegian–Swedish–British expedition that will leave South Africa next month for frozen Queen Maud Land in the Antarctic.'[44]

By the time the article appeared, however, Law had already left for Cape Town, where he was to board the expedition ship, the *Norsel*.

Notes

1. S. A. C. Campbell's Preliminary Report, 23 January 1948, ADH.
2. Law to Tim Bowden, ABC, 30 November 1987, ABC:SHU.
3. Norman Bartlett, 'Life of Antarctic Weathermen', 1950.
4. Law, *Antarctic Odyssey*, p. 40.
5. Jacka to Daniel Connell, ABC, March 1988, ABC:SHU.
6. Campbell-Drury's Diary, 22 January 1949.
7. Ibid.
8. Campbell-Drury's Diary, 5 February 1949.
9. Jacka to author, 8 August 1990.
10. Ibid.
11. Campbell-Drury to author, 17 October 1989.
12. Law to Bowden, ABC, 30 November 1987, ABC:SHU.
13. Law, After Dinner Speech, CSIROSIP Dinner, 13 November 1987, LP.
14. Ibid.
15. Law, *Antarctic Odyssey*, p. 54.
16. Burton to Heath, Antarctic Division, 26 February 1949, LP.
17. Law to Lennard Bickel, 19/20 April 1975, ANL.
18. Law, Unpublished draft notes for *Antarctic Odyssey*, LR.
19. Smith to Bowden, ABC, 2 December 1987, ABC:SHU.
20. Law to Bowden, ABC, 30 November 1987, ABC:SHU.
21. G. McKinnon and D. Twigg to author, 24 June 1989.
22. Law to Lennard Bickel, 19/20 April 1975, ANL.
23. Collings to author, 5 July 1990.
24. Paper presented to EPC Minutes, 3 June 1949, ADH.
25. Law to Lennard Bickel, April 1975, ANL.
26. Various expeditioners to author, 1989–1990.
27. Law to Bowden, ABC, 2 December 1987, ABC:SHU.
28. Ibid.

29. *Daily Telegraph*, London, 18 April 1966.
30. Law to Lennard Bickel, April 1975, ANL.
31. 'Communicating with Antarctica', *ANARE Personal Communications Booklet*, Antarctic Division, Department of Science and the Environment, First Edition, October 1980.
32. McKinnon to author, 24 June 1989.
33. Fay Butterworth (ed.), *WYTOY, WYSSA, The Antarctic Wives and Kinfolk Association of Australia, An Overview of 25 years*, 1990.
34. EPC Minutes, 3 June 1949, ADH.
35. Law, *Antarctic Odyssey*, p. 197.
36. Law to Lennard Bickel, 19/20 April 1975, ANL..
37. Sir Arthur Tange to author, 6 July 1990.
38. R. Huntford, *The Amundsen Photographs*, 1987, p. 9.
39. *Bohemia*, vol.5, no.5.
40. 'The October Meeting was a Winner', *Bohemia*, Melbourne, 1 November 1949, vol.5, no.5.
41. Law, Lecture Notes in 1949/50, LR.
42. Lecture given to Royal Empire Society, 7 July 1949, LR.
43. *Bohemia*, vol.5, no. 5.
44. *The Australasian Post*, 24 November 1949.

7. Australia's 'Mr Antarctica', 1950–1951

1.

DURING 1949 LAW HAD PERSUADED THE ORGANISERS OF THE NORWE-gian–British–Swedish Expedition (NBSE) to allow him to go as an Australian Observer on the round trip from Cape Town to Antarctica and back to Cape Town. He believed, and convinced the Australian Government, that he would gain invaluable experience about logistics, huts, clothing and aircraft on such a trip. He had also requested Government approval to fly to Europe at the end of the voyage to continue the search for a suitable ship and to investigate clothing, tents and other supplies appropriate for any future Australian Antarctic expedition.

The NBSE came about thanks to the efforts of Professor Harold Sverdrup of the Norsk Polarinstitutt in Norway, Dr L. P. Kirwan, Director of the Royal Geographical Society of Great Britain and Professor Hans Ahlmann, the world famous Swedish glaciologist. The plan was to set up a base in Dronning Maud Land and for scientists to spend two years investigating climatic, glacial and geological conditions, including the theory that the Antarctic was gradually getting warmer and causing profound changes to the climate in the Southern hemisphere.[1] The voyage was to be undertaken in a new 700-ton, diesel-powered ship, the *Norsel*, which had been built in Hamburg specifically for sealing in Greenland waters. The Antarctic trip would be her maiden voyage and she was to be commanded by a Norwegian, Captain Jakobsen, a man well experienced in Arctic conditions. The Expedition Leader was to be Captain John Giaever, also a Norwegian.

After weeks of hectic preparation for his own trip and for Heath's two relief voyages to Heard and Macquarie Islands, Law left Melbourne on 17 November 1949. He would be away for over five months.

The *Norsel* sailed out of Capetown at 6 p.m. on 28 December 1949. It had not been due to leave for another three hours, but since part of its cargo was a large amount of dynamite to blast its way out of the ice in the event of being trapped, the Harbour Master, nervous about the dynamite, had sent a tug to push the *Norsel* out before the appointed time.

Law was pleased to find that conditions on the *Norsel* were excellent. He 'shared a two berth cabin complete with running water and washbasin, writing table, settee, reading lamps, curtains around bunks, wardrobes and drawers.' However, the food, by comparison, made the *Wyatt Earp* seem like a gourmet's paradise. Law's diary entries included regular scathing comments about the meals and he told Nel that he nearly starved the first week. By the fourth day out he lamented that his diary was 'becoming a list of menus!' and it continued that way throughout the voyage.

By Tuesday, 10 January 1950, the *Norsel* was approaching the South Sandwich Islands. Little exploration, or collection of rock samples had been done there, and most of the Expedition members were keen to land and collect samples. Captain Jakobsen, who Law privately thought was keen to get back to Greenland for the sealing season, refused to spend the time on this exploit. 'Once again we have here the set-up of divided motives of Expedition and Captain of ship,' Law mused and resolved, 'more than ever I am determined to have a ship and Captain completely under my control.'

Being such a small ship, the *Norsel* was unable to carry all the supplies essential to set up an Antarctic base camp. An arrangement had been made for a Norwegian whaling-factory ship, *Thorshovdi*, to carry five men, forty-seven huskies, three weasels and several important pieces of machinery to the fringe of the pack-ice, where they would be transferred to the *Norsel*. A few days out from Capetown, however, *Norsel* was advised that *Thorshovdi*, instead of being at 40° east, had moved to a position 41° west. This meant a detour across the South Atlantic from Africa to South America; a detour that would cost them three weeks of precious Antarctic summer.

When they finally encountered *Thorshovdi*, on 12 January, she was a curious sight with seven whales in tow and two on deck, whilst myriads of birds screeched around the ship or swooped at floating offal. 'To leeward of the ship the smell was something like that at the Flemington abattoirs with the reek of whale blubber thrown in for good measure', Law wrote. Fierce storms and heavy seas made it impossible for the two ships to come close enough to make the transfer of goods. For two days they waited for calmer conditions. On Saturday 14 they decided to risk an attempt behind the shelter of a large iceberg. The whale-factory manager was reported as saying 'It usually works out all right, sometimes, at any rate',[2] which did not inspire confidence in the heart of Captain Jakobsen, who already took a gloomy view of the prospect of the transfer operation.[3] Two dead whales were used as fenders between the ships as they carefully drew together 'with 500 pairs of eyes watching from the ship's rails, from port-holes and ventilators, and 500 heads shaking doubtfully'.[4] With thousands of Cape pigeons crowded around picking parasites off the whales, the men, fifteen tons of whale meat, howling dogs and equipment were winched across in cases onto the *Norsel's* deck. 'It was a stylish performance', Captain Giaever, the Expedition Leader, reported.

The *Norsel* was now heavily laden, both above and below decks, with the two precious Auster aircraft, weasels (over-snow tracked vehicles), cases of machinery, tractor-sledges and forty-seven huskies, all surrounded by, or buried in, tons of whale meat. Law, too, had admired the expert way the supplies had been loaded onto the *Norsel*, but was disgusted with the resultant conditions on the ship. 'Now there is not a square foot of deck space that has not a case or a dog or other cargo on it. You cannot step out of the saloon door without falling over three dogs and to go forrard or aft is a continuous struggle against churning dogs.' He hoped that by the time the dogs had 'pissed and crapped all over the decks and we have tramped it around a bit more on our boots' the men would be used to the smell and might not notice it.

Moving 'heavily like an old woman with a bad heart, dirty as a Gypsy and smelling even worse',[5] the *Norsel* sailed south-west along the polar ice floes of Weddell Sea, following the ice edge as closely as possible. The weather was 'gloriously calm—we are having excellent luck with weather just when we need it.' Icebergs and growlers dotted the sea but did not hinder their progress. By Thursday 19 they were moving through sparse pack-ice, with occasional thick pack. Law was delighted with *Norsel*'s ability in the ice:

> Stuff up to one foot high it just sails straight through at 8–10 knots, but two foot high it rises up on (with engines turned off) and breaks through with its weight. It is a most effective ice ship. It would give the Captain of an ordinary steel ship the horrors to see the way we charge at pack ice and to hear the crunch of ice on the ship's sides and to feel the vessel lurch sideways as it strikes a more solid piece.

They now began to see seals, which the Norwegians usually shot. Some were saved because they had been scarred from the teeth and claws of the sea-leopard, which made their skins almost valueless. 'These Norwegians can't resist seals and other living creatures. It sickens me', Law wrote disdainfully. At one stage ten of the rare Ross seals were sighted. Although only fifty had ever been seen before, they shot four of them.[6] Disgusted though Law was at this slaughter of the animals, he was a pragmatist, and a hungry one, and he cooked the seals' brains to augment the detested Norwegian food. 'I bet I'm the only man to have ever eaten Ross seal brain', he boasted. Later on in the voyage they saw many more of the Ross seals, which turned out to be not as rare as had originally been thought. The Norwegians continued to shoot them.

Whalemeat was often used for meals and Captain Giaever reported: 'It was amazing how many palatable courses the cook could create from those uninviting lumps of meat. Our English friends talked about "very nice steaks," and the Swedes were delighted.'[7] Giaever had obviously not spoken to the Australian passenger, whose opinion was that the meals deteriorated as the voyage progressed. Law had found out that the Expedition had chartered the ship and the owners had supplied the food. He concluded: 'No doubt the catering is on the cheapest possible lines.' He had also discovered that Norwegian sealing companies were notoriously mean with victuals, so much so that the Norwegian Government had legislated to ensure that sealers and sailors on such ships would be adequately fed. Pasted on the wall of the *Norsel's* galley was a copy of the official statute, specifying the minimum level of provisioning that had to be met. This turned out to be exactly what they had been receiving. It was another valuable lesson for Law and he resolved that 'food should be supplied by the Expedition.'

On January 19 the *Norsel* passed into the Antarctic Circle and a 'Crossing the Line' ceremony was performed. Soon they could expect to see land. Instead they encountered thick pack-ice, thicker than previous explorers had ever experienced in the area. For days they tried to penetrate it, with the *Norsel* continuously charging and backing, but little progress was made. After five days even Law became despondent:

> At about 9am we headed due south into the pack and soon ran into trouble. Although the floes were not particularly high—one foot to two feet above water—they were loosely packed—10/10ths cover— and such spaces as existed between them, no more than one or two feet wide, were densely choked with thick sludge. As a result, when the ship tried to pass through there was nowhere for the ice to be pushed. One floe would jamb against the next and so on until the ship, pushing in effect several miles of ice, comes to a halt. Looking back there is no sign of a track—everywhere is closed up again ... Back and forth, back and forth we went, each time gaining a few yards. Very tedious and rather hopeless—this is the limit of what we can penetrate. We shall have to wait until wind or tide or currents open up something a little.

Unusually pessimistic, Law must have had the *Wyatt Earp's* abortive voyage on his mind for he questioned himself, 'Am I a Jonah? Too bad if this is my second unsuccessful trip! But I don't think so—I'm not worried yet—we have only just started to try.'

So far, Law had been recording the conditions of the ice, the ability of the ship and the techniques used by the Captain to break through the ice. He spoke with Jakobsen about designs for ships, read books on Antarctica and compiled a list of those he would buy for the Antarctic Division library. He was pleased to have the time to think and work on the articles he was writing on Heard and Kerguelen Islands. He also talked with Giaever and the expeditioners about clothing, showing them the suit he had designed and concluding that the hood needed to be larger. He discussed the medical equipment with the expedition doctor, interviewed the glaciologist and recorded that he was 'gradually reducing the number of subjects requiring attention.'

The ship crawled along for three more days, with the barometer still

Station at Heard
Island.

Station at
Macquarie Island.

Unloading at
Atlas Cove, Heard
Island.

Right: Fred Jacka.

Below: George Smith (1959).

Below right: Richard Thompson (1954).

The *Norsel* at Maudheim (1950).

Law, Mrs Casey, Mr R. G. Casey, Lem Macey, Doug Leckie and Ray Seaver at 1954 send-off ceremony.

Digging out the beset *Kista Dan.*

Captain Hans Christian Petersen.

Kista Dan beset.

high and the good weather continuing, but on the morning of 27 January the ship could go no further. 'And so here we lie', Law wrote, disheartened, '"as idle as a painted ship" ... with the coast tantalizingly 50–60 miles south, and all this good landing weather going to waste!' Later in the day the ship made another attempt to move, but to no avail 'engines full ahead then full astern—and we didn't move even a fraction of an inch. So here we are really stuck!'

They were beset for two days, with everyone on board hoping and praying for a storm, or at least some wind to create a swell to loosen the pack, but the barograph stubbornly recorded a straight horizontal line. On Sunday 29 another attempt was made to move the ship:

> She is now backing and charging with remarkably little result. ... The sound of the jagged claws of ice clutching at the side of the ship is quite terrifying. The pack is so close there is practically no give at all, and when we go through the only way the ice can move is upwards. So great cakes of it tilt up and fall over beside the ship and grind and press on the sides as we pass.

The *Norsel* soon gave up the struggle and was still again. The weather remained placid and perfect. Time was running out. The expedition could only afford to spend another two weeks searching for a suitable landing area. Finally, the Auster aeroplanes, equipped to use floats, skis or wheels, were sent up in the hope that a way could be found through the pack-ice. It was to no avail.

Eventually, on 30 January, the ship was able to start up again. This time, however, it was not heading through the pack-ice but was going out to sea, first north then west. It was on February 2 that the *Norsel* once more entered the ice-pack and headed south again. Day followed day with the ship ploughing through the ice, but with no sign of a suitable landing place. Giaever later wrote:

> Searching for somewhere safe for the expedition to land, the *Norsel* sailed for days, mile after mile along the fortress of perpendicular ice that stands, inviting but unassailable, at least 30 yards high along Queen Maud Land. Sometimes we thought we had found a landing place, but on closer examination it would prove to be impracticable.[8]

A sighting of land always brought a rush of excitement, 'it is amazing how electric the atmosphere becomes when one gazes at last on the object of one's quest', Law wrote, but the coast always proved impenetrable.

An air of determined and desperate resolve had settled over the ship. 'If we don't get in it will not be Jakobsen's fault—he has taken every possible risk with the ship', Law noted, obviously impressed with the audacious Captain's efforts. On one occasion what they thought was a perfect spot was found, with a natural wharf and a nine-foot-high ice ledge. Their spirits rose, only to be dashed when the Auster flew over the region and the pilot found that the slope was a gigantic crack where a huge ice area was breaking loose from the ice shelf. To set up a camp there would be to risk floating out to sea on a vast iceberg.

The two Auster aircraft proved invaluable for reconnaissance purposes. Whenever a plane took off all those on the ship waited expectantly for the pilot's report. The flight controller kept contact between the pilot and the chart-house on the ship. The Captain peered through binoculars, trying to keep visual contact with the aircraft. In the chart-room the plotter marked off distances, courses and bearings on a chart. A radio operator tape recorded the messages as they were transmitted and another one noted the exact time at regular intervals. These remarks were heard over the loudspeaker by all the members of the ship.

It is a fascinating experience listening in while the plane is away [Law wrote]. There we are, helpless at sea level, eager to know which way to go and what is in store for us. Somewhere within 50 miles is the plane, and his voice comes clearly and concisely through the loudspeaker '127 to *Norsel*, my course is ..., my altitude is ... my air speed ... the radio compass bearing is ... I am flying over a bay which extends to starboard ... I am going down to have a closer look at it. I shall contact you after this reconnaissance and give you my new course.'

Men gathered in the saloon when the pilot returned and, using the plotter's rough map, he explained the details of his flight, playing back the tape recorder to refresh his memory and to check details. Too often what he had found was unsatisfactory for landing and the ship continued on day after day, sometimes ploughing through the pack, at other times just cruising or drifting with the wind. Twice they had to 'skedaddle' away from icebergs bearing down and threatening to crush them. Their search was complicated by winds and snow and they anxiously searched the coast in the few minutes it became clear. The initial excitement of the search settled into monotony.

By 10 February Giaever decided they could spend only one more week searching, then they must depart. They had just entered a large lane of ice-free sea, swept free by the wind and the current. The pilot wanted to investigate a chasm valley he had seen on a previous flight but, with intermittent snowfalls, it seemed unlikely the aircraft would be able to fly. Without aircraft reconnaissance there was little chance of finding a break in the inhospitable ice cliffs. By lunchtime the conditions had eased and the pilot took off to investigate inland. Giaever later told the story:

I shall never forget his voice telling us over the radio: 'I can see a spot in there. The edge looks very low and there is a slope rising slowly up towards a vast area of flat inland ice. I would like to take Captain Giaever to have a look at it. This may be just it.'[9]

And so it was. The *Norsel*'s search had ended. Everyone was 'rewarded by the sight of a beautiful ice quay of just the right height with a slope leading up to the plateau.'[10]

Queen Maud Land is encrusted with continental ice which stretches for miles out to sea so this particular site was not on land as such, but on a floating ice shelf. Before a base could be set up, the area first had to be inspected to ensure there was no danger of the ice breaking off from the mainland and floating away. Law had been selected as a member of the ski-patrol and it immediately went ashore to check the site and to mark a crevasse-free route for the weasels:

We skied inland for three miles ... Weather dead calm, visibility good. It was a terrific thrill to be pushing along on skis over this vast unbroken plain of snow. But what a boring place to be left for two years! Utterly featureless.

The view when we returned to the cove was glorious. The ship lay hard up against the side of the cliff which was, I suppose 6–10 feet high. The opposite side of this little harbour was a cliff face 60 ft. high. ... Strung out in a long line [on the snow] were the dogs. A busy weasel chuffed importantly back and forth towing gear as it was unloaded from the ship. Snow fell softly over everything and there was no wind. Men worked quietly at the winches and on the fore-deck, or on the ice beside the ship.

They worked till midnight, by which time the bay, which had been ice-free a few hours earlier, was completely choked with thick pack-ice. 'It is absolutely incredible,' Law recorded, 'how quickly and silently a bay two miles x one-and-a-half miles can be covered without one noticing it happen.' Had the icing-over occurred earlier in the day it is unlikely the *Norsel* would have attempted to come in. 'We were damn lucky,' Law wrote, but with a momentary apprehension noted, 'I hope we can get out of here 10 days hence!'

The next week was spent erecting the huts and establishing the camp. The unloading was back-breaking, 'I have been working like a cart-horse and am quite knocked up', Law wrote. The men often worked from 5 or 6 a.m. until 10 or 11 p.m. Law kept notes on the design of the huts and the tents, learned to build an igloo, continued to grumble about the *Norsel*'s food and flew in the Auster over the base and surrounding area, a 'magnificent sight'. He noted when and why there were hold-ups in the unloading, when and why inefficiencies occurred, and concluded that the Australian organisation was superior to Norwegian:

They rely completely upon the initiative of the men themselves—no direction at all from Giaever. Their initiative is superb, but there are a number of things which would go better if someone directed them and got them organised better.

Law also confirmed his low opinion of the official professional photographer. 'He is never in the right place at the right time and even at the wrong time his camera is generally empty!'

The weather proved unkind to the party for, during the first few days, there were many heavy snow showers which made it difficult for those men building huts and for the weasel drivers to find their way to the base, three miles from the ship. But within eight days, 450 tons of equipment had been discharged from the *Norsel* and transported to the Maudheim base. The first hut was completed and a second hut, a motor house, workshop and meteorological hut were well on the way to completion.

Now that the safety of the men who would remain at the base was reasonably assured, the *Norsel* could stay no longer for fear of being stranded for the full year. On 20 February, after 'much shaking of hands, group photographs, individual photographs, cheering and waving,' the *Norsel* slid quietly away leaving a 'forlorn little group, clustered around their weasels on the desolate shore', to make her voyage back to Capetown.

Although the expedition had managed to penetrate the formidable barrier of ice, the Antarctic was not going to let them depart peacefully. By 8 p.m. they had already entered thick pack-ice and the next day dynamite had to be used to blast their way out. The use of dynamite to free a wedged ship is a delicate operation and the experience prompted Law to later write an article assiduously detailing the technique involved:

A quantity of dynamite, varying from two to six sticks, is fused and tied to the end of a bamboo pole. A hole is made in the ice with a crowbar about eight feet from the ship's side, and in a position where the wedging appears worst. The engines are set going in the forward direction and by the use of poles as much ice as possible is pushed from around the ship to the stern where it is carried away in the wake.

The engines are then set full-speed astern, the fuse is lit and the bamboo is thrust down the hole and well under the ship. A few seconds later there is a dull boom and the ship shudders as though from a 'near miss'. The explosion may shatter the ice or it may merely produce a surge and a lift of the ship. In either case the chances are that the straining propeller will drag the ship clear. If not, poles are again used to clear loosened ice from around the ship and the process is repeated. Sometimes three or four charges are exploded simultaneously along one side of the ship or even on both sides.[11]

By Wednesday morning Law recorded that it looked as though they would never get out of the ice. 'Practically no breaks—just occasional pools six to eight ft. wide and 20–30 yards long covered by thick three to four inch black new ice ... However, I have no doubt that something will open up if we wait a day.' Jakobsen was now playing a waiting game—waiting for conditions to change from the now unwanted calm. But there was to be no change and the ship often became wedged so that dynamiting had to begin again in an effort to keep the *Norsel* in a pool of free clear water. Law decided to spend this waiting time more profitably by studying astro-navigation, and so 'thrashed around with the help of the Nautical Almanac, books of tables, and Brown's "Air Navigation".'

The calm weather continued so that by 23 February Captain Jakobsen had become alarmed that the ship would be beset. But Law had more faith in the Captain's ability to get them out of the predicament than Jakobsen did himself. Nonetheless, Law did take the time to contemplate the possibility for himself:

> If we are beset life will not be pleasant. We may not have enough
> fuel to keep the warming system going and shall get very cold. But,
> what is worse, there is very little food on board—God knows why!
> With strict rationing and additional meat from seals, penguins etc.
> we might last nine months. Otherwise we would be faced with a trip
> 120 miles across hummocked sea-ice without tents to the Base at
> Maudheim.

Friday brought no cheer. 'There is no free water visible anywhere. What were open pools are now covered with black ice four to six inches thick.' And there was an eerie silence, for the birds had left. Later in the day the rudder was damaged by the ship backing into the ice. 'Sheered off bolts and bent things a bit', Law wrote. 'Can only turn three or four degrees to starboard. A bit worse and we could not have negotiated our way out of the pack! Ya gotta be lucky!'

The next day they were all heartened by a mile long and half-a-mile wide stretch of clear water and for two hours the ship made excellent headway. Later on the ice closed in but, since it was new ice only a foot or two thick, with a lot of backing and charging they were able to push on to the expected ice edge. But the ice seemed never-ending:

> It looks as though the ice edge, which should be right here, may be
> 100–150 miles further on. If so we shall need to cross that distance
> pretty damn quick or the freeze will beset us. Another six inches of

ice on the bottom of this and we would be dead slow or stationary.
As it is we are making only two to four knots!

Relentlessly the ship pushed ahead and the continuous ice sheet broke
up into separate floes separated by sludge. Law jubilantly recorded, 'We
are getting along famously through this, although it covers the sea
10/10.' Soon the sea began to swell, large stretches of open water
appeared and, by 12 noon on 26 February, the last traces of ice had disappeared. They had used fifty kilograms of dynamite to release them
from the pack, but they were now heading 'full fahrt!' for Capetown.

In the first open water encountered for four weeks, the *Norsel* hit a
strong north-easterly blow and swell. Law immediately became seasick
and couldn't find his Dramamine tablets. 'A dead loss. Missed dinner
last night, spent a lousy night altogether with the ship performing the
most amazing convolutions. OK lying down but sick as hell if I rose and
walked about.' His thoughts now turned to Nel and he was impatient to
arrive at Capetown to receive her letters 'I feel as though the world has
gone on without me,' he wrote, 'and I am standing in the middle of the
road crying in the dust watching it disappear over the hill.'

The weather did not improve, the ship continued to roll and Law felt
'like hell'. He became impatient, resenting the wasted time. 'Writing [is]
almost impossible, reading most tiring, sleeping difficult and work out
of the question. ... the day becomes an intolerable vista of hours, leading
to an equally intolerable night.' Law used the time, as best he could, to
make a list of the 'sum total of different dishes served during the trip,'
with terse comments beside them such as 'Storm soup—dreadful, thick
storm soup—even worse, corned beef—uneatable, salt pork—not too
bad early in the voyage, now getting yellow and "high".'

The *Norsel* arrived at Capetown on Tuesday, 7 March and Law 'had
that glorious free happy feeling which comes from knowing a job is finished and successful and that there is for the moment no other worry in
sight, only the anticipation of comfort and pleasure.'

The expedition had been, for Law, a wonderful apprenticeship. The
ship had traversed 2 300 miles in the pack-ice zone, 1 500 miles of that
through thick pack. Law had gathered invaluable information, from a
man whom he believed was a 'first class ice captain', about handling a
ship in Antarctic conditions. His diary and note books included sketches
of proposed landing areas, and reasons why they were not suitable, his
impressions of each of the fifteen men who had stayed at the Maudheim
Base and general and scientific information gained from the Expedition
Leader and the scientists aboard. He had also gained specific information about the type and quantity of stores and equipment needed, and
an understanding of the conditions to expect, when setting up a base in
Antarctica. Furthermore, Law now knew far more clearly what he

required of the ship for Australia's Antarctic attempt and had decided that the *Norsel* was too small.

During the *Norsel* trip Law had received approval to go to Europe to look for a ship and other supplies. Immediately after the *Norsel* docked, Law flew to London, where he arrived on 15 March 1950. He stayed at 'Mayfair 8166' in Park Street, a Government hostel used for accommodation for visiting Government dignitaries from various parts of the world. He was 'living like a Lord', he told Nel, and obviously loving it:

> I have a private bathroom in black and cream tiles and a good bedroom with the softest bed and pillows and a lovely eiderdown quilt ... If I leave clothes around I return to find them neatly stowed away.

Like many Australians, Law was both delighted and intrigued with London and, in a long and enthusiastic letter to his 'grandpassion, my patient and ever-loving grass widow, my adored Nelw,' told her:

> It is really terrific—but I'm not sure why. Partly I think because of all we have heard. Every way one looks one sees names and places that bring one to a gasping halt. I still can't feel it is real—just glorious Technicolor and soon it will be interval and we'll go out for a smoke.[12]

He promised her he would bring her to London, even 'if I have to save up for the rest of my life!' After the crowded life on the *Norsel* he was enjoying the luxury of his own company and told Nel, 'How I love being alone! I'm growing as bad as you in this respect.'

During the next five weeks Law visited countless people and institutes in England and Europe, building on his knowledge of all matters relating to Polar work. He met with the Polar expert, Brian Roberts of the Scott Polar Research Institute and, for days, examined the Institute's filing and library systems. He traipsed around shops and manufacturers investigating the availability and costs of various pieces of equipment unobtainable in Australia. He compared camping and mountaineering equipment, checked boots, ice axes, climbing ropes, primus and other burners, alpine tents and windproof materials. At one manufacturer in England he found a warm cotton windproof cloth called 'Ventile', which later proved unequalled as a material for parkas and tents, particularly in the wet-cold conditions at Macquarie Island. He visited ship builders in Glasgow, inspected detailed plans of ships and wrote specifications for Australia's requirements.

In France he visited the French Polar explorer, Paul-Emile Victor, who had set up the semi-private organisation 'Expéditions Polaires Françaises', and gained information about the availability of weasels, the over-snow tracked vehicles he had seen used on the NBS expedition. In

Norway, he visited Professor Harald Sverdrup, the Director of the Norsk Polarinstitutt, who had been chairman of the organising committee of the NBS expedition. There he was able to gain more information about the field equipment, including dog and cargo sledges, which the Norwegians had used in the NBS expedition.

He was in high spirits about what he was learning, and told Nel:

I am more and more certain that the thing to do is to build a new ship! And I think I can sell the idea to the Govt! My god, the Cabinet will wonder what has hit them when I put all my elaborate plans on the table! Oh well, if it doesn't work we can get that holiday a bit sooner. But they'll buy it, I'm sure, or most of it!

He ended his letter exuberantly:

God this is a fascinating business. And already I know more about it than anyone I meet. Just give me three years to work it all out![13]

Confidence Law certainly had, but it was not a shallow or superficial confidence, for it was based on the hard grind of his accumulation of information about every aspect of Antarctic work. His attention to detail, similar to that paid by Roald Amundsen before his expedition to the South Pole, is unequivocal.

2.

Whilst Law had been away there had been a change of Government in Australia, in December 1949, to a Liberal-Country Party coalition with R. G. Menzies as Prime Minister. Menzies, Law always maintained, had little interest in Antarctic Division affairs, but three other appointments brought men into roles which would impinge on many aspects of Australia's future involvement in Antarctica. Alan Watt was appointed as Secretary, DEA, Charles Kevin was made Assistant-Secretary (Administration) and later, in 1951, Richard Casey became Minister for External Affairs.

Law and Watt seldom saw one another, but the departmental files and Law's comments about their relationship display a certain warmth and sensitivity on Watt's part to both Law and the Antarctic Division in general. Watt made some administrative changes to the structure of the DEA, bringing in a system of three Assistant-Secretaries: two to deal with matters of policy and one to handle administrative matters. It was the Assistant-Secretary (Administration), who would be a vital link between the Antarctic Division and the DEA:

The Assistant-Secretaryship (Administration), [Watt said in his autobiography] was designed to ensure that a senior diplomatic officer, who had himself served overseas, would have responsibility for all 'housekeeping' matters ... dealing with such mundane matters as salaries, allowances, movement of staff, housing, leave, health, family, educational problems etc.[14]

Even Watt admitted that this position was a 'thankless post' and concluded that 'no one in this position ever achieves fame or glory ... He can only do his best and await the day when he will be given an interesting post abroad, where he can join the critics of his successor.'[15]

Unfortunately for Law, Charles Kevin was appointed to this position. Law's and Kevin's relationship was never good and their mutual animosity was only lightly masked by the stilted, impersonal language used in their memoranda.

Law was concerned that the new Government might not give the same support to the Antarctic activities as its predecessor had done. He was also concerned by the recent activity in Antarctica by USA, Chile, Argentina, Norway and France. He believed that the interest being shown by other countries in Antarctica created a major and urgent reason for Australia to establish a continental station so as to consolidate its claims. He presented a proposed resolution along these lines to the May 1950 EPC meeting. Mawson supported Law's proposal, stating that 'it was important to safeguard Australia's territorial rights in Antarctica' and that 'permanent occupation was ... the best basis for territorial claims.' After much discussion the members unanimously agreed that a resolution should be submitted to the Government, through the Minister for External Affairs. The EPC Committee recommended that:

(a) a permanent station be established on the Antarctic Continent.
(b) a long–term programme of scientific research be commenced.
(c) the existing stations at Heard and Macquarie Islands be maintained.[16]

Law also used the opportunity to gain the EPC members' commitment to Australia building its own ship suitable for Antarctic conditions. Mawson again supported Law's proposal, the members agreed and a recommendation was made that, to give effect to the previous recommendations, a new ship of special design will have to be built.[17]

Law followed these recommendations with a personal approach to the Minister for External Affairs, Percy Spender, and on 2 June Law wrote to all the EPC members and advised them that the Minister had promised support for the proposals put forward in the Committee's resolution.[18]

A week later Law asked permission from the Secretary, DEA, to grant interviews to two journalists who, Law maintained, had requested information on Australia's proposed plans for Antarctica. Law pointed out that the journalists could then 'compose first class accounts which they will submit to us for approval' and, by the time the Minister was ready to release his official press release, the journalists would 'burst into print with these pre-prepared articles.'[19] Charles Kevin replied that the Secretary felt that 'for the time being it would be better if no interviews were granted.'[20]

Always eager for publicity about the events of the Antarctic Division, Law used journalists in a way similar to how it was said the Prime Minister used them—as unpaid extras.[21] He had a standing arrangement with local journalists that, if they were short of news, he would always be able to find some Antarctic Division activity that was newsworthy. But a few weeks after the DEA's refusal for him to be interviewed by the journalists, the Antarctic Division received unexpected publicity that Law could well have done without, but which gave added impetus to his quest for Australia to have its own Antarctic ship.

On 20 July 1950 Law received a message from the OIC at Heard Island that the Medical Officer, Dr Serge Udovikoff, had appendicitis. As no other expeditioner was capable of performing the operation, Udovikoff's situation was critical. With no ship at the disposal of the Antarctic Division, Law immediately requested assistance from the Navy, but 'they refused point blank to go ... middle of winter ... they said they had no ship suitable and they couldn't spare one anyway.'[22] Law then arranged for an SOS to be sent to all ships within a certain distance of Heard Island, asking if they could divert to Heard Island via the Cape.

This story hit the headlines and, by Saturday, 21 July, it was reported that a passenger steamer, *Port Phillip*, travelling from Australia to London, had answered the call and was heading toward Heard Island and would arrive on Monday. Meanwhile Law had been advised that Udovikoff intended to operate on himself. Law radioed Heard Island and told the OIC that a Medical Adviser at the Royal Melbourne Hospital advised Udovikoff not to operate because he would probably kill himself, but to use other more conservative methods. Despite this advice Law received a message, at 3 a.m. on Saturday, that Udovikoff had decided to operate on himself with the aid of the two Heard Island biologists. Law waited anxiously for news, but later heard that Udovikoff, after setting up all the apparatus, had decided not to go ahead. Later in the day the newspapers reported that the Captain of the *Port Phillip* could not continue the dash to Heard Island because he could not risk his ship, a passenger vessel, in Antarctic waters in dangerous weather conditions.[23] The Captain had told Law that the ship encountered heavy seas, the passengers were all complaining, the furniture was getting broken and the piano had broken loose.[24]

By Sunday, 22 July, another ship, the *Perthshire*, had responded to the call and was steaming towards Heard Island and expected to arrive by Thursday. The two doctors on board the ship were standing by 'day and night to broadcast detailed directions to the expedition should Dr Udovikoff decide to remove his own appendix.'[25] The press were lapping up all this drama. On the same day the *Sunday Telegraph* even carried headlines that 'Doctor with Knife Poised, Stops Own Operation.'[26] By 24 July Law, with characteristic control, reported that Dr Udovikoff's condition, was 'satisfactory. An appendicular abscess had developed as had been expected. An operation would be necessary but there was now no extreme urgency.'[27] By midnight on 25 July a message was received that the *Perthshire* too had abandoned the mercy dash because of high winds raging in the region. At 5 a.m. the following morning sunspots prevented any radio communication with Heard Island 'cutting the island's last link with Australia and the world'.[28] Law then again approached the RAN for help.

The weeks of this saga were a nightmare for Law who was under continual pressure, as he later told an interviewer:

> The 'phone almost didn't stop ringing with in-coming and out-going calls and me sending cables down to Heard Island and Heard Island sending cables back to me and me ringing the hospital and so on. So, for a fortnight, I just slept in cat-naps. Nel shifted my bed-clothes all out onto the lounge in the lounge-room next to the telephone and I sort of lived there and worked with this immense pressure to try and cope with this problem ...

Finally the Navy decided to help and, on 27 July, it was reported that the *HMAS Australia* was being sent at 10.30 that evening 'on her 3200 mile mercy dash to Heard Island', with two doctors aboard.[29] Law had been contacted two days earlier by the Navy and asked to 'have everything ready, and arrange cold weather clothing for the crew':

> So here I am in Melbourne [continued Law] and I've got to outfit some 150 men. So we descended on Myers and Buckley and Nunn's and London Stores. We bought all their Long Johns and their woollen singlets and tried to get enough cold weather clothing for these blokes and tried to get everything done in a period of 36 hours.[30]

The *HMAS Australia* left on schedule, with extensive publicity surrounding the mercy dash. It was reported that 'an atmosphere of urgency obsesses every man aboard,' as she headed towards gale-swept Heard Island. By 1 August, 35–foot waves were breaking across the bows of *HMAS Australia* and on 2 August the ship received a message from Heard Island that they were experiencing one of the year's worst blizzards, with wind gusts reaching 100 m.p.h. and heavy snow falls.[31] By Monday, 7 August, the seas were calm enough to transport Udovikoff to *HMAS Australia* where he greeted the officers, who had just come more than 3 000 miles, with 'Hullo! Sorry I'm such a bother' and, to confound everyone, walked the length of the ship to the sick bay. He also walked off the ship when it arrived in Australia. Law, ever vigilant over the image the Antarctic Division portrayed to the public, was furious about this blatant display of health:

It was a good four weeks since the appendicitis first struck. So, by then he was pretty well recovered and what they should have done was carry him ashore on a stretcher for the benefit of the cameras and everything. But naturally when the cameras all photographed the arrival [and] he *walked* ashore there was an uproar by ignorant people, and the media in some respects, querying whether in fact he had ever been sick.[32]

One outcome of this month-long episode was that no medical doctor was later accepted for Antarctic service unless he had previously had his appendix removed. This ruling caused trouble with the Australian Medical Association, which considered it unethical to remove an appendix from a healthy person. When asked how he overcame their objection, Law responded 'We just ignored it,' adding that, 'it did curtail the number of people who would apply for the job, because not everyone is prepared to walk *cold* into a surgery and have his appendix out just to get a job in the Antarctic.'[33]

The need for Australia to own its own Antarctic ship was even more pressing as a result of the Udovikoff episode, nevertheless, Law was still hopeful that he could, by using a chartered vessel, mount an expedition to the Antarctic Continent in the summer of 1951–52. But, at the September 1950 EPC meeting, another obstacle was raised. This time it came as a result of the invasion by North Korea of South Korea. The Committee expressed concerns about the advisability of going ahead with the plan in view of the uncertain international situation and fears of war resulting from the Korean incident. Law had anticipated this and advised the EPC members that he had already spoken to the Secretary, DEA, who had informed him that this was a question for the Minister, if not for Cabinet itself. Law suggested that the EPC should confine its discussion to the practicability of the plan that had already been drawn up by the Antarctic Division. He got his way. The Committee resolved to recommend to the Government that a ship be chartered in 1951 to set up an Antarctic research station and, in the meantime, that a sub-committee be appointed to prepare detailed specifications for the new vessel.[34]

A sub-committee including Law, Sir Douglas Mawson, Captain Davis and Commander Peter Peek, RAN, met for their first meeting on 14 December 1950.[35] During the next two years this sub-committee worked painstakingly with a designer from the Australian Shipbuilding Board, Claude Barker. The general requirements for the proposed ship were that it be capable of breaking three-foot thick sheet-ice, could carry fifty passengers and fifty crew, include a helicopter deck and have space for an aircraft, amphibious vehicles, laboratories, oceanographic winches and other equipment. Within two years complete specifications for an

Antarctic ship, 'right down to the furniture and the crockery' had been completed and approved by the sub-committee.

3.

During this period Law was gathering around him highly qualified staff, whom he both respected and trusted. They were men skilled in their specific areas and, like himself, were also 'outdoor men', usually capable skiers or bushwalkers or climbers.

Law not only wanted to build up the Antarctic expertise in the Division, he also was looking for someone whom he could groom to take over his own position, if ever the need arose. He had been particularly impressed with Joe Jelbart, the young physicist who had worked with him on the cosmic ray equipment at Hotham Hut and who had spent a year at Heard Island. After discussions with Jelbart, Law arranged for him to gain Antarctic experience by accompanying the Norwegian-British-Swedish Antarctic expedition for its second year at Maudheim.

Law had also gained approval for additional staff appointments in the light of the proposed program for the permanent Antarctic station. He had been able to arrange a position as Senior Scientist for Fred Jacka, the other physicist who had worked with him at the Cosray Hut and who had spent a year on Heard Island with Jelbart:

> His [Jacka's] tasks were to direct the research programs in upper atmosphere physics, act as liaison officer with the Tasmanian physicists working on cosmic rays and supervise the scientific programs in general.

Of Jacka's personal qualities Law later wrote:

> Possessed of a fine intellect and a highly developed critical faculty, Jacka was also a remarkably wise person, with the capacity to think deeply and philosophically ... He was a prodigious worker, a clever and innovative experimental physicist and a good mathematician.[36]

The Antarctic Division's Supply Department, although established by now, still needed to be controlled by a person who could develop and operate the foolproof logistic supply system upon which men's lives could depend. The Division had already had some supply mishaps. Although not serious, these mistakes had been disappointing for the men on the Islands, as Law recalled:

> Walter Lindrum donated a billiard table to each station, a wonderful gesture, but all the billiard cues went to one station and all the billiard balls went to the other one.
>   On another occasion we had sewing machines sent down and all the needles went to one place and all the cotton went to the other.[37]

Apart from food, drink, medical supplies, clothing, and building materials for the year, each expedition needed thousands of spare parts for radios and diesel engines, pumps, generators and scientific equipment. Meticulous attention needed to be given not only to purchasing, but to packaging, listing, resupplying and reordering. The position was advertised and, from a large number of applicants, Richard (Dick) Thompson was selected. Thompson's appointment, Law later maintained, 'was one of the best I ever made.'[38]

He was previously a clerk in the PMG's Department and was studying for a degree in Commerce at Melbourne University part-time. A number of my friends in skiing circles knew him personally and had spoken enthusiastically of his dynamic energy and physical toughness. He had worked ... to build the Australian Postal Institute ski lodge at Mt. Buller, and he had the sort of experience and multi-faceted competence that is valuable in Antarctic situations. Further, he had served with the Royal Australian Navy during the war and knew a lot about ships and boats and seafaring generally.[39]

In Law's opinion Dick Thompson 'transformed the whole supply situation.' Jacka too, can remember the difference that Thompson made to the Supply Department which, until then, had been fairly ineffectual:

After Dick's appointment it started to hum. Dick was very energetic. He was very keen to find out what everyone was trying to do and he was dedicated to setting up structures and organisation that would achieve what he perceived to be needed.[40]

The admiration was mutual. Thompson thought working at the Antarctic Division was 'absolutely marvellous'. Even though he was many years younger than Law, they quickly established an excellent working relationship. Both men were enthusiastic and energetic and Thompson knew his ideas were listened to:

I was working in an exciting place where you were doing things [recalled Thompson] where the things that you suggested were not rubbished as being that of a younger person and who, therefore, knew nothing, but as something that he [Law] could put into his enquiring mind and accept or not accept ... We were able to talk pretty straight to each other, although I was, in the early days, respectful, just because of the public service hierarchy. But we were always very straight to each other.[41]

Lem Macey, who had been in the RAAF during World War II, and had also been the radio-officer-in-charge on the 1948 Heard Island expedition, joined the Antarctic Division as its Technical Officer. Macey was also an excellent seaman and Law regarded him as:

a good example of the capable technical all–rounder. There was nothing he could not fix—radios, engines, vehicles, huts, boats— and he possessed considerable innovative skills. Like Dick Thompson, he had spent World War II in the Royal Australian Navy and his seagoing experience was of great value to us.[42]

Law had managed to move Trevor Heath, the Secretary, out of the Antarctic Division, not without some personal anguish on both sides, but it was generally agreed by staff at the Division that Heath was not capable of doing the job. Law told Thompson that he thought he would like an older man in the position, one who was accustomed to working in the Public Service, and who would be able to advise Law on how to handle the public service system. They found a person who fitted the role perfectly:

Jeremiah (Jerri) Donovan, ... joined the Division in 1951 with the title of Administrative Officer. He was a permanent Commonwealth public servant then aged 53 ... He was one of the band of early skiers that put the sport on the map in the 1930s and he was still participating actively. He brought to the Division a wealth of knowledge of Commonwealth Public Service procedures and a wise, balanced and conservative approach to administration that counterbalanced the less mature and more ebullient style of the younger staff, including myself.[43]

Thompson and Macey worked closely with George Smith out at the Tottenham Store, 'nutting things out ... making things, devising things'. Thompson said that the Antarctic Division 'consumed' their life.

Everything was tied up with the Division. My social life. Macey, George and I would work weekends ... One year, in between voyages, Macey, George and I worked through Christmas Day and Boxing Day out at Tottenham physically remaking things.

But, Thompson added, 'I suppose it would not have [consumed my life] if I didn't believe it was worth doing and if I didn't believe the Director was worth working for.'[44]

Law indeed had an eye for character and an extraordinary ability to select skilled individuals. He moulded these men into a team and enthused them with the same sense of commitment to the invisible mystique of the Antarctic as his own.

By now the Antarctic Division's goal to set up Australia's first base on the Antarctic continent was in sight, and Law tackled it with the same enthusiasm and sense of purpose with which he approached the other aspects of his life. Characteristically, he planned each strategy in detail, anticipating obstacles, either circumventing or scaling them, and consistently built up an image for himself and the Division that gained public support on many levels. The Antarctic Division staff were now capable of handling the thousands of administrative and technical details to design, supply and land an Antarctic expedition. But, without a suitable ship, Law's mission was still impossible.

4.

Parallel with Law's quest for a ship, the annual relief of the Island parties had to proceed. With no alternative available, and despite his apprehension about the suitability of the *Labuan*, he had to again use it for the Heard Island relief voyage of 1951.

The *Labuan*, under the command of Lieutenant Commander I. Cartwright, left Melbourne at 9 a.m. on Tuesday 16 'to the noisy farewells of about 100 friends and relatives of the men on board.'[45] By the time it departed from Albany in Western Australia, on Monday 22 January, it was minus two of the crew who had 'shot through' because they were sure 'the ship will never get there'.[46] They were to be proved wrong, but this particular voyage was to point up, even more graphically than the Udovikoff episode, the need for an appropriate Antarctic Expedition ship.

The next few days were fine and uneventful, but by Thursday 25, the weather had deteriorated and high seas had forced the ship to slow down. On Friday the turbulence caused the deck cargo to shift and the ship had to heave-to whilst it was relashed. On Saturday 27 the weather was the same: 'strong wind, moderately rough seas, grey and overcast'. Law went to bed by 10.30 p.m. and 'slept rather well' despite the *Labuan's* terrifying vibrations. Prophetically, in light of later events, Law then recorded 'it is a wonder the ship continues to take such treatment!' Next day the weather was even worse. By 10.30 a.m. the gale was blowing at force 7 and the ship again had to heave-to into the wind whilst the bosun tightened the chains around the drums again. In the evening, Law noted that: 'weather growing worse, if possible.'

On Monday 29 Law recorded the events of the previous night:

Spent a very bad night. The ship took a dreadful bashing—I don't know how it stands it! The half-dozen or so bucks that she gives as she unkinks herself after balancing on a high wave amidships are almost violent enough to buck one out of bed.

Awoke to seas 40 ft high. Progress has been deadly slow for six days now. Captain is becoming worried about fuel and lubricating oil. If we don't have a better run soon we shall have to cut our stay at Heard Island and may even have to abandon Kerguelen altogether!

I'm still optimistically hoping for good weather on arrival—it can't go on like this indefinitely, or can it?

That evening he went up onto the bridge, an event he enjoyed, 'Most fascinating and thrilling. Hurricane force wind—60mph with gusts up to 90mph—a pitch black night, mountainous seas.'

It was so dark that he could not see the water in front of the ship and 'hoped fervently there were no icebergs about.' Only by watching the spray that shot high into the air and was swept horizontally back along the ship could he tell whether or not the vessel was still heading into the wind:

> The Captain remained on the bridge most of the night in case a sudden change of wind direction necessitated a change of course. If the ship were once to turn broadside on to these waves I doubt that she would remain afloat. It does not do at such times to think of possible engine or steering failure.

During the night a curious episode occurred which Law, years later, regaled to a meeting of the Shiplovers' Society of Victoria:

> Our men were quartered in one of a number of large bunk-rooms situated alongside the large cargo compartment which comprised the main volume of the LST [*Labuan*]. With them were a number of sailors. In the middle of the night our men awoke to find no sailors in the bunk-room. They went and looked in the next, which was also empty. Then they panicked, thinking they had been deserted in an abandoned ship, so they dressed and rushed back aft. There, in the mess decks, fully clothed and with packed kit bags, they found most of the sailors, who apparently had reasoned that if the ship was going to break in two, they might as well be in the half that had the engines in it![47]

By Tuesday the storm was abating, although seas were still high. Law was pleased to see that 'our team of men is very happy and all seem to get on well together.' The men were equally pleased with Law, as Campbell-Drury recorded in his diary:

> The unloading program should go with a swing. Phil has every detail and every man organized and briefed in his respective duties—most efficient leader, and efficient because of his popularity amongst the men. No matter what anybody has to discuss with Phil, and no matter how seemingly insignificant—he always has time to stay and talk the matter over. He treats everybody alike.[48]

Saturday's weather was bad, with waves again of 40 ft, and in the afternoon the steering broke down and the crew were forced to work in shifts, steering manually by the emergency gear.

They eventually sighted the dome of Big Ben, Heard Island, at 4.40 a.m. on Monday, 5 February, amidst comments from the new wintering-over party such as 'so that's why no one has ever climbed Big Ben—who would want to?'; 'isn't it magnificent' and 'I think I'll go back to Australia—St. Kilda will do me.'⁴⁹ They arrived at Atlas Cove at 7.47 a.m. in reasonably calm weather, but unloading could not begin as pounding of the heavy seas on the bows had damaged the ramp, which could not come down when the doors were opened. So the DUKWs had to be laboriously brought up to the deck and hoisted overboard.

Law, fed up with waiting, took six of the ANARE men, the mail and fresh food and went ashore in a LCVP (Landing Craft Vehicle and Personnel). It began to rain heavily and continued without a break all that day, registering the highest fall, 179 points, since the 1950 party had arrived the previous February.

The first DUKW did not arrive at the Island until nearly 3 p.m. and only a few loads were able to come ashore before a swell caused the unloading to cease. As usual, Law fretted at the wasted calm weather of the morning. Eighteen men, including Law himself, had to remain on the Island to sleep the night. The weather worsened and at 9 p.m. the *Labuan* put out to sea in a NW gale. 'Things look bad,' he recorded, 'the Captain informed me he would have to leave on Friday owing to fuel shortage. This gives me a helluva chance to complete my programme!'

On Tuesday 6, Law was up at 3 a.m. for a scheduled radio contact with the ship but the weather was too bad for the *Labuan* to come in and by 7 a.m. reported 'the worst blow of trip and was hove-to into it off the Island.' Law's plans for unloading and the building of the huts had to be altered. A message later in the day from the Captain advised Law that the ship's fuel position was not good and they would have to sail from Heard Island on Saturday. Writing his diary at 11 p.m. Law noted despondently:

> Ship still at sea, weather still bad and barom[eter] going down! Ship to sail Saturday, which leaves me three-and-a-half days! Gee! Still hoping each hour for a moderation of weather.

His hope was realised. The weather did moderate and unloading continued during Wednesday, but at such a slow pace that Law became exasperated. 'One DUKW now seems to have gone down the far end of the beach and got itself bogged', he moaned into his diary. 'Altogether things at present are bloody gloomy.'

And they got worse. The Captain sent Law a message to say the ship's condenser tubes were leaking and allowing salt water to pass into the fresh water. The ship's supply of fresh water was now running short because cracks had also opened in the hull and salt water had polluted some of the fresh water tanks. The captain advised Law that they would have to leave at midnight to go to Kerguelen for water and, if the weather permitted and the ship were in seaworthy condition, he would return later to Heard Island to unload the remaining stores.

This was Law's first personal experience of the problems of dual control arising from the disparate objectives of an Expedition Leader and a ship's Captain. Law's aim as Expedition Leader, in this particular case, was the successful change-over of the Heard Island men. But the Captain was responsible for the safety of the ship, its crew and passengers and he had to answer to the shipowner, in this case the Naval Board, for any damage to the vessel. Although the Expedition Leader is in charge of the overall expedition, a ship's Captain has the right by law, when the safety of the ship is at stake, to override an Expedition Leader's decison.

Law pointed out to the Captain that many of the supplies still on board were essential to the survival of the Heard Island men during the following winter, but the Captain was adamant that the overall safety of the vessel was more important.

The general feeling was that the ship would not survive the trip and Law felt forced 'to work on the assumption that there was a possibility that we might not return and that all essentials should therefore be put ashore.' Faced with the imminent departure of the *Labuan*, he again changed the landing plans. He sent a priority list of essential stores to the ship, then everyone 'worked flat out to try and land all of our minimum requirements' for the wintering-over party.

Inefficiencies continued and criticisms were rife about the bosun, mainly from the sailors, but the DUKW drivers 'were pretty caustic also'. Law, still on shore, sent the bosun a letter telling him which particular drums were required. Irked at receiving instructions from the Expedition Leader, the bosun abused the messenger and told him that 'he was not going to take letters, that he took his orders from the Captain.' Law assuaged his anger, as usual, by writing. He snarled into his diary that not only was the bosun 'a blustering, inefficient ignoramus', but that the crew were an 'unskilled, untrained lot of sailors'.

Blustering bosuns and untrained crew were only part of the problem. In the morning Law received a message that the Medical Officer had had his leg crushed between the DUKW and the ship when climbing up the side. An X-ray found that there were two clean breaks in the foot and it was agreed that he could stay on for the year on Heard Island.

Unloading continued through the night, 'sailors and men ashore worked splendidly', although not through altruistic motives. 'Every crew member wanted to get the hell out of the place', Law later reported. 'They hated Heard Island. They were frightened stiff about the ship and everything to do with Heard Island.'[50] One can well imagine why.

At 12.30 a.m. Law was taken back to the *Labuan*, 'damn tired ... we had been working since 4.30am and it has been a day of crisis after crisis.' But even this splendid work had not completed the unloading and some essential items were still on board, including coke, liquid fuel and huts.

Their desperate attempt to make a return visit to Heard Island unnecessary had failed by only a few hours.

The party arrived at Îles de Kerguelen in the evening of Friday, 9 February, with Kerguelen showing off its 'usual glorious scenery' with 'perfect colouring and cloud effects'. Law's last visit had been in 1949, when the Island was uninhabited. Since then the French Government had established a permanent station and Law was eager to see what they had done. The ship's Captain and the ANARE group went ashore where they were introduced to the forty-five men in the French party and were officially welcomed with a short speech followed by a champagne toast. In the meantime the LCVP returned to the ship for the rest of the crew. While the main group were looking at the new quarters, 'the rest of the lads, plus sailors, got stuck into more wine—vin rouge—and were all very high when we returned.'

By the time the group was ready to leave Law and a few of the more sober men had to round up the others and get them to the wharf.

It was like droving sheep without a sheep dog [Law wrote]. As soon as one would get one group of men shepherded towards [the] harbour, one would find several others had gone back for another drink at the camp.

Law did not know that this 'sheep dog' act would become one of the annual rituals of the ANARE. In the following years the expeditioners would use the visit to Kerguelen as a 'let down' exercise after the exacting work at the other stations. Law later likened these visits to a 'Melbourne football team flying off on a "junket" trip to some exotic place at the conclusion of the football season.'[51]

The following day Law enjoyed a long walk around the beautiful Kerguelen Island with its abundance of wildlife, seals, penguins and many species of birds. He took his rifle to do some duck shooting and returned at 6 p.m. with 'blistered heels and very tired'. On the deck of the ship he found a bird which had stunned itself flying at the searchlight. Thinking that Norm Favaloro, the Ornithologist, would be interested, Law took the bird to Favaloro's cabin, only to find when he arrived 'six other chaps there, all with a bird in hand, and as we laughed others kept arriving with birds, culminating in the Captain coming with one in each hand.'

In the midst of the uproar of a huddle of men, feathers and screeching birds, Favaloro, almost overcome with the excitement, threw his arms up in the air and smashed his light, adding further to the pandemonium. Campbell-Drury, almost hysterical with laughter, reeled backwards and sat on something soft which he later found, when the light globe was replaced, was Favaloro's prized collection of stuffed birds. As stealthily as possible he 'bent them all back into shape—and shot through.'[52]

Sunday's weather was beautiful and, as Law was to often notice later, brought with it an uplift in morale. Some repairs had been done to the *Labuan*, fresh water had been pumped aboard and the Captain told Law they would be able to return to Heard Island.

The *Labuan* left Kerguelen on Monday 12 and Law was delighted to accept a farewell gift of a bottle of 50-year-old Cognac. They arrived back at Heard Island at 4 p.m. on Tuesday 13. The weather still was reasonably good and, not wanting to waste such an opportunity, Law arranged for the men to work on into the night. By using flood lights and torches, the ship had been emptied by midnight. The wintering-over party now had all their essential supplies and Law could heave a sigh of relief. The major job completed, Law now hoped they could spend some time helping the men with the building program, but the weather was so bad the ship was unable to come in, and the Captain would not risk sending in a DUKW with men and timber.

Frustrated with 'cautious captains' who, 'like all very cautious people cannot make use of the breaks when they come,' Law spent much of the time photographing the Island. He loved the unique and rugged scenery of Heard Island with its magnificent craters, rich chocolate cliffs, and the glacier with its crevasses and rookeries, but it could not compensate for precious days lost when so much could have been achieved.

By Saturday 17 the weather cleared sufficiently for the group to be picked up from the Island. The *Labuan* then set sail for Australia. The very next day, however, it stopped because the steering broke down again. One of the crew devised an impromptu gadget to replace the faulty steering and things looked more optimistic. On Monday the sun broke through, the sea was calm but the engine stopped running for an hour.

The weather stayed calm on Tuesday but, this time, the engines stopped for approximately eight hours. Law now knew that the ship would need to undergo repairs both at Fremantle and Melbourne. This, coupled with the slowness of the trip, began to worry him because the relief voyage to Macquarie Island still had to be carried out. It now looked as if it would be April before they could get to relieve the 'poor Macquarie-ites'.

More mishaps followed. On Wednesday 21 the main boiler-room fan broke down and the *Labuan* remained stationary for eight hours while repairs were made. 'The absence of noise, the absence of the throbbing engines was uncanny', Campbell-Drury wrote. 'It was the still quietness of a dead ship.'[53] Law was told that a crack had opened up, right across the steel deck. This added to everyone's anxiety, particularly those who knew that a number of LSTs had broken in half during the war in heavy storms. The Captain had asked for a tug to be sent out to the ship. So they waited. The weather, luckily, remained calm.

Law spent Thursday debriefing each of the men from the 1950 Heard Island expedition. He had previously advised them that he wished to

spend time with each expeditioner and had requested that he see the
photographs they had taken, as well as their diaries, if they were willing,
and to discuss any suggestions they might have had to improve any
aspect of the expedition. He was pleased with the results:

> This system is fine—I get a knowledge of exactly what is going back,
> either official or personal, goods, records, diaries, films etc. etc. Very
> glad I organized it.

Still they waited. By Friday water was restricted to drinking only, and
then only at meal times. On Saturday the sea was flat calm and Law was
thoroughly sick of the ship and impatient to get home.

By Sunday Law was 'feeling lousy' after three days with the stringent
water restrictions. Beer was available instead of water but beer made him
feel 'three times as bad as I feel now'. Conditions were fast becoming
intolerable, and by Monday the Law Luck had deserted him. The refrig-
erator broke down and many of Favaloro's bird specimens from Heard
and Kerguelen were lost.

During the day Law received the tragic news that Joe Jelbart, the
young physicist whom he had nominated to go as the Australian
observer with the Norwegian–British–Swedish Antarctic Expedition, had
been killed. Jelbart and two other men, whilst driving a weasel in fog,
had driven over the ice cliffs into the sea near the base at Maudheim.
That evening Law recorded simply, 'Am very upset.' But by Tuesday, he
wrote:

> I am still numb with the shock of Joe's death. Why do the finest and
> best men always seem to go in this fashion? I can hear myself reas-
> suring his mother and father on the ship at Port Melbourne as he
> left, telling them how safe it was down there—'Nothing happens to
> men these days in the Antarctic'.

Despite the sorrow Law must have felt about Jelbart's death, expressing deep, personal feelings, even into the privacy of his diary, was not his
style, and this small paragraph is the only indication of his grief.

Later in the day, the engines stopped again.

> We are rolling idly at the mercy of the swell (fortunately it is fine
> and calm) waiting for a tug to steam 120 miles from Fremantle to
> take us in tow ... I suppose we are really lucky to have got this far!

Without any steam they could not pump water, either fresh or salt,
and so they could not wash, nor clean their teeth. There was now no
drinking water at all, only beer, and:

> no flushing at the heads! The WCs stank to high heaven and why we

were not provided with a rope and bucket so we could flush them that way after use I don't know ... the places were so choked up that you couldn't go any more.

By now Law had lost his appetite, could no longer sleep, had a bad head-cold and was feeling 'thoroughly depressed', but with stolid optimism concluded, 'Will come out of it I suppose when I get to Perth.'

By 10 p.m. on Tuesday a tug had finally arrived, but it was decided not to hook it up to the ship until the following morning. By then the very last thing to break down on the ship had done so, for the lights went off and the ship was left in darkness. They were now without water, power, pumps, toilets and light. 'A decent storm at that time,' Law later said, 'like any one of the dozen or more we had passed through, would have rolled us over.'⁵⁴ Miraculously, the weather stayed calm.

The next day the boiler had been fixed and Law jubilantly recorded that the ship was 'steaming towards Perth, without the use of the tug, at about five knots. Whoopee!' But not for long for, 'No—engines stopped about 6am—fire in the boiler room!' Later still 'no—was not a fire apparently—looked like.' The *Labuan* finally arrived at Fremantle after dark that day, but it was not permitted to dock. One hundred gallons of fresh water were sent out to the ship. On Thursday morning, 1 March, the *Labuan* limped into Fremantle dock, with the help of tugs, and berthed.

The following day, Law flew to Melbourne where Nel met him and he was 'whisked off in car to have lunch at the Ritz Cafe.' Even though he had not seen her for over six weeks, there was little time to enjoy the release from the tensions of the voyage. He now had another anxious, and distressing, duty to carry out; he had to break the news of Joe Jelbart's death to Jelbart's relatives in Ballarat. Fred Jacka, who was even more distressed than Law because of his close friendship with Joe during their year at Heard Island, went to Ballarat with Law. Jacka recalls the circumstances:

I really was extremely upset then and I really found enormous difficulty in coping with that situation. Phil coped with it admirably ... masterly handling. I would think that it was the first time that he'd ever been confronted by that sort of problem. Very great sympathy was apparent and, at the time, very great control.⁵⁵

Jacka had lost a close friend and Law had been deprived of the man whom he had selected to train to take his position if ever he left the Division. Law now decided that Jacka, whom he had always held in high regard, 'would be my obvious successor' should he ever leave the Division.⁵⁶

The news of the *Labuan* was depressing. She spent some weeks undergoing repairs in Fremantle and survived the trip to Melbourne, where further repairs were carried out. Finally, she sailed to Sydney, where she was tied up and never put to sea again. Law was once again without a ship and the Macquarie Island changeover was well overdue.

5.

In a desperate attempt to find a vessel Law, during the following four weeks, wrote to or interviewed every organisation controlling private shipping around the Australian coastline, but without success. Many ships were suggested, but for one reason or another, all proved inadequate for the Macquarie trip.

Finally the Australian Shipping Board offered ANARE the *River Fitzroy*, a 9 000-ton ship used for transporting iron ore for BHP. It was by far the largest ship ever to visit the island and was quite unsuitable for the job. With no other alternatives available Law accepted it gratefully. He was also thankful for the Army's offer of two rather dilapidated DUKWs to replace the good DUKWs that were still on the *Labuan*.

On the *Labuan* the Navy personnel had had the responsibility for landing the stores, but now, with a commercial ship, the ANARE personnel would need to take over this duty. Law hoped he had the perfect man for the task in Dick Thompson, the Supply Officer. One of the reasons Thompson had been appointed was his experience with ships, boats and seafaring generally whilst in the Navy during the war. Law now appointed him as his second-in-charge, with specific responsibilities to handle the landing operations.

The *River Fitzroy* finally sailed at 12.30 p.m. on Saturday, 28 April 1951. Law had been so delighted with the Dramamine anti-sea-sickness tablets on the Heard Island trip that he had issued them to all the men and was pleased to report 'no-one was ill.' This blissful state of affairs apparently did not last long, for Jacka—who was on the round trip as a supernumerary and who shared the cabin with Law—recalled that 'Phil was hideously sick.'[57]

The trip to Macquarie was made in moderate weather, except for the last twenty-four hours which were 'very rough ... strong wind ... beam swell, waves up to 35 ft. high'.

Law's record of the trip shows a fair degree of understatement, at least compared to Jacka's recollections, which were that 'it was just an awful trip.' Law and Jacka were lucky, they at least had a cabin, but the other expeditioners, including Thompson, were housed in quarters near the forecastle. The conditions there, Jacka recalls, were appalling, 'The din of the clanking chains and hefty gear rattling round each time it hit the wave was colossal. And the stink! The ventilation was almost non-existent.'[58] With Law so sick, Jacka acted throughout the trip as the messenger between Law and the men's quarters.

Macquarie Island covers less than half the area of Heard Island and is twenty-one miles long and three miles wide and runs from north to south. From the coastal beaches a steep escarpment rises to a plateau.

There is varied vegetation on the Island: grasses, mosses and lichens, but no bushes or trees. Sir Douglas Mawson's earlier attempts to have the Island proclaimed a sanctuary were achieved on 17 May 1933 and it now provided a breeding area for thousands of seabirds, penguins and elephant seals.

It is a dangerous place to approach by ship, exposed as it is to the constant westerlies of the Roaring Forties. The first sight of Macquarie Island is of precipitous slopes, covered in tussock grass, rising to a plateau that is usually obscured by cloud. The weather pattern on the Island is consistent: either fog or rain for 300 days of the year. Coupled with this are strong winds, grey skies, and snow squalls. The men on the station become accustomed to the scream of the unceasing winds and the roar of the surf. Silence is more noticeable.

Although further south than Heard Island, the climate is not as severe and the snow on the highlands melts in the summer. Its climate is classed as 'wet–cold' with little seasonal variation in temperature, as Law described:

> The temperature swings from about 27–28 degrees F. minimum in winter to a maximum of about 40–42 degrees F. ... It's very easy to get dreadfully wet, and it's pretty miserable and it can be pretty cold physically. ... But at least at Macquarie you could always go out, even in the middle of winter.[59]

The ANARE station nestles on an isthmus at the foot of a low rocky promontory at the northern extremity of the island. The unloading is hampered by tangled kelp, pounding surf, shingle beaches and underwater rocks.

> Macquarie Island landings are hairy [Law later told an interviewer]. The Army DUKW people have never in their army experience had anything like unloading stores at the side of a ship. And the ordinary normal landing place at Macquarie Island is ... through Niggerheads, and the DUKW only has about six foot clear on each side, and it's quite a job ... to steer and get it right. You've got to keep pretty high power on the engines, you can't just float in because the wind is broadside, tending to drift you sideways onto the rocks, so you've got to take it fairly fast, and again you get picked up by a big wave and you've got your engines roaring trying to keep the speed on the thing so you've got steerage way while this great wave takes you in and then you surge through this narrow gap between the Niggerheads and get ashore.[60]

On 4 May, the *River Fitzroy* dropped anchor in Buckles Bay, Macquarie Island, close in to shore, but the party were unable to go ashore. The following morning, Saturday, 5 May, Jacka investigated the motor cutter and found that it had been badly damaged in the storm the night before they arrived at Macquarie. This left them solely dependent on the dilapidated DUKWs. 'There goes our only auxiliary power transport,' Law recorded, 'I hope the DUKWs don't break down!'

After frustrating delays with the unloading of one of the DUKWs, it was finally lowered 'swinging dangerously' into the water and Law was able to go ashore with several of the men:

> I experienced the usual thrill as we raced ashore through a slight
> surf and sprang down to the beach to shake hands with three or
> four of the 1950 party who had come to meet us.
>   It is grand to meet these chaps again at the end of their long
> sojourn down here.

They continued unloading throughout the day until it was dark, and later had a 'good dinner of steak and onions, date tart, excellent Seppelts claret and hock—best of their stuff I've ever tasted!' Finally Law held a meeting with the men, explained the program for the next days, allotted bunks for the night, sent several radio messages to the ship and at 10 p.m. wrote up his diary, 'Am very tired—my muscles are not used to lifting heavy cases. I shall sleep soundly tonight.'

On Sunday, 6 May, with a screaming 45 m.p.h. NW gale, rising sea and swell, Law laconically reported that it was 'not a good day'. The two DUKWs went out to the ship at 8 a.m. 'Both returned smartly, but the first one broke down with a spluttering engine before it completed its run along the shore to the Station.'

His apprehension over the condition of the DUKWs had not been unfounded. The other DUKW went back to the ship, taking six of the men to shift cargo from one hold to the other, 'However, it returned almost at once, empty, having had great difficulty negotiating rocks with a fairly heavy swell and surf coming in parallel with the beach and a NW wind blowing crosswise.'

By 10.30 a.m. the swell at the ship's side was approximately eight feet 'and with one DUKW out of commission I couldn't risk cracking the other on rocks or having its engine fail out at the ship.' So Law reluctantly abandoned the unloading for the day.

So badly had the weather deteriorated that by 3.30 p.m. the ship had to put out to sea, taking with it the ANARE men who had been helping in the ship's hold. This left Law in the same predicament as at Heard Island: unable to unload, and the vital men needed for the shore work stranded on the ship. Irritably he recorded:

> I cursed having been tricked into losing six more men out on the
> ship idle, when they could have been working ashore. It seems to
> happen to me no matter how I try to plan against it.

By evening the sky had cleared and his optimism returned, 'I am hopeful that it will be SW when we awake tomorrow morning. Two good days and we will get a bit of this stuff ashore.' But the crew's working hours were galling him:

> Regular meal breaks for the crew make the game hard. With *Labuan* we would stagger all meals and keep the job going. These drongoes don't start before 8, stop 12–1 for lunch and then stop at 5pm. Not much of a day's work by our standards.

Law always had difficulty coming to terms with the fact that other people were not as committed to the Antarctic work as the ANARE men. He resolved to ask the Captain to arrange for the crew to stagger their meal times and work into the night if required.

The following day, Monday 7, began well with the six ANARE men on the ship being brought in early, but then the good DUKW's engine failed half way out to the ship and the men had to spend precious time rescuing it with the other DUKW. The delay this incident caused was serious:

> We persuaded the crew to work shifts over lunch-time and this kept things going. I have now asked (actually the First Mate suggested it!) that we work on into the night till 10pm while the sea is fairly calm. The Captain is at this moment discussing it with the crew.

The crew agreed to work and they unloaded until 9 p.m. Law was pleased with the day's achievements, 'Things are now moving as they ought to!' and, satisfied, he wrote, 'bed at 11.30. Very tired but fit and well after much carrying of cases.'

The unloading continued satisfactorily, and by Wednesday, the sea was calm enough to begin to unload the heavy forty-four gallon drums of fuel. 'That's a dangerous business,' years later Law described to an interviewer:

> ... having drum hooks clasp three drums and lower them into a DUKW with the ship rolling and bashing the drums against the side of the ship and the DUKW coming up and down. On occasions the drum hooks come loose and the three heavy drums drop, and men throw themselves backwards out of the DUKW into the heavy sea, to avoid being crushed.[61]

On this occasion the operation went without mishap, Law was pleased to record that evening.

On Thursday 10, the sea was smooth and Law hoped that they would be able to get the new replacement tractor ashore. Afraid of damaging the ship whilst lifting the tractor intact over the side, the Captain requested that the tractor be dismantled. Law refused because he thought it would be a useless exercise and, 'anyway I can't spare an engineer for two days!'

Later the Captain suggested a scheme for getting the tractor off and said he was willing to give it a go. Law heaved a sigh of relief: 'Thank God for that—I don't mind if they try and fail, but I would be annoyed if they simply said it couldn't be done.' Failing was bad enough, in Law's eyes, but not trying was intolerable.

Law scrutinised the crew's struggle with the tractor through binoculars from the shore for nearly an hour and later reported that he could see that what they were doing would not achieve its purpose.

> The boys who were out at the ship say that the whole operation was dreadfully slow—a lot of inefficient mucking about. If we lose out on this chance it will be due solely to the tedious delays and snail pace of this afternoon's work on the ship.

In the end, the darkness closed in and they had to halt their efforts to get the tractor into the DUKW and so it remained on the ship. Law's frustrations are evident:

> With all the work to be done and the need for haste we had eight men out there who were not allowed to lift a finger to help out, [and who] had to stand around and watch the work going along at that deadly rate.

On Friday the wind was too strong to make another attempt to move the tractor and Law was advised that the ship would unload drums. The first DUKW went to the ship at 10 a.m., but had to return empty handed as the men were almost washed off the DUKW when they tried to hook it to the ship's sideline. They decided to return to the beach. As they turned they faced straight into a gale. The thrill Law felt at these escapades, is well captured in his description:

> The spectacle of that DUKW returning was magnificent! Once per second she struck a choppy wave, sending a white cascade of water and spray 30 ft into the air which the wind whipped back for 50–100 ft behind the DUKW. One man, [Hugh] Oldham [a geophysicist], stood in the DUKW, head and shoulders above the windscreen, with these dashes of icy water whipping his face, to direct the driver, who could not see a thing. From the shore the DUKW was only occasionally visible—all one could see were these regular bursts of white spray with a dark blur beneath, out of which a figure stood upright.

The men spent the morning skinning a seal, packing, hanging frozen foods, repairing engines, making recordings of hut noises in the gale on the wire recorder and preparing lines to assist the pontoon when it arrived with the tractor. Only the DUKW drivers were unemployed, waiting for the gale to abate. This it refused to do, but the DUKW was needed for a rescue mission:

> More excitement. This afternoon about 3.00 p.m. the anchored pontoons broke away from their moorings and began to drift very rapidly out to sea. I spotted them, so did Thompson, and in a few minutes we had a crew of McCormack, Thompson, Bunt, Jacka in one DUKW which set out to chase the pontoon ... The gale was at its height with 60 mph gusts, no swells, but a terrific choppy sea with the tops of the chop whipped off by the wind. Going out was OK— they caught up with the pontoon ... They got a line on it. Thompson and Bunt stood on the pontoons and they turned for home. From then until they reached the shore we hardly saw them ... Clouds of spray deluging the DUKW, spray and green seas sweeping over the pontoons where Bunt and Thompson stood, dimly seen as two dark uprights occasionally through the white whirls of spray.

Thompson was certainly proving his worth as a seafaring man. An hour later the wind suddenly dropped, the sea became calm and drum unloading continued. By 11 p.m. the ship was almost empty and the main part of the operation had been successfully concluded.

Writing his diary that evening, Law, seldom reflective, pondered on some of the potential dangers in the incidents of the previous few days:

> It has been very worrying having DUKWs out at night in these high winds, which blow off shore and would drift a disabled DUKW to sea very rapidly, as shown by the pontoons. When a DUKW is half way between the ship and shore it is difficult to tell whether it is moving or not and its engine could stop quite a long time before we discovered it. On the misty nights we would not discover it until a prolonged absence of a DUKW at both the ship and shore ends made me apprehensive.

After giving the 1951 group 'instructions ... advice and congratulations on their fine work this last week', Law and the 1950 party went back to the ship at midnight.

By Saturday 12, with little swell at the ship, the Captain was willing to try to unload the tractor again. Although pleased to have another opportunity to get the tractor ashore, Law was faced with another day of unplanned activity, something that frustrated him:

> Today will be one of those awkward messy days when nothing is clear cut, everything depends upon circumstance and how other

things proceed, and at some stage I must make a decision regarding how much longer we can stay here.

Thompson had arranged for three long pontoons to be lashed side by side and heavy timber decking was fitted to them to create a broad raft on which to place the tractor. The DUKW that was still working went to sea, picked up the pontoons and towed them to the ship's side, and the tractor was hoisted outboard and allowed to slide down the side of the ship onto the pontoon raft. If the work Thompson had already achieved during the landing had not established his later reputation as a landing expert, this episode of bringing the tractor in would. The DUKW slowly pulled the pontoons and tractor ashore through choppy seas. Law recorded:

> It was lucky to reach the shore because one pontoon was leaking and the whole load was well down on that side. When it hit shore the trouble started. In heavy surf we waded to and from the pontoons and rigged ropes. By hauling in various directions as seas came in we got them swung around facing the beach and grounded at the front. Men were frequently immersed in heavy surf.

Finally the men, half wading and half swimming, in the freezing, pounding waves, managed to get the tractor ashore. By now the pontoons were so badly holed they could not be floated back to the ship. This meant they were forced to leave the old tractor behind at the Island and had to spend the rest of the days dismantling the pontoons.

On Sunday, 13 May—nine days since they had arrived—Law awoke and found the landscape transformed by a heavy snow-fall, 'picking out in brilliant relief the eroded gullies and gorges of the plateau and softening the harshness of the isthmus and station area'.[62] The combination of snow and the wind blowing from the south-west meant 'a good day!' Law wrote at 5.45 a.m. But his optimism was misplaced and the dramatic events that occurred prevented him from recording in his diary for two days.

'So much has happened in so short a time', wrote Law the following Tuesday, as he set down the events of the previous days:

> We arrived off Lusitania Bay [to land a load of cased cargo] at about 3pm [on Sunday] with No. 1 DUKW taking in water so rapidly that the use of the motor pumps plus one man baling, were necessary. We loaded up No. 2 DUKW ... then we [11 men] cast off and headed for the shore.

As they approached the beach they had to make a choice between two alternative landing spots. They selected a narrow entrance flanked with ugly looking rocks, but they had barely straightened up to steer toward what seemed the clearest part when:

> the swell picked us up and we found ourselves running in like a surf boat towards the sand, shingle and rocks that formed the narrow beach.
>
> About 6–10 yards out from the beach we stuck fast on rocks and succeeding swells, breaking over us, slewed us around broadside to the surf. At this stage we unloaded all the cargo and waded ashore with it. John Bunt, who was pretty exhausted, was washed out with the backwash while trying to rescue a floating case, but was washed in with the case on the next wave.

For the next hours the men tried desperately to move the DUKW up onto the beach. They ran a hawser from the DUKW's winch to a rock on shore. Then, by rocking the DUKW alternatively in forward and reverse gears, and hauling with the winch, it looked as if they would get it moving. But just as success was in sight, the clutch failed. Without the clutch, neither the wheels, propeller, winch nor pumps could be operated. The immobile DUKW quickly filled with a foot of water covering the engine, and they had to abandon their attempts to save it:

> We carried all the items still higher on the beach then lit a bonfire out of old packing cases. Inside the hut we lit lamps and a kero. stove and cleaned everything out of the hut. We then had tea— tomato soup, beef stew, plum pudding. Some of the men gathered around the bonfire, some stayed in the hut, and a bottle of whiskey quickly disappeared. We held our garments out to the fire and became relatively dry.
>
> Beds were made up about 10.30–11 pm and we turned in. Eleven men in a hut about 8'6" x 10'. Very nice packing—they looked like sea-elephants in a mud wallow. Luckily we had plenty of blankets.

For Thompson, who seldom drank alcohol and never drank spirits, the combination of exhaustion and whiskey was too much for him and he went to sleep early in a dark corner of the hut under one of the hammocks:

> About 10pm while were we talking, he [Thompson]started up wildly screaming 'I can't see where I bloody am,' ... and followed up with 'Am I safe? Am I safe.' Troy said "You're OK old man—hold onto this" and gave him a handful of wood-wool from a packing case. Whereupon Dick clutched it firmly in both hands and lay down again, comforted, to resume his slumbers. We nearly laughed our heads off!

In fact Thompson, who had spent much of the last ten days working from dawn to dusk in hard, dangerous, wet and miserable conditions, was suffering from exposure and exhaustion, which was diagnosed when he finally returned to the ship.

The next morning, with the narrow entrance they had previously used now blocked by the stranded DUKW, the men had to tackle the problem of how to be rescued from the Island. Law inspected a beach further north but 'found heavy surf bashing over rocks and kelp. A hopeless approach.' Eric Shipp, the biologist from the 1950 party, found a reasonably protected approach further south and at 8 a.m. they signalled the ship and gave those on board a code for signals.

We arranged to fly an orange flag (two Mae West life jackets on a pole) to show them the landing beach and signals with two white flags ... for directing the whaler.

About 9 a.m. the ship came close in and dropped the whaler a mile further up the coast from where the men were waiting, then headed out to sea. The Second Mate was at the rudder of the whaler and four men wielded the oars. The wind was rising and it had begun to snow.

They came in around the point and proceeded to just about the breaker line. There they let out the bow anchor but did not turn about. Instead they rowed straight in and swung around broadside at the beach. Luckily it was a lull period for breakers and we waded in and held the boat to stop it from drifting onto rocks, which were 10 ft. off either end.

I directed men to pull the stern and push the bow at the same time detailing a man to haul on the bow anchor rope. She came around beautifully, all of us scrambled aboard, and we rowed out.

'Dick was amazing,' Jacka recalls, 'he was obviously still absolutely blind [drunk] and yet once he got onto the whaler, he got hold of an oar and pulled.'[63] They rowed out a mile to where the ship was waiting for them.

That evening Law took stock of the relief voyage:

Very glad to be on board again ... The loss of the DUKW was unfortunate but we were lucky not to lose any men in the two landing operations—DUKW and whaler. Anyway the whole program we set ourselves to do has been completed for the loss of 1 DUKW, 3 pontoons, one stove-in cutter, and a tractor left behind.

The *River Fitzroy* was now headed back to Port Kembla and Law had a 'lousy night's sleep owing to the ship rolling like buggery all night.'

For the next few days, with the changeover well and truly behind him,

Frank Morgan repairing Auster 200 on the fast ice beside the ship.

Horseshoe Harbour from air (1954).

Rescuing Dovers' weasel which had broken through fast ice off Horseshoe Harbour.

The 1954 Mawson party, from left to right: Georges Schwartz, Lem Macey, Bill Harvey, Bob Dovers (OIC), Bill Storer, John Gleadell, John Russell, Bruce Stinear, Bob Dingle and Bob Summers in front of Explastics hut.

The 1954 Mawson party gathers on fast ice in Horseshoe Harbour to farewell *Kista Dan*.

Law raises the Australian flag and officially names Mawson Station in the presence of the wintering party, 13 February 1954.

Kista Dan at Scullin Monolith.

Law and Richard Thompson on Magnetic Island, Vestfold Hills, first landing (1954).

Law shows Sir Douglas Mawson the first published picture of Mawson Station after his return to Australia.

Law immediately began to plan for the work that would await him at Melbourne. He sent 'a spate of telegrams to Donovan,' the Administrative Officer in Melbourne, to organise various appointments for his return; he filled in customs declarations, held discussions with each of the returning Macquarie Party and arranged their complicated travel arrangements.

The party arrived in Port Kembla on 19 May 1951.

6.

During the *River Fitzroy* trip Thompson had established himself as an excellent 'off–sider' to Law, not only at Headquarters, but in charge of landings on expeditions. It was the first of many trips they would do together in the following years and the success of their working relationship was often commented upon by other expeditioners:

> I think they were an excellent team [maintained Jacka], they worked together extremely well. I think Dick was very important in the leadership on the voyages. His importance derived from three main facts: one, he was a highly intelligent fellow; secondly, he had great abilities in handling practical affairs and he was never intimidated by the circumstances; and the third was his ability to communicate with everybody. [64]

And Budd, a Medical Officer, remarked: 'They were both very intelligent and forceful personalities [with] an intelligent understanding of their respective roles. The combined effect was greater than the separate parts.' Budd went on to say that Thompson had the ability to knock around with the boys on the lower deck[65] whereas Law, although always available to talk with the men, was more aloof; 'Phil was your Chief.'[66] They each gained commitment from the men, but again in different ways. 'Phil was a "carrot" man and Dick was a "driver"', was a distinction another expeditioner made.[67] Thompson agreed with this, and explained:

> I am fairly famous, or infamous, as a driver, but a fairly cheerful one. I would get up at 4am to look at the weather and decide whether we could work that day. I was discharging cargo, building huts and so on.
>
> So Phil would write, or take photographs, or work on scientific problems. I would make a judgement as to whether we could work that day and if we could I'd go around saying "DUKW in five", or whatever and I'd get them out of bed—a lot of cheerful noise to get them up. I was impatient, I was intolerant and I would tell them so, if they weren't ready. And physically I worked. I ran that unloading.[68]

Law, many agreed, 'sometimes asked the impossible, and Dick almost achieved the impossible.'[69] It was also agreed that Law did not ask anyone to do what he would not do himself.

In just over two years Law had built up the Antarctic Division with highly motivated people who not only handled jobs of a comparatively routine nature at the Antarctic Division office, but who were also capable of the highly dangerous work of safely landing men, equipment and supplies on the sub-Antarctic islands. These triumphs were bare testimony to his superior administrative talents. In July 1951 Law was featured in *The Argus Magazine* as Australia's 'Mr. Antarctica,' where his 'zeal and courage' was compared to that of Captain James Cook.[70] He received a bit of ragging at the Division about the title, but it reflected the way he was seen by many, as Campbell-Drury attests, 'He is a man who knows what he is talking about—he is the only man. He is "Mr. Antarctica" as far as we are all concerned.'[71]

Notes

1. 'Australians Take Part in Three National Antarctic Expeditions', *Sun*, Friday, 28 April 1950.
2. Captain John Giaever, 'Into the Antarctic—The Norsel's Eventful Voyage to Queen Maud Land', *The Times*, 10 April 1950.
3. Captain John Giaever, *The Times*, 19 April 1950.
4. *The Times*, 10 April 1950.
5. Ibid.
6. Ibid.
7. Ibid.
8. *The Times*, 11 April 1950.
9. Ibid.
10. Ibid.
11. Law, in *The Antarctic Today*, 1952, pp. 231–6.
12. Law to Nel Law, 17 March 1950.
13. Ibid.
14. A. Watt, *Australian Diplomat, Memoirs of Sir Alan Watt*, Angus and Robertson, 1972, p. 164.
15. A. Watt, op.cit., p. 165.
16. Minutes of EPC Meeting, 18 May 1950, ADH.
17. Ibid.
18. Letter to Members of the EPC, 2 June 1950, ADH.
19. Law to DEA, 9 June 1950, LP.
20. Kevin to Law, 23 June 1950, LP.
21. Lindsay Nance, *Prime Ministers of Australia*, Bison Group, p. 67.
22. Law to Bowden, 30 November 1987, ABC:SHU.
23. 'Antarctic Mercy Ship Turns Back, Critical Decision for Sick Doctor,' *Herald*, Saturday, 22 July 1950.
24. Law to Bowden, 3 November 1987, ABC:SHU.
25. 'Freighter in Dash to Sick Doctor,' *Sun*, 22 July 1950.
26. 'Doctor with Knife Poised Stops Own Operation,' *Sunday Telegraph*, 22 July 1950.
27. 'Ship Taking Two Doctors to Heard Island', *The Age*, 24 July 1950.
28. 'Radio Fails: No Word of Island Patient', *Herald*, 26 July 1950.

29. 'Stores Rushed for Cruiser's Mercy Trip', *Herald*, 26 July 1950.
30. Law to Tim Bowden, 30 November 1987, ABC:SHU.
31. '100 m.p. h. Blizzard Sweeps Heard Island,' *The Age*, 3 August 1950.
32. Law to Tim Bowden, 30 November 1987, ABC:SHU.
33. Ibid.
34. Minutes of the EPC Meeting, 21 September 1950, ADH.
35. Minutes of Meeting of Ship Sub-Committee of the ANARE, 14 December 1950, ADH.
36. Law, unpublished draft of *Antarctic Odyssey*, LR.
37. Law to Lennard Bickel, 19/20 April 1975, ANL.
38. Law, unpublished draft of *Antarctic Odyssey*, LR.
39. Ibid.
40. Jacka to author, 8 August 1990.
41. Thompson to author, 9 July 1990.
42. Law, unpublished draft of *Antarctic Odyssey*, LR.
43. Ibid.
44. Thompson to author, 9 July 1990.
45. 'Labuan Stole the Limelight', *The Age*, 17 January 1951.
46. Campbell-Drury's diary, 23 January 1951.
47. 'Tribulations at Sea', Talk given to Shiplovers' Society of Victoria, 11 May 1966.
48. Campbell-Drury's diary, 2 February 1951.
49. Campbell-Drury's diary, 5 February 1951.
50. Law to Bowden, 30 November 1987, ABC:SHU.
51. Law, Dinner Speech at CSIROSIP Dinner, 13 November 1987.
52. Campbell-Drury's diary, 1951.
53. Ibid.
54. Law, 'Tribulations at Sea', 11 May 1966.
55. Jacka to author, 8 August 1990.
56. Law, unpublished draft of *Antarctic Odyssey*, LR.
57. Jacka to author, 8 August 1990.
58. Ibid.
59. Law to Bowden, 30 November 1987.
60. Ibid.
61. Ibid.
62. Law, Voyage Report.
63. Jacka to author, 8 August 1990.
64. Ibid.
65. Budd to author, 7 July 1990.
66. Stinear to author, 8 July 1990.
67. McKinnon to author, July 1989.
68. Thompson to author, 9 July 1990.
69. Stinear to author, 8 July 1990.
70. Norman Dunbar, 'Mr. Antarctica', *The Argus Magazine*, 27 July 1951.
71. Campbell-Drury to author, 17 October 1989.

8. *Director, Antarctic Division, 1952–1953*

1.

DURING 1951 LAW REQUESTED THAT HIS TITLE BE CHANGED FROM 'Officer in Charge' to 'Director'. His request was granted and, from then on, Law was always referred to as 'Director', although the position itself was still officially an 'acting' one.

In addition to this change in Law's title, the Division itself was relocated. Over one weekend the staff shifted the entire office furniture and equipment to the prestigious address of 187 Collins Street, Melbourne. By now the number of staff at the Antarctic Division had grown to eighteen with Law as Director, Jerri Donovan as Administrative Officer, Fred Jacka as Physicist in charge of a small staff of scientists, Dick Thompson as Supply Officer, Lem Macey as Technical Officer, George Smith as Storeman at Tottenham, Alan Campbell-Drury as Photographic Officer, Mynwe McDonald as Cables Officer, a librarian and two or three typists.

Staff likened the structure of the Antarctic Division to a 'wheel' with Law as the 'hub'. Although statements abounded at the time, and continue to do so today, that 'Phil treated everybody the same,' and there were no 'men and boys' or 'chiefs and Indians', everyone knew that Law was boss. 'He had that command right at the outset ... He directed and he knew what he wanted and by Jove you did it too',[1] is a typical statement.

Law used, what staff referred to, as an 'open door' policy. They felt free to go to him at any time with their personal or work related concerns. This method of operation, whilst glibly advocated in management texts as a technique for democratic leadership and team building, is equally often questioned because of its propensity to interrupt the work of the manager. In Law's case, this did not happen. 'Phil had a sort of split mind', one staff member recalls, 'he could hear, listen to you with one ear and keep concentrating on what he was doing.' Furthermore:

> You could just tap on the door as you'd go in. And he would say 'Yes, what do you need?' In you would go and tell him what the problem was and he would just keep on writing away ... and he would hear you out. Then he would put his pen down and say 'Right, I'd suggest you do this—One, Two, Bang, Bang, Bang'. And then you would walk out and say 'Crikey, that's fantastic'. It was just

like that. He had an instant come-back. Then he'd just go back to what he was doing.[2]

Dividing his attention and thinking quickly came naturally to Law, but other leadership skills still needed honing, as he knew himself. He deliberately spent concentrated periods of time on 'thinking about leadership, the problems of it, reading books about it'.[3] He never attended any courses in administration or leadership but he studied and read the biographies of all sorts of leaders, particularly Polar explorers.

As a child he had noticed how other boys flocked around his brother, caught up in the excitement that Geof generated on whatever project he had undertaken. Law had never had Geof's personal magnetism, but he did have the sharp intelligence, the vision and the driving force necessary to foster a culture within the Antarctic Division where all staff were involved with and committed to the major aim of getting scientists onto the Antarctic continent. Of this particular ambience he created, Dick Thompson maintains:

> Phil added an atmosphere, a dimension of excitement into what we were doing by having everybody involved one way or the other ... You had no doubt that you were working in a very, very interesting organisation compared to elsewhere in the Public Service.[4]

Law believed that, above all else, a leader must be competent and maintained that a leader 'must be better at most of the jobs in his field of leadership than most of his followers. If he is, he will gain the respect that confidence engenders.'[5] Law did not confine his need for competence to the exercise of leadership, he expected it from his staff as well. They all soon learnt to expect Law to drop in on them at any time to discuss, in depth, their particular line of work, and to question them about their objectives, the expenditure they needed, how they were using the money and their progress. He seldom interfered with how they achieved the desired results, as Graham Budd, a Medical Officer and scientist, explained:

> Phil always selected good people and then he trusted them. He didn't keep looking over their shoulder. He let them get on with it. He realized they would want to make a lot of their own decisions and he just gave them complete support and loyalty and defended them whenever necessary. And that is the way to get loyalty back. It certainly worked.[6]

Others remembered that he simply treated them as professionals. Jacka particularly appreciated the discussions Law had with him on various intellectual matters:

Phil and I had long talks about *how* science progressed. He was very much interested in the philosophical point of how best one, or how ought one, to conduct research in science. I certainly thought about it much more as a consequence of his questioning me than I would have otherwise. It certainly influenced me in formulating my own philosophy and indeed, I would go further than that, it has always done so ever since.[7]

Law also set a great store on appointments being kept and tasks being completed on time. 'He wouldn't take any lateness ... you had to be there', Campbell-Drury recalls. If a staff member was unable to have a job done on time he made sure he had a 'damned good excuse why not'.[8] Or, as Eric Macklin an expeditioner and later full-time Antarctic Division staff member recalls, 'When Phil wanted things done he expected them to be done and he'd want to know why they weren't done. People jumped when Phil wanted things done.'[9]

Likewise, if a staff member failed to perform to the standards Law expected then his staff knew they could expect to 'wear Phil's wrath ... his controlled sort of emotion ... severe reprimand'.[10] These occasions were apparently rare, for some members who had been with Law for ten or more years could not remember ever having seen him angry. 'Curtness' or 'abruptness' were more likely to be descriptions of Law's expression of displeasure.

There were two reasons why Law mostly remained emotionally detached when things were not carried out to the standards he expected. One was that he usually blamed himself, 'I get so angry with myself when things go wrong, because it usually means it was my fault, because I did not give precise enough instructions.' Secondly, Law admired men who could be 'coldly calculating' and he deliberately tried to control his responses, apart from enthusiasm, to any issues. Law would no doubt agree with Nikolai Lenin, to whom some have said he bears a strong physical resemblance,[11] when Lenin commented that 'the emotions are not skilled workers.'[12]

Whenever Law did reprimand a staff member the Antarctic Division staff believed that he 'didn't hold it against you later.'[13] The same could not be said about his attitude towards troublesome Antarctic expeditioners. At the end of each year's expedition the Officer-in-Charge presented Law with a report and it was generally believed that the name of any trouble-maker went into Law's mental black book and Law never gave him the opportunity to go to Antarctica again.

Law believed that until staff had had first-hand experience of the conditions under which the men were living and working at the Antarctic stations, they could not fully appreciate the importance of absolute dedication and efficiency in the work at headquarters. To this end he insisted that all full-time male staff, regardless of their official job, act as 'supernumeraries' on the yearly relief voyages to Antarctica. Law saw these 'summer cruises', as they were later euphemistically known, as an essential part of the work. He also expected all headquarters staff to be involved in the organisation and planning for the expeditions:

> Most people were trying to do things better [Thompson recalled]. There was no resting on your laurels. There was always this desire to improve things, to do things better, to make it stronger, or lighter, or faster.[14]

Discussions about improvements were often held over working lunches, when, several times a week, Law and a few staff members would meet at a local hotel or restaurant. Their talks were general but usually centred around what Law described as the 'five things that are of fundamental importance in an Antarctic expedition—good nutrition, shelter, suitable clothing, efficient transport and friendly relations between the men.'[15]

Like Amundsen before him, Law went to incredible lengths to put these principles into practice. High quality, nutritious food was regarded as vital for both the physical and mental well-being of the expeditioners, who were already deprived of family contacts and general social life, sex and diverse entertainment. Having suffered with poor food on various voyages, Law was determined to get the best possible meals for ANARE men. Thompson had devised a high calorie ration scale, patterned on a military one, of the nutritional requirements of each person each day, taking into account the cold climate. This formed the statistical basis for the quantity and type of food for the expeditioners. But the individual tastes of the men were also catered for by Division staff holding 'tasting sessions' for cordials, jams, sauces and tinned fruits. Past and future expeditioners attended the tasting sessions to establish which brands were the most popular.

Special supplies had to be prepared for men on field trips and particular effort was put into developing a biscuit made of 100 per cent wholemeal flour and butter, that was solid and did not crumble easily. After many experimental batches, made by one of Law's skiing friends, Fred Derham, who was head of the firm Swallow and Ariell Ltd, a biscuit, called the 'Sledge Biscuit,' was finally marketed.

Law was concerned about some alcohol problems that had occurred at the stations and ruled that there was to be no hard liquor and, instead, supplied a variety of wines. He placed liquor supplies under the strict control of the Officer-in-Charge of the station and abolished the 'ration per man' system. The accepted practice was that sherry and dry red and white flagon wines were placed on the sideboard in the mess room for each meal. Better quality bottled wines replaced flagon wines on Saturday nights, or on special occasions, and port and beer were also available. Later on these supplies were supplemented by the men brewing their own beer with equipment and supplies provided by the Antarctic Division.

Whenever they applied for expedition positions, men were advised, that if they could not exist for a year without a whisky or a gin they should withdraw their applications. Law was already a wine enthusiast himself, but many of the men, in the early 1950s still regarded wine suspiciously, as Budd recalls:

> A wine bar was where the 'old plonks' and 'deros' would go. On one occasion when we had some nice wine on the table one of the men looked at me very sternly and said 'Jeez Doc, I likes me drop of piss as well as the next man, but I draws the line at plonk.'[16]

To overcome this antagonism Law arranged for some wine firms to supply a range of wines and he held wine tastings with men from previous expeditions. Each man was given a score card to rate the samples. Those wines the men rated most highly were ordered for the expedition. Despite one expeditioner's bitter remark that 'if PGL wants to educate men in drinking, the Antarctic is not the place to do it', Law and others thought that the campaign to reform the drinking habits at stations was successful.[17]

Safe, comfortable huts were also essential for the well-being of the expeditioners. These had to be easy to construct, because of the difficult climatic conditions under which they were erected. The huts developed in the early 1950s were made from panels with a core of 'Onazote' insulating material 4 in. thick with sheets of 5–ply bondwood glued to each side of this core. The panels were assembled by bolting them to a frame. Unfortunately, this model of hut was more difficult to erect than they had hoped. Late in 1951 a new hut was made by a Melbourne firm, Explastics Insulations Pty Ltd, manufacturers of cold rooms and refrigerated storerooms. The panels were again made of 'Onazote' and plywood but the frame was dispensed with and the panels bolted together with brackets on the outside. This model proved more successful and each hut took only one day to erect.[18] The ANARE was the first Antarctic organisation to introduce individual bedrooms for men instead of bunk room accommodation.

The men's recreation and reading requirements were also well catered for with supplies of 78 r.p.m. records and record players and sets of chess, draughts and other popular games. Law was particularly keen to ensure the men had a good library, including classic and popular novels, 'an Encyclopaedia Britannica to settle any arguments'[19] and second-hand copies of first editions of the polar classics which he found in second-hand shops when on his European trips. 'We did not have that much time to read,' said one of the expeditioners, 'but when you did it was a very good place to read about your predecessors.'[20]

Law was personally very interested in the development of effective Antarctic field clothing. The 'Ventile' cloth he had discovered on his first visit to London proved unequalled for parkas and tents. Much detailed work by the staff was involved with the design of the Ventile windproof suits; the length of the parkas, the shape of the hoods, the width of the trouser legs which needed to be wide enough to be removed without first taking off boots, the selection of zips, buttons and draw-cords. Boots had to be tried out under differing conditions, for what suited the 'wet-cold' of Macquarie Island did not suit the 'dry-cold' of the Antarctic continent.

Protection for the hands proved to be the most difficult exercise in design. Insulation that did not greatly impair the men's ability to carry out their work was needed. In the end the best solution was to use three layers—silk gloves, woollen mittens and heavy outer gloves with wind-proof surfaces. With this array a man could, for a limited time, carry out quite delicate work by removing the outer gloves. However, when the air temperatures were very low their hands had to remain fully protected and warmer shelter had to be sought before a job could be performed.

The Antarctic Division staff knew that the efforts they put into the designing and organising of better facilities for the expeditioners was important work, not only for the well-being of the men concerned, but indirectly, for cementing Australia's Antarctic claims. With this knowl-edge came a sense of purpose and cohesion:

> We prided ourselves upon our esprit de corps [Law later com-mented], our vigour and enthusiasm, our rate of work and output, and our freedom from red tape and frustration. We considered our-selves unique in the Commonwealth Public Service.[21]

Law was determined to have the Division working as little like a Public Service Department as possible. Rules existed but the staff were willing to break them, particularly approaching sailing dates, when they would cut corners in order to get supplies onto a ship. In fact, Law did encour-age staff to stick to the rules if possible and justified 'red tape' as 'only doing things in a systematic way'. It was noted, though, that he did not always follow this injunction himself.[22] His frustrations with what he saw as the intransigence of the Commonwealth Public Service were evident, as Jacka recalls:

> Phil used to have almost continuous battles with the bureaucrats in Canberra at various levels from the middle ranks to the top, some-times to the Head of the Department and quite often to the Minis-ter.[23]

Law referred to these battles as his 'wars of attrition', which he often won simply by 'hammering away' and waiting, sometimes years, to get what he wanted. Another tactic he used was, what he called, 'the frontal attack mode'. He maintained he could often achieve more by this method than by being devious:

> Not that I had any moral objections to being devious [he explained] it is just that most people in the Public Service seemed to work in that mode and the 'powers to be' had ways of handling it. They were not as prepared for the frontal attack, so that I often got what we wanted because people tended to make all sorts of allowances.

On occasions, Jacka recalls, Law would discuss with the Antarctic Division staff the problems he was having with the DEA or the PSB but 'most of the time Phil would have made quite positive efforts to shield me and most of the people from getting involved in a lot of this. It was a hell of a waste of time. He had to do it as Director.' Instead Law vented his frustrations by his now well established practice of writing about the issue:

> He would be absolutely furious about something [Jacka continues] and he would sit down for perhaps a day, maybe more, and he would write furiously, trying to develop an argument and post a letter urgently to Canberra to try and persuade them to do this or that. But it was very common that at the end of this he would say 'Oh well, I have got it off my chest now' and he wouldn't send it. This happened many times.[24]

Although stories of Law's conflict with public service departments have become legion amongst Antarctic Division staff, his working relationship with the Canberra departments was, at least in the early years, generally cordial. Evan Collings, the Commissioner of the Public Service Board at that time, recalls Law as:

> a nice fellow, gently spoken and yet persistent. You couldn't just wipe him off and say 'You are not getting that Phil, go away'. [You could] talk perfectly sensibly to him and say 'Phil I don't know where you got that idea from but it just ain't on' and he would say 'well what is on?' and then you could work it out together.[25]

Arthur Tange, who became Secretary of the DEA in 1954, describes Law's approach as 'blunt' but explains:

> Everybody who needs government money ... has to be a petitioner, it is just in the nature of things ... He [Law] was pretty blunt with me ... blunt about what he wanted. An enthusiastic advocate for it ... he naturally tended to see things from the point-of-view of the Antarctic Division and Antarctic expeditions. That's the sort of enthusiasm

that gets people places. It sometimes has to be curbed because of other prior claims for money and staff.[26]

Law's main complaint throughout his years as Director was that DEA lacked any real appreciation of matters regarding the science, technology or logistics associated with the Antarctic Division. 'So if we wanted a new tractor or a new bit of machinery or a workshop, we had to go through an interminable amount of interrogation and paper work.'[27] But, as Tange pointed out, DEA also had to go to Treasury for its budget and to the PSB for staff positions and salaries. Tange maintained he had great admiration for the courage and skill of Law as leader and of other expedition members; nevertheless he agreed that there was limited understanding on the part of the DEA of the practical problems encountered by the Antarctic expeditioners. One reason for this, he believes, was because the Antarctic Division was the only 'operational' division under the DEA's control, 'there was really no natural affinity between Antarctic exploration and the conduct of Australia's diplomacy and the management of our Foreign Service', he explained. Further, Tange reasons, the problems were exacerbated by the difficulty of communications at that time between the DEA in Canberra and the Antarctic Division in Melbourne. Seldom could they sit down and talk across the table together. Meetings, in the late 1940s and early 1950s, usually entailed, as Tange recalls, 'dependence on unreliable air schedules or, worse, a trip in lousy, cold draughty trains, where you had to change trains in the middle of the night or early morning at Albury.'[28]

Although a nation's presence was seen as the overriding factor in claiming Antarctic territory, and Tange later claimed, 'you wouldn't send people down there to do nothing', staff of the Antarctic Division are still of the opinion that Law had to constantly battle to ensure scientific work was carried out in Antarctica. One opinion that reflects others, is Eric Macklin's: 'They [the DEA] were quite happy for us to sit down and do nothing. They didn't want to have the hassle. Phil was a goer. He was doing things ... he could see the opportunity.'[29]

There was never any doubt in Law's mind that an Australian presence had to be supported by ongoing scientific endeavour. A great deal of his time as Director was, therefore, spent talking with scientific organisations, persuading them to be involved with the Antarctic research, writing articles and making the arrangements necessary for worthwhile scientific work to be carried out.

The scientific programs were designed by a committee of scientists and approved by the EPC. In the early years, those scientists would have only a few weeks to prepare for the work they were to do at the Antarctic stations, but Law imbued in them the belief that the research they conducted was an essential part of the justification of Australia's claim on the Antarctic region:

And that's very important [Budd, a Medical Officer and Officer-in-Charge recalls]. When conditions are trying it is very easy to think 'oh well, gosh it is hard enough just surviving at the moment, forget about the science.' In fact, many people did go to great lengths to see they made the observations on time, that is why we were there.[30]

During 1951, the Government appointed Richard G. Casey as a replacement for Percy Spender as the Minister for External Affairs. Casey's appointment was, for Law and the Antarctic Division, the most satisfactory appointment that the new Government had made. Some Antarctic Division staff go so far as to say that Law would not have been as successful if he had not had such a supportive Minister in Casey.

Casey already had a history of involvement with Antarctic work, beginning when he was stationed in London, during the 1920s, as Australian Political Liaison Officer. There he had been associated with Sir Hubert Wilkins, the Australian naturalist and Polar explorer who was, in April 1928, the first man to fly over the North Pole and who, on 16 November of the same year, made the first flight ever to be carried out in the Antarctic. Wilkins later named one of the several ice-filled channels that he encountered during this flight the 'Casey Channel' after R. G. Casey himself.[31] Whilst in London in 1928, in his capacity as Australian Political Liaison Officer, Casey had also dealt with issues involved with Mawson's BANZAR Expedition. And later, in 1937, when he was Australian Treasurer, Casey was chairman of a Polar committee that recommended to the Imperial Conference in London that the dominions co-operate in setting up one or more permanent meteorological stations in the Antarctic.[32]

Although W. J. Hudson's biography of Casey does not recognise Casey's great contribution to Australia's Antarctic work, it does maintain that Antarctica was one of Casey's lifelong interests.[33] Sir Arthur Tange also attests to Casey's 'unbounded enthusiasm for the Antarctic Division'. As part of this general enthusiasm for Antarctic matters, Casey was both open to and offered suggestions, 'some of which were useful', Law maintained, but others were 'equally often quite impractical'.

As a qualified pilot Casey, who had been named the 'flying diplomat',[34] always supported Law's efforts to use aeroplanes in Antarctic exploration. After Casey's retirement it was many years before aerial support for ANARE was to reach the same level.

Another point on which Law and Casey agreed was on the need for favourable publicity. Hudson maintains that 'it was typical of Casey that the first administrative issues to engage him were the need for the department to recruit a journalist able to improve its public relations.' Casey actively courted the press, 'dining with editors, giving background briefings to newspaper executives, keeping in touch with columnists, having department officers prepare articles on current events for publication over his name'.[35] This penchant for publicity and promotion suited Law, although he always preferred to have press statements released from the Division in Melbourne rather than from Canberra, because he believed this was faster and more effective.

Much of the success of the Casey era of administration can be attributed to the fact that Casey's office was in Melbourne. During this period Law saw Casey every few weeks. When Casey departed, Law saw his successor in Canberra only once or twice a year.

2.

By the end of 1951, however, there was still no chance of the establishment of an Antarctic continent station, for again there were no ships available. Even the relief voyages to Heard and Macquarie Islands were proving a problem since the *Labuan* had broken down and the *River Fitzroy* had proved unsuitable. As late as 20 December 1951, Law had to report to the EPC members that he hoped negotiations were almost complete for the charter of a Norwegian sealer, the *MS Tottan* to relieve the Heard and Macquarie stations. As the result of a complex agreement between ANARE and Expéditions Polaires Françaises to share the ship over the summer season, the *Tottan* was ultimately obtained.

In February and March 1952 the two Island stations were finally relieved, accompanied by the usual squalls, storms, break-down of machines, near accidents and frustrating delays.

Eric Macklin, a radio operator and a first time expeditioner on the Macquarie Island trip, has vivid memories of his impressions of Law's leadership style during the changeover operation. 'Phil was driving the boys all the time. We worked very long hours. He would push, push, push ... Phil annoyed everybody ... but he certainly got things done.' Macklin recalled that, after all the stores had been landed and the men were settled on the island, Law gave lectures on various aspects of Island life. 'He'd brief the new and the old party pretty well really', Macklin continued. 'Before he left he would tell us what he expected of us during the year.' During one session Law began to explain the finer points about the wine that had been so carefully selected and supplied. But, as Macklin pointed out, 'There was no fresh food, it was all canned stuff [and] nobody had heard of wine in those days':

> Phil was telling us what to drink with different meals. One fellow yelled out 'Hey Phil, what sort of wine do you eat with bully beef?' That brought the house down.

Law followed this talk with one on the need for economical use of the supplies:

> He told us the Division wasn't made of money [Macklin continued] it was scratching for funds all the time. And he said, quite seriously

'When I was a boy we never had toilet paper in our lives, we'd use a telephone book, we'd cut up paper. Now I come down here and I find they have run out of toilet paper and I go outside and I find they are using Kleenex tissues AT TWO BOB A BOX.' That brought the house down too.[36]

Industrious enthusiasm was the one raw emotion Law allowed himself to show and many of the expeditioners, often 'fresh out of World War II, THE man's world', were somewhat taken aback by this. 'At that time they didn't know how to take Phil', recalls Macklin. This was particularly evident with those men who had had little opportunity to meet Law in circumstances other than during the expedition. 'All the Antarctic business was about being in a man's world', Thompson reflected and, at that time, Australian men were expected to be 'taciturn' or 'off-hand', 'they wouldn't give anything away, wouldn't show their feelings. And enthusiasm was something you would try to hide.' But not Law. 'Phil was an overt enthusiast ... Phil had to be out there being the lead Husky.' Thompson, also an avid enthusiast for anything Antarctic, disguised his own feelings with 'rough men's talk',[37] and was seen as 'one of the boys'.

Law was never accorded the Australian male accolades of being 'one of the boys' or a 'mate'. He was involved with all the practices that bind a group in mateship, but he was always slightly apart from the men and, as he admits, never became very close to any of them because all his relationships with men had an element of competitiveness. The expeditioners respected Law for this aloofness, as one commented: 'That is something I always give Phil credit for. He was the Director and as a Director it was better that he didn't show his feelings. ... In those early stages he felt for his men, I know that, but he never showed it.' One outcome of this deliberate separateness was also highlighted by the same expeditioner, and reflects similar comments by others, 'I always regard Phil as a personal friend, but I didn't know him.'[38]

Law now included Dick Thompson and Lem Macey on all of the relief voyages. The combined abilities of these two men proved invaluable in organising the loading of supplies and the hazardous work entailed in the landings. With each voyage they became more proficient and took over more of the hands-on work and close supervision of the men, leaving Law free to direct the operations.

The *Tottan* expedition was mainly memorable because of a discussion which occurred whilst on the ship. During the return trip Law, Thompson, Macey and Hannan (the returning Officer-in-Charge) discussed the idea of building up a reserve of people with interest, enthusiasm and competence in Antarctic affairs. This discussion culminated in the birth of the ANARE Club. Jacka drew up a rough constitution and, later, an inaugural meeting was held at which Law was elected President and Alan Campbell-Drury became the first Honorary Secretary. By the 1980s the club had grown to more than 1 000 members, with branches in each capital city in Australia. Ad hoc meetings are held throughout the year on items of interest and two major functions are held annually, the Mid-Winter Dinner and the Farewell Party for expeditioners leaving for the stations at the end of the year.[39]

Whilst on the *Tottan* Law sought approval to again visit Europe. On this occasion he obviously thought a devious approach would be more successful than the frontal attack mode. His manipulation of the system to gain an overseas trip, appropriately filed in the Antarctic Division files under 'Future Planning',[40] is an excellent portrayal of his use of this approach.

It had been two years since he had been overseas, and there were many Antarctic matters he wanted to investigate and discuss with various people in England and France. At the December 1951 meeting of the EPC he advised members that two separate conferences on Antarctic matters had been mooted in Europe for the following year. 'Mooted' is not quite the correct word, implying as it does that these conferences had already been discussed. In fact Law himself was just about to moot them. On the way to Macquarie Island in the *Tottan*, on 27 March 1952, he arranged for a cable to be sent to the Scott Polar Research Institute (SPRI) in England stating: 'I suggest conference this year on Antarctic Research Development etc. between NBSE FIDS Expolaires ANARE would be most valuable. I am considering visiting Europe June or July and would welcome such conference to review progress and plan future work.'

A day later he received a reply from the Director of the SPRI reading, 'Your plan Antarctic conference seems excellent to me. Will quickly discuss with others concerned. Suggest Cambridge best place. Regards Bertram.' Obviously delighted, Law cabled back that Cambridge was ideal and suggested that June would be a suitable date. In the meantime he had also sent a cable to the Ministry for Overseas, France:

> I would like discussion with you concerning scientific research and other co-operation between respective stations in South Indian Ocean. A letter from your Department suggesting such a meeting in Paris would assist me to obtain approval for my visit.

On 23 April 1952 the French Embassy duly requested the DEA to allow Law to proceed to Paris with a view to studying with the French Services how collaboration between France and Australia, with respect to the Southern Antarctic expeditions, could be effected.

During May a string of memos, submissions and telegrams crisscrossed between the Antarctic Division and the DEA regarding approval for Law's visit. On 7 May, Kevin advised Law that it was most unlikely that approval would be given for anyone from Australia to go to the SPRI Conference and that the Minister felt that the visit to France could not be undertaken at the present time. Law had also received a letter from the SPRI to say that the earliest date they could organise a conference was in May the following year, 1953.

Undeterred by what might have appeared to others as overwhelming odds, Law went to see Casey. On 19 May Law wrote to the DEA advising them that the Minister had approved his proposed visit to England and France in June–July 1952. He attached a submission for his proposed trip to Europe, which now was slightly altered to include the visit to England to 'confer with the Director of the Scott Polar Institute, at their suggestion, to make arrangements for an Antarctic Conference.' Law pointed out that he hoped to leave Australia on 12 June.

On 28 May Law sent a telegram to DEA enquiring 'Any decision yet regarding my Europe visit?' Two days later he received a reply stating that the Prime Minister's Department wanted more information, although they were not sure, as yet, what additional information was required. On 6 June Law was advised that the Prime Minister's Department had not approved his visit. As time had run out, he cancelled all overseas arrangements.

Then he went on the attack again. Suspecting that no action had been taken by DEA, Law demanded, on 12 June, that DEA advise him whether all the information he had submitted had been placed before the Overseas Travel Committee. On the same day, Casey spoke with Kevin in Canberra. Later that day Kevin advised Law that the Overseas Travel Committee had convened in order to review their decision.[41] Law waited. On 18 June, Kevin—clearly fed up with what he referred to as Law's 'irascible letters'—wrote a 'Personal' memo to Law about many current issues, one of which was Law's overseas visit. The memorandum began:

I can reply to your messages officially, in which case I would speak of the tone of them as well as the content, or I can reply personally, which I propose to do.

One would assume he meant 'unofficial', but in fact a copy of that particular memorandum was placed in a 'Confidential' DEA file on Law.[42] In this same memorandum Kevin pointed out that the 'Antarctic Division is only one of many divisions and sections in a large organisation ... bound by the same rules and must share in the same practices' and that 'I give as much attention as I can to your requests and queries.' Kevin then advised Law that the committee would meet, for the first time, the very next day to consider his proposed overseas visit. They met on 19 June but still Law heard nothing. It duly met again on 27 June and Law was invited to present his case. Two members approved the trip but the Treasury representative dissented. Law was not advised of the outcome. He went ahead, anyway, and made tentative arrangements to leave Australia on Monday, 7 July.

By 2 July he had still heard no answer and he cabled Kevin: 'Please press for decision one way or another today. I have only two business days left to complete arrangements.' On the same day Casey, presumably after Law's urging, again spoke to Kevin about the matter, but still Law was not given an answer. Later that day he received a telegram advising him that directions from the Acting Prime Minister were that 'the matter should be referred to the Prime Minister [Menzies] on his return.'

On 4 July Casey wrote to Menzies outlining Law's case and concluded that 'I assume the policy of maintaining Australian interest in the Antarctic regions is supported, and on this basis I feel that Mr. Law should be allowed to accept the French invitation.' Law had still not been given a decision by 7 July, although he was packed and ready to go if approval came through. It did not and he again had to cancel his flight booking.

Shortly after, the Prime Minister returned and, by 12 July, he had personally approved Law's visit to France and the United Kingdom.[43]

That hurdle over Law now raised another one. He immediately approached the DEA with a proposal that he add the USA to his itinerary because, he reasoned, 'Although I have excellent contacts in France, Norway and the United Kingdom with the foremost Antarctic experts, I have, as yet, no personal contact with any of the Americans.' Not surprisingly, his request was refused.

Law went to France and, whilst in London, he wrote to the Antarctic Division on 5 August, advising them that he was leaving London in ten days' time to go to the USA. He asked them to tell Nel about the new arrangements. He did not advise DEA of this change of plan until the day he left London, 15 August, when he sent a cablegram stating that he was 'leaving today for return via United States at own expense.' Watt, Secretary DEA, received this cable the next day and scrawled a note across the bottom which read 'Law is a trier!'

When Law finally returned to Australia he sent a memorandum to Watt enclosing an eight foolscap page, single-spaced report of his visit. In his accompanying memorandum he stated 'A perusal of the report relating to my U.S. visit will, I think, show that the stay in America was well worthwhile.' He then requested that 'I be considered to have been on official duty for this visit.' On 10 September Law was advised that the cost of a round world ticket for his recent trip abroad, including the fare for return via USA, had been accepted as an official charge.[44]

Law's manoeuvring and persistence had been successful. In addition to the practical information he had gained on Antarctic expeditions, he had also established links and laid foundations which later earned him an international reputation as an authority on Antarctic exploration and scientific research.[45]

His growing international reputation was also enhanced by the outcome of another proposal he put to Casey to form a committee to handle the approval of place names for Australian Antarctic Territory. Historically it had been the internationally accepted practice that the explorer who discovered a feature had the right to name it. In more recent times the nation which discovered the feature had prior right to its naming.[46] Law found that, as Director of the Antarctic Division, he was in the position of being the sole arbiter of names in Antarctica and believed that 'no man should have this sort of power uncontrolled.'[47] He knew of the methods used by both the United Kingdom and the USA and suggested a similar system be set up in Australia to decide on formal procedures for approving names both on Heard and Macquarie Islands and the Antarctic continent. The Minister agreed and the Government approved the establishment of 'The Antarctic Names Committee of Australia' (ANCA) to 'advise the Minister for External Affairs upon all matters relating to place-names in Antarctica.'[48] ANCA held its first meeting on 21 October 1952. The membership consisted of Law as Chairman, Sir Douglas Mawson, B. P. Lambert, the Director of National Mapping, Captain G. D. Tancred, the Chief Hydrographer of the Royal Australian Navy, and A. A. Wilcock, Senior Lecturer in Geography at the University of Melbourne, was appointed as the Secretary. Law remained Chairman of the Committee for almost thirty years. This position necessitated close contact and discussions with those other nations which also claimed territory in Antarctica.

Despite his international reputation, Law was still only 'acting' head of the Antarctic Division. The DEA had made no attempt to create a permanent Officer-in-Charge position, as had been contemplated when Law had first been employed. It was not until 1951 that Law broached the subject with the PSB, pointing out that the job had increased during his years as Director 'by a factor of at least two ... [and] the whole organisation has been rebuilt.'[49] When nothing was resolved by February 1952 he appealed in a 'personal and confidential' letter to Watt. 'If I had known as much of Public Service procedure three years ago as I do now,' he wrote, 'I have no doubt that I could have made sufficient nuisance of myself to have had this cleared up long ago.'[50] At the same time, Law also negotiated a claim to have his salary at the OIC range paid retrospectively to 1949. He was refused the retrospective salary adjustment, but was appointed to the position of 'Officer-in-Charge' Antarctic Division on 27 March 1952, more than three years after he had taken up the acting position.[51]

If the DEA had been reluctant to take the step to appoint Law in the permanent position of head of the Division and Leader of the ANARE, the Antarctic staff did not have the same qualms. They were adamant that Law was 'a very fortunate choice for those formative years of the Antarctic Division,' as Budd recalls, 'Phil had that combination of drive and personal vision as to what it should be like. He was ready to do battle with his masters in Canberra for what he thought was right ... They were very necessary battles.'[52]

Near to a ship's sailing date, this spirit often became too demanding and those who stayed back in the office heaved a sigh of relief when the ship sailed from Australia. Once Law was out of the way they could settle down and catch up on their work. But this respite was short-lived for, once the ship left the Island and turned for home, Law's attention would immediately be focused on what needed to be done when they arrived back at headquarters. Radio messages would be sent to staff at the office to 'get this done', 'look up this', or 'just find this out'. Law took the opportunity, whilst on the voyages, to sketch out articles on various issues and he would radio the men at the Antarctic Division to look up technical information to 'fill in the spaces'.[53]

Once back in Melbourne everyone turned their attention to tying up the loose ends of the previous expedition. Data gained during the year had to be sent to appropriate authorities, including maps and survey data to the National Mapping Division, scientific data to the Weather Bureau, Bureau of Mineral Resources, universities and CSIRO; photographs were processed and records compiled; expeditioners' reports were read and recommended actions were taken; reports had to be written and edited for the ANARE Scientific Reports or other professional journals; public relations work was carried out; lectures were given and ongoing liaison continued with other nations' expeditions.

Combined with this termination of the previous expedition's work was the never-ending job of caring for the needs of the men down on the stations. There was a constant flow of radio messages between the expeditioners and headquarters that had to be handled, including personal cables from the men at the stations to their relatives and details of scientific research. Talks had to be prepared and were broadcast over the ABC to the stations each Friday. These included special announcements, music and personal messages. And whilst all this went on, planning was beginning for the next year's expedition.

During 1952, and just as the plans for Australia's new ship were nearing completion, Law was advised by Westralian Farmers Transport Ltd, that a Danish shipping firm, J. Lauritzen Lines, had just built a new ship, the MV *Kista Dan*. They thought the ship might be of interest to Law. Law immediately cabled Lauritzen and found out all details. The *Kista Dan* was almost perfect for the ANARE's needs. He proposed to Lauritzen that, rather than tying up the *Kista Dan* during the northern winter, they should agree to charter it to ANARE for work during the southern summer. Lauritzen agreed with the principle.

Law's next move was to persuade the members of the EPC to give approval to charter the *Kista Dan*. He approached the September meeting with his usual forethought and paved the way before presenting this new proposal. First he reported to the Committee that the Government had decided to defer construction of a new Antarctic ship for the time being. Each member was then given a chart showing the present staffing and organisation of the Antarctic Division. Law pointed out to the members that the 'administrative machinery functioned exceptionally well in

the case of the present Island Stations' and, with little subtlety, concluded that 'it would be a pity if an opportunity to make use of such facilities for the despatch of an Antarctic expedition did not occur soon.'
Later in the meeting he reminded the members of the circumstances
which had led up to the establishment of Heard and Macquarie Island
stations and the factors which had mitigated against the earlier establishment of a station on the Antarctic continent. Only then did he draw
their attention to the papers which detailed the proposals for charter of
the *Kista Dan* for an Antarctic Expedition in the summer of 1953–54.

After much discussion about the importance of both Heard and Macquarie Islands the meeting finally 'strongly recommended' that, as the
original purpose for the founding of an Antarctic Division was the establishment of a base on the Antarctic continent, 'This Committee therefore urges that an expedition to establish such a base be despatched at
the earliest opportunity.' Members also stated that they attached such
importance to the establishment of an Antarctic station they would 'even
be prepared to consider a reduction in the programme at the Islands, if
the financing of the three stations proves impossible, in order that the
Antarctic station should be set up.'[54]

By agreeing to reduce the programs at one of the Island stations Law
was using tactics that he would later describe as 'start small and gradually build up and then no one feels the hardship of a sudden splurge.'[55]
Law had already anticipated that he would have to cut back on one of
the Island stations to gain approval for a a permanent Antarctic continent station. That had been his reasoning behind his manoeuvre to get
the French interested in Iles de Kerguelen, close to Heard Island, thus
giving him more leverage to shut down Heard Island if needs be. The
minutes of any meeting Law chaired always reflected where Law wanted
the Antarctic Division to go and the minutes of the EPC meeting on September 1952 were no exception.

The Australian Government approved the proposal on 6 February
1953[56] and, on 21 March, it was announced in the press that the Government had decided to send an expedition to the Antarctic continent
during the next summer to set up a scientific research station in the Australian Antarctic Territory.[57] Casey sketched out what would be done at
the projected station and concluded: 'Today the Antarctic is a challenge—which cannot be ignored—to Australian courage and imagination, and the proposed expedition shows that we will grasp our opportunity.'[58]

The Government's plans were also endorsed by the Leader of the
Opposition, the Rt Hon. Dr H. V. Evatt, who remarked that 'this territory
is of great strategic importance in the confused state of the world
today.'[59] 'Such unanimity of political opinion', the Antarctic historian, R.
A. Swan, commented, 'boded well for the future of Australian Antarctic
activity.'[60]

3.

It was fourteen years since Law had written to Nel 'The Law Luck is just aching to show what it can do.' With the assurance of an Antarctic ship he now had the opportunity.

Law's efforts were now devoted to preparation for the Antarctic continent expedition and, for the first time since joining the Antarctic Division, he did not lead the relief expeditions to Heard and Macquarie Islands. Instead Jerri Donovan, the Administrative Officer, supported by Thompson and Macey, successfully completed the changeovers, again using the *Tottan*, during February and March of 1953.

By 1953 the Antarctic Division had been sending expeditions to Heard and Macquarie Islands for five years and had set up an organisation specifically designed to run expeditions.

'Establishing an Antarctic base', Law told an audience at the time, 'is like a combined services operation at a beachhead in wartime, but on a smaller scale—and with climatic hazards instead of bullets!' The one overriding factor is the irrevocable deadline of the departure of the ship and everything revolves around that date. Firstly, activities were listed that had to be completed before the ship's departure. Times were then allocated to each of the activities and placed in the sequence in which they had to be completed, 'It is no good thinking in broad general terms,' Law maintained, 'the only thinking worth anything is <u>detailed</u> thinking, down to the last small article, the last small move, the last remote possibility.'[61]

The Antarctic Division's planning system was set out in a monthly timeline and began in April, as soon as Law had returned from the changeover operation. Plans, forward estimates of costings and budgets were prepared for the next expedition. Staff positions were created and approvals sought. The ordering of overseas supplies began. During May the design of new, or the overhaul of old, buildings, radio equipment, engines, vehicles and aircraft began and continued throughout the year. Advertising for the staff required for the following year's party started in June. The budget was prepared and presented to Treasury. Ordering of Australian supplies began and continued throughout the year.

In July Law visited the capital city of each State to interview prospective expeditioners and, once back in Melbourne, the appointments were finalised. During this month the original planned program for the following year was altered in line with the amount of money approved by Treasury. Orders were received from the Island stations during August for the resupply of food and equipment which were then lodged through the various suppliers.

During September, Operations Manuals were written or updated, itineraries for the ship were worked out and passenger lists prepared. Training of the new personnel began during October. Trial erection of new huts was carried out and men began the packing of stores for the stations. Stores packing and training continued throughout November. The ship sailed sometime during December.

In the early years of the Antarctic Division there was little training, apart from two men attending the Royal Melbourne Hospital to learn basic anaesthetic and nursing techniques to assist the doctor, and the cook learning bread baking. Soon after Dick Thompson was employed as Supply Officer he attended a Public Service residential course for administrative officers. He returned to the Antarctic Division committed to the concept of training the men to handle the conditions they might encounter in Antarctica. He put a proposal to Law, who agreed, and from then on the training of expeditioners became far more comprehensive.

In addition to the medical training for two men, and bread baking for the cook, there was specialist training arranged for the Medical Officer in dentistry at the Dental College; mechanics received special instruction on engines, alternators, electric wiring, tractors, switchboards and refrigerators, and radio men were given experience on the transmitters and receivers which they would be using. Selected men were given training in the use of explosives and under-water work. One man of each party was appointed official photographer for his station, supplied with official cameras and film and Alan Campbell-Drury briefed him on specific photographic techniques suitable for Antarctic work.

To prepare expeditioners for many important aspects of working in Antarctica, compulsory indoctrination sessions were held in November of each year at the University of Melbourne. This week-long program consisted of lectures on the aims and ideals of the expedition, survival and first aid, hygiene, fire precautions and the use of fire extinguishers, Antarctic clothing, how to travel by tractor and dog sledge, details of scientific programs, films of life at a station, photographic techniques, supply problems, re-ordering, stores procedures, administration and how to deal with morale and psychological problems.

Concern for the psychological well-being of the men was equalled by the concern for their physical safety. The hazards in Antarctica were numerous. There was the danger to ships from hurricanes, pack-ice, icebergs, submerged rocks and dangerous coasts. Once at the site the dangers came from the ever present possibility of accidents occurring during the unloading of stores under difficult conditions. Ashore there was frostbite, snow-blindness, fire, carbon monoxide poisoning, the danger of slipping and falling on ice and accidents when the men were handling vehicles, tools and aircraft. During overland travel there are the hazards of crevasses, becoming lost or disoriented, the failure of equipment, lack of visibility due to white-out or drifting snow and the dangers associated with moving over sea ice of an impermanent nature. During aerial exploration flights there was the likelihood of equipment and instrument failure through the intense cold, white-outs and blizzards which could occur with little warning and dangerous landings on ice.

Training for, or awareness of, these hazards to reduce the risk of accident was aimed at creating a healthy respect for the dangers without over-stressing them to the point where men would become so anxious they might not want to participate in field trips:

> We, therefore, strive to increase men's awareness of what can happen by lecturing them on the hazards and dangers [Law explained to an audience]. We show them how these dangers can be minimized and we drill them on safety rules. ... We encourage their enthusiastic contributions towards all safety precautions. Then we enforce rigid discipline, accepting no excuses and allowing no exceptions.[62]

The greatest hazard was fire, for any Antarctic party whose station is destroyed by fire is in a desperate situation; without shelter, fuel and stores, men would have little chance of survival. To lessen this hazard, the huts are physically separated so that, in the event of fire, only the particular burning hut would be destroyed. Reserve equipment, food and clothing are normally stored away from the main supplies and fuel dumps are isolated from living quarters and other buildings. Scientific records are removed each month from working huts and stored in sealed steel drums outside. Automatic fire alarms are installed in the huts, no smoking is allowed in bed and one expeditioner in each party is selected as Fire Officer.

As part of the training routine instituted, Thompson took the men to Port Melbourne for trial runs to gain experience in landing the amphibious craft and the use of the rockets and lines. Despite the tameness of conditions at Port Melbourne, compared to those they would experience in Antarctica, these dummy runs gave recruits some valuable experience in how to handle the craft. Law and Thompson conducted gymnasium classes in the early evenings twice a week at the YMCA. Not all the expeditioners viewed these classes with the enthusiasm Law would have liked. Some even thought he organised them to keep them out of the hotels, which closed at 6 p.m. in those days. Jacka recalls, what he refers to as, 'those hideous gymnasium sessions':

> I really hated them. But Phil was absolutely insistent that we had to climb up this bloody rope or some other equally horrible thing. I tore the skin off my hands, my arms ached and Phil would say 'Come on, more, more, more'. In retrospect, of course, I realize that it was desirable. It would have been hard to convince me then that it was essential.[63]

Law and Thompson also took the expeditioners to Mt Hotham for five days' instruction in snow conditions, preparing meals in tents, and survival and skiing techniques. The Mt Hotham stay also gave them the chance to talk about leadership issues, working together as a team and handling some of the problems that arose before they encountered the isolation in the Antarctic. It is likely that Law would have given the men the same advice about leadership which he later gave at a public lecture:

> In Antarctica one has no disciplinary powers. A man must lead by enthusiasm, drive and energy; he must move in on a job himself then look back over his shoulder and say, 'give us a hand with this, Joe'. He must lead from in front, not push from behind. But he must lead![64]

Law had selected nine men to set up the first Antarctic base. The majority of these were familiar with the type of life and work that would be expected of them. The OIC was Robert Dovers, a surveyor, who had been a member of the Heard Island pioneer party in 1948, and who had spent six months at Macquarie Island and twelve months at Adélie Land as the Australian observer with the third French Antarctic expedition. Lem Macey, the Technical Officer, had been a member of the same Heard and Macquarie parties. John Russel, an engineer, had also been on both sub-Antarctic bases. William Dingle, a weather observer, had been on Heard Island and William J. Storer, a radio operator, had been on Macquarie Island. Robert Summers, the Medical Officer, was a University Ski Club member; Bruce Stinear, a geologist who had had experience in the NZ Alps; Jeff Gleadell, the cook, born at South Georgia, had accompanied Sir Hubert Wilkins' expedition to Graham Land; and William Harvey, a carpenter. An official French observer, Georges Schwartz, a seasoned Polar traveller with experience in Greenland and Adélie Land was to join the party when it reached Iles de Kerguelen.

There would be 400 tons of cargo, including approximately 20 tons of food, to be packed onto the *Kista Dan*. Amongst the cargo were four different types of huts. The first, of pre-cut timber construction, was a living hut that included sleeping, messing and recreational quarters for the party. Law had bought this hut from the NBS Expedition in 1950 in anticipation of using it in Antarctica at some future date. There was a work hut—the first of the prefabricated 'Explastics' huts—for radio, meteorological and survey personnel, which also included the surgery and photographic dark room. Another pre-cut timber hut, made at the Tottenham Store, would also be used as an engine room and workshop and two smaller prefabricated store huts for supplies and equipment. All the huts had trapdoors built into the roofs to provide entry and exit whenever the expeditioners were snowed under and all but the storage huts were insulated and warmed by electric space heaters. Because of the constant concern for fire it was planned that the huts would be separated and any connecting passageways would be made of galvanised iron and fitted with fireproof and smokeproof doors.

Snow vehicles, called 'weasels', manufactured in USA during the war and which had been bought from the French expedition, were to be used to explore the Antarctic hinterland. The weasels would haul a 'caravan', designed mainly by Bob Dovers, in which the men could work, sleep and eat whilst in the field. Solid Norwegian hickory sledges would be used to transport the men and supplies in the field and would be hauled by husky dogs, which were already being bred and trained at Heard Island.

Law had arranged to buy the two Auster aircraft from the NBS Expedition when it concluded in 1952. These aircraft were small enough to be carried on the deck of the *Kista Dan* and were being taken to both help guide the ship through the pack-ice and to conduct aerial surveys. The RAAF undertook responsibility for the aircraft operations during the voyage with Flight Lieutenant Douglas W. Leckie in charge. Both aircraft needed extensive renovation and modification for ANARE's use. Leckie, an RAAF pilot with experience with floats, had been selected as CO. He, in turn, selected Sergeant Morgan, the rigger who had carried out most of the rehabilitation work on the Austers, to accompany the voyage. Morgan was to prove an excellent choice. The two other men were Sergeant Pilot Raymond K. Seaver and Sergeant Kenneth W. Duffel, a Fitter. The aircraft were modified so they could be fitted with wheels, skis or floats.

Law believed that for worthwhile scientific work to be carried out at the Antarctic base it needed to be conducted over several years. But, because he felt the Government was not willing to spend large amounts of money on scientific work in the Antarctic, he drew up three plans successively: 'elaborate, modest and downright cheap'. He chose to work on the 'downright cheap' plan for several reasons. He preferred to see modest plans completed thoroughly rather than to have ambitious plans only half completed and also because of the fact that:

We are going to unknown places, facing a number of unpredictable hazards and taking a number of chances beyond our control. The less we risk the less we can fail; the smaller the plan the more flexible it is and capable of adjustment to suit unexpected conditions.[65]

The expeditioners' job was to build a solid station which would last for many years and to establish a modest program of meteorology, biology, geology and exploration.

Exploration was to be carried out in two ways. The inland exploration—designed to fix the exact positions of all major landmarks, capes, islands, mountains and bays within 300 miles of the base—would use sledges and husky dogs, backed up by caterpillar-tracked snow vehicles. The coastal exploration entailed the Auster aircraft flying along the coast taking continuous photographs, then later making landings at strategic points for a group of scientists to take astrofixes and magnetic observations.

With his usual thoroughness, Law had added to the regular 30 clauses in the *Kista Dan* Charter Agreement, 27 of his own. Of these new clauses two were those he had years earlier vowed to include, whenever he had the opportunity to lead his own expedition. One was to ensure that the expedition supplied its own food. He went one step further and arranged that the expedition should not only supply its own food but also its own cook, who was to have the free use of the galley in co-operation with the ship's cook.[66] His other vow, 'to have a ship and Captain completely under my control,'[67] was, of course, impossible.

The problem of divided command between the Captain of the ship and the Leader of the Expedition had already arisen between Law and Lieutenant Commander Cartwright whilst on the *Labuan* voyage in 1951. But the problem was not just one confined to Law and ships' captains. Many Antarctic explorers and Antarctic sea captains had found themselves in this unenviable predicament. Shackleton had experienced it with Captains Evans and England,[68] and the problems between Mawson and Davis, and to a lesser extent, between Mawson and MacKenzie, on the two BANZAR Expeditions,[69] were well known. Law hoped to overcome some of the problems before they arose by setting down clear guide-lines for himself and the Captain of the *Kista Dan*. The clause Law included in the Charter Agreement read:

All movements of the ship are finally the Captain's responsibility and he is justified under the charter to refuse to take any action which he considers is prejudicial to the safety of the crew, the ship and its boats. The Captain of the ship is to carry out the operational instructions of the Director, Antarctic Division, or in his absence the instructions of his deputy, except under circumstances when the Captain considers that obeying such instructions will endanger the crew, the ship and its boats. In such a case the Captain must make a full written report of the circumstances, setting out his reasons for not obeying his instructions, and lodge it with the Director of the Antarctic Division at the earliest opportunity. At the conclusion of the charter the Captain is to provide the Director, Antarctic Division, with a fair copy of the ship's log written in English.[70]

From the Australian Embassy in Washington Law had obtained a set of photographs of the coasts of MacRobertson Land and Kemp Land that had been taken by the USA Naval 'Operation Highjump' in the summer of 1946–1947. He spent hours, sometimes with Mawson, searching through the photographs, with the aid of a magnifying glass, to determine what they hoped would be suitable locations. Finally he selected an area on MacRobertson Land, about Long.63°E. The area was a horseshoe-shaped outcrop of rock on the coast between Mount Henderson and the Masson Range. The aerial photographs showed an interesting mountain range inland, an area rich in rock formations, accessible from the sea and offering great scope for exploration and scientific work. It appeared to have everything wanted for a site, but part of the reason for its selection was political. MacRobertson Land and Kemp Land had been sighted from the sea by Mawson's BANZAR Expedition of 1929–1931 and landings had been made at Scullin Monolith, Proclamation Island and Cape Bruce. Since that time the coastal aerial mapping done by Lars Christensen, a Norwegian, in 1937, and more recently by the United States, had overrun the Australian work. If Australia's claim to this section of its Antarctic territory was to stand up, the original reconnaissances of Mawson's BANZAR Expedition would have to be consolidated.[71]

Law planned first to conduct coastal surveys along Princess Elizabeth Land in the vicinity of the Vestfold Hills and then to go westward along the coast to MacRobertson Land. At the EPC meeting in November 1953, Mawson agreed with Law's proposals, but suggested that the plan should be reversed, pointing out that the landing of the Antarctic party and the building of the station was the first duty of the expedition and should be completed first before the coastal survey was conducted. After some discussion the Committee agreed with Mawson and approved the recommendation along those lines.[72]

The plan was to leave Melbourne in mid December to relieve the Macquarie Island station and to then return to Melbourne and load the ship with stores and supplies for both Heard Island and Antarctica. At Heard Island the 1954 party was to be left ashore with the 1953 party, except for seven men who were to go on to the Antarctic to augment the working strength of the Antarctic establishment party. Three teams totalling 30 huskies would also be picked up at Heard for use at the Antarctic base. From Heard Island the ship would proceed to Iles de Kerguelen to take on water, petrol and diesel fuel and pick up Georges Schwartz and Dr André Migot, a French Observer later to write the accounts of this voyage under the title *The Lonely South*.[73] With these two men, the party now totalling 24, they would proceed to Antarctica.

Notes

1. Campbell-Drury to author, 17 October 1989.
2. Twigg to author, 24 June 1989.
3. Moodie to author, 7 August 1990.
4. Thompson to author, 9 July 1990.
5. Law, Lecture Notes on 'Character, Leadership and Training', LR.
6. Budd to author, 7 July 1990.
7. Jacka to author, 8 August 1990.
8. Campbell-Drury to author, 17 October 1989.
9. Macklin to author, 4 May 1989.
10. McKinnon and Twigg to author, 24 June 1989.
11. John Hetherington, *Australians, Nine Profiles*, F. W. Cheshire, Melbourne, 1960, p. 127.
12. Cited in A. F. Davies, *Skills, Outlooks and Passions, A Psychoanalytic Contribution to the Study of Politics*, Cambridge University Press, Melbourne, 1980, p. 291.
13. Campbell-Drury to author, 17 October 1989.

14. Thompson to author, 9 July 1990.
15. Law, 'Nutrition in the Antarctic' The Annie B. Cunning Lectures on Nutrition before the Royal Australasian College of Physicians in Melbourne on 11 October 1956.
16. Budd to author, 7 July 1990.
17. Law, *Antarctic Odyssey*, p. 194.
18. Law, *Antarctic Odyssey*, p. 246.
19. Budd to author, 7 July 1990.
20. Ibid.
21. Law, *Antarctic Odyssey*, p. 202.
22. McKinnon and Twigg to author, 24 June 1989.
23. Jacka to author, 8 August 1990.
24. Ibid.
25. Collings to author, 5 July 1990.
26. Sir Arthur Tange to author, 6 July 1990.
27. Law to Bickel, 19/20 April 1975.
28. Sir Arthur Tange to author, 6 July 1990.
29. Macklin to author, 4 May 1989.
30. Budd to author, 7 July 1990.
31. R. A. Swan, *Australia in the Antarctic*, p. 178.
32. Swan, op. cit., p. 224.
33. W. J. Hudson, *Casey*, Oxford University Press, Melbourne, 1986.
34. Hudson, op.cit., p. 35.
35. Hudson, op.cit., p. 230.
36. Macklin to author, 4 May 1989.
37. Thompson to author, 4 May 1990.
38. Bruce Stinear to author, 8 July 1990.
39. Law, *Antarctic Odyssey*, p. 209.
40. 'Future Planning—Antarctic Conference Proposals', AA:CRS P1469 (1951–1963) .
41. AA:CRS P1469 (1951–1963) Future Planning.
42. AA:CRS A1838/246 1251/X, P. G. Law.
43. AA:CRS P1469 (1951–1963), Future Planning.
44. Hanfield to Law, 10 September 1952. AA:CRS P1469 (1951–1963), Future Planning.
45. Citation for PGL's appointment as a Commander of the Civil Division of the Excellent Order of the British Empire on 31 December 1960.
46. Law, *Antarctic Odyssey*, p. 260.
47. Law to Bickel, 19/20 April 1975.
48. LP Minutes of First Meeting of Australian Committee on Antarctic Names, 21 October 1952, LP.
49. Law to Public Service Board, 6 December 1951. AA:CRS A1838/245, P.G. Law, pt 1.
50. Law to Secretary, DEA, 6 February 1952. AA:CRS 1838/245, P. G. Law, pt 1.
51. *Gazette*, 27 March 1952.
52. Budd to author, 7 July 1990.
53. McKinnon and McLeod to author, 1989 and 1990.
54. Minutes of EPC Meeting, 29 September 1952, ADH.
55. 'Trying to bring a heritage in from the cold', *The Age*, 3 October 1983, p. 11.
56. Law, 'The Australian 1954 Antarctic Expedition to MacRobertson Land', *Geographical Journal*, vol. 120, 1954.
57. *Herald*, 23 March 1953.
58. Cited in Swan, op.cit., p. 265.
59. Ibid.
60. Ibid.
61. Lecture Notes 'Planning an Antarctic Expedition', Constitutional Club, Monday, 30 March 1953, LR, Series 7.
62. Lecture Notes, 8 August 1960, LR, Series 7.
63. Jacka to author, 8 August 1990.
64. Lecture Notes, 'Some Polar Leaders', LR, Series 7.

65. Lecture Notes, 30 March 1953, LR.
66. Ships for Charter *Kista Dan* 1953/1954, Uniform Time–Charter 1912, 27 March 1953, Clause 50, AA:CRS P1469 (1951–1963).
67. LD, Tuesday, 10 January 1950, LP.
68. R. Huntford, Shackleton, p. 197.
69. Jacka, *Mawson's Antarctic Diaries*, xlv–xlvii.
70. Ships for Charter *Kista Dan*, 1953/1954, Uniform Time–Charter 1912, 27 March 1953, Clause 35, AA:CRS P1469, (1951–1963).
71. Law, *Antarctic Odyssey*, p. 14.
72. Minutes of EPC Meeting, 25 November 1953, ADH.
73. André Migot, *The Lonely South*, Rupert Hart-Davis, London, 1956.

9. Antarctic Explorer, 1954

LAW HAD HIS FIRST VIEW OF THE *KISTA DAN* ON 11 DECEMBER 1953, AND 'a very fine ship she looked, too, coming up the Yarra.' He went on board and met Captain Hans Christian Petersen, Kristen Mikkelsen, the Chief Officer, and Vilhelm [Bill] Pedersen, the Second Officer. Captain Petersen had had extensive ice experience with the Lauritzen Company on the Greenland coast. He had also already sailed the newly launched *Kista Dan* to Antarctica, in the summer of 1952–53, to make a film 'Hell Below Zero'.

Compared to other vessels, Law thought the *Kista Dan* was a very 'pucka' ship and, at the beginning of the trip, was concerned about the formality of the regulations for times for watches, hours and overtime which the Captain had set down. Law hoped that 'when they get to know us we can strike a more informal note in which our men can mix in and help without too much toeing the line set down in the regulations.' Overall Law was feeling relaxed and optimistic: 'My cabin is very comfortable and I feel I am going to enjoy this voyage!'

The changeover at Macquarie Island was completed in less than five days, a record time. Law was pleased with the ANARE men on the ship and was sure their exemplary behaviour had created a very favourable impression with the Captain and crew. He was equally pleased with 'the highly efficient management of the *Kista Dan* by her Captain, officers and crew.'

The short time they had taken for the Macquarie Island trip meant they could now leave three days earlier for the Antarctic. Law was delighted. Not so the Antarctic expeditioners, who had had their Christmas holiday period reduced by three days. 'The wives are the trouble,' Law grumbled into his diary, 'I am used to working at nights when the pressure is on but these married blokes won't do that.' Since Antarctic work was always paramount in Law's mind and Nel did not complain about his erratic hours, Law had little sympathy for those men who, on rare occasions, put their family before the Antarctic Division.

The week before the departure of any expedition was always hectic but, added to this, the men were edgy about the amount of work that now had to be completed in even less time. The situation was compounded by the wharf labourers refusing to work on two of the afternoons. Law then upset Bob Dovers by announcing at a staff meeting that

Thompson was to be his Second-in-Charge on the ship. Law placated Dovers by finally agreeing to call Thompson 'his Lieutenant'. Unfortunately for Thompson this title stuck and was, Thompson later said, 'a phrase I never liked'.[1] Dovers also objected to Law appointing the Second-in-Charge of the Antarctic Station, a right Law insisted on retaining. 'All rather petty,' was Law's pronouncement and concluded that, 'D[overs] is exceptionally egotistical and has always resented my control. No doubt the publicity I have had lately has irked him considerably.'

Both Law's and the expedition's public relations had been good and many articles appeared in metropolitan daily newspapers. Casey stated that 'a new era of Australian activity in the Antarctic would begin on Monday'[2] and, on Saturday, 2 January 1954, *The Age* made a dramatic announcement that:

Years of Government planning—and generations of explorers' slaving and suffering—climax on Monday when nine men sail from Melbourne intending to set up Australia's first permanent base on the Continent of Antarctica.[3]

More than 300 people assembled at North Wharf on 4 January 1954 to farewell the expedition. Law later recorded that when he arrived he

walked into a maelstrom of noise, confusion and people. Three tape-recorder fiends from broadcasting stations lay in wait for me, reporters grabbed my arm and tried to drag me off for interview or photos, friends clutched my hand and murmured good luck and other wishes, the loading continued, a public address van set up on the wharf made arrangements to amplify the Minister's speech.

Despite his protestations, one gains the impression that Law was in his element.

The *Kista Dan* finally pulled out from the wharf at 4.30 p.m. amidst a 'last minute flurry of tears, cheers and breathless farewells'.[4]

Conditions on the *Kista Dan* were much more comfortable than on any of the other ships ANARE had used. Law had a single berth cabin, just below the bridge on the port side, with a toilet and shower in the nearby passage. One half of the men were in 3 or 4–berth cabins in the accommodation aft, but eleven of the others, including Thompson, were in the forecastle.

For the first few days the weather was good but from then on it was consistently and unpleasantly rough and Law, as usual, felt 'lousy'. By Thursday 14 he had 'given in and taken pills'. This left him less squeamish but lethargic, a condition he also disliked. 'I am all right, but I can't force myself to work ... I guess from some points of view my enforced idleness constitutes a rest for me,' but he nevertheless concluded, 'I'd far rather be working hard ashore.'

At least the meals were good. The arrangements Law had made to have the ANARE provide their own cook and Australian provisions were, Law believed, working well. Thompson's opinion differed. He thought the arrangement was a 'great inefficiency and uneconomical' especially when the ANARE cook was sick, which occurred on the return trip from Heard Island and many subsequent voyages, and Thompson himself had to do the cooking.

The *Kista Dan* arrived at Heard Island on 19 January with a 'most unpleasant' 25 knot wind blowing. Even Law found the Island uninviting in those conditions: 'Heard certainly looks a grim place in rough seas, screaming wind, lowering clouds beneath which the bottom slopes of glaciers, highly crevassed, and great black rock cliffs plunge into the sea.' The changeover was more than usually difficult because of continuous bad weather, squalls and a blizzard, but the work was completed in three days and the *Kista Dan* sailed for Kerguelen on Thursday 21.

The following evening, 22 January, the ship anchored off Port aux Français, Iles de Kerguelen, and met the Chêf des Missions, Monsieur Francois Armengaud with several of his staff, including the French Observer, Dr André Migot who was to do the round trip on the *Kista Dan*, and Georges Schwartz, the French dog-handler who was to join Dovers' winter party.

During the next few days Law and his men arranged for the loading of 600 drums of fuel, 40 tons of water, the weasels and over a hundred cases of rations and equipment that the French had taken to Kerguelen to relieve the pressure on the limited hold accommodation on the *Kista Dan*. The loading of most of the supplies continued without too many mishaps, although 25 drums of fuel were lost when a pontoon capsized on the way to the ship, and the loading of the fresh water proved far more difficult than had been anticipated. The seas were rough and it was not until Wednesday 27 that they had all their supplies aboard. The support which ANARE received from the French, for which there were no charges, was only surmounted by the superb meals and wines they supplied. 'I cannot speak too highly of their friendliness, co-operation and generosity', Law stated in his official report. The *Kista Dan* sailed at 8.25 p.m. on Wednesday 27. Law wrote until 10.30 p.m. then 'fell into bed exhausted.'

The following two days were uneventful and on Saturday, 30 January, they sighted the first ice for the trip, 'a small bergy bit about 5 m[iles] to starboard'. A little later the men saw the first Antarctic petrels. By the following morning, two icebergs, more Antarctic petrels and some white chinned petrels had been sighted.

There now was a chill in the air, but it was more than counteracted by the glow of excitement from the men: 'a keen sense of anticipation evident everywhere.' The French Observer, Migot, was a little disappointed at how quickly they had arrived at this destination, latitude 64°S:

> If we kept up the same speed we should be in sight of Mac-Robertson Land the next day and ready to land. ... I had been looking forward so much to the prospect of steaming through the pack-ice, to the splendid scenery, to the difficulty and excitement of it all, and to the adventure of a polar expedition that I had dreamt of so long, that I felt that I should be cheated if we arrived too quickly and met no obstacles on the way.[5]

Migot was not to be disappointed. That evening they encountered open scattered pack-ice, 'from one to four yards across and from two to eight feet thick.' The Captain reduced speed to dead slow until daylight.

On Monday, 1 February, Law noted: 'most of the floes old, hard hummocked, from two to four metres thick and averaging about 10 metres across.' He went to the crow's nest to speak to Captain Petersen about the ship's future movements. They decided to push straight ahead into the thicker pack towards a large tabular iceberg. If the ice proved difficult they planned to return to open water for an aerial reconnaissance. A little later they saw their first penguins for the trip, two Emperor and six Adelie.

As the *Kista Dan* pushed toward the iceberg the pack became thicker. Law was pleased with the *Kista Dan*'s performance, 'It is indeed a thrill for us all', including Migot, who wrote:

> The *Kista Dan*'s bow was specially shaped in a gentle curve just above the water. When she hit small floes or lumps of iceberg she merely brushed them aside without trouble, but when she came upon a more solid mass of ice she slid up on to it like a sledge. When the ice was thin she broke it with her own weight, but when it was too thick the ship was jammed in the ice and could go no further. So she went astern and charged the ice again, gradually driving a sort of furrow across the floe, until finally it gave way and broke in pieces, letting the ship subside heavily into her natural element.[6]

Antarctic wildlife was now in abundance: 'Cape Pigeons, Snow Petrels, Antarctic Petrels, Wilson Storm Petrels, Penguins, Crabeater seals.' Dovers shot one of the seals for food for the dogs.

The going was slow with a long, hard battle against the pack-ice and, by the evening, they were in very heavy floes and their position 'lay astride the Antarctic circle at approximately longitude 63°E15 and were in very heavy floes.' For once Law wished he had been more cautious and stayed in the open water and used the aeroplane, but 'I optimistically pushed ahead—and the Captain too!'

The next day, from the crow's nest, Mount Henderson and the Masson, David and Casey Ranges on the Antarctic continent, were sighted. There was clear water between the pack-ice and the ranges. Law was elated. 'There is now nothing to stop us', he recorded. 'I shall rush down for a spot of breakfast and go back to the crow's nest with my cameras and field glasses.'

At 12.30 p.m. the ship passed through a large expanse of water surrounded by pack-ice. As the water was calm Law wished to take the opportunity to have the aeroplane launched, and asked the Captain to stop the ship. But Captain Petersen was 'most difficult ... said he couldn't anchor—it was too deep—and complained about wasting time.' Law insisted and 'the Old Man got sulky but went and anchored the ship against a floe' and Law and the pilot, Leckie, proceeded to 'tog up ready for the flight in our survival suits.' After some difficulty getting the aircraft airborne they were away. At 3 000 feet altitude the view was superb, but disheartening, for the open water Law had seen earlier in the morning did not extend to the coast, but continued for only another three miles before it was replaced by fast ice that stretched on for some 16 miles to the shore.

Law's elation of the morning suddenly vanished. But they had found the rocky harbour, shaped like a horseshoe, that Law had chosen as a possible station site from the 'Operation Highjump' photographs. From the air it looked an excellent place for a station. He was, though, surprised and disappointed by the surrounding area, 'the highland behind looked terribly forbidding—blue crevassed glacier ice with no snow or firn cover.' They arrived back safely, 'Leckie made an excellent landing' and later in the evening Law spent some time in the crow's nest with the Captain, guiding him through a lead they had seen in the open sea whilst on the flight. Law noted in his diary that evening that the Captain was 'in quite good humour again'. But Law was 'too tired to describe the magnificence of the aerial scenery or the enjoyment I had from the flight,' for he still had to write a press release for the Australian Associated Press (AAP).

Law, of course, was eager to receive both good and extensive press coverage for the expedition. He had received a cable from the Antarctic Division to say that his AAP report had been given a good press, but later had heard that the Melbourne daily newspaper reports were now totally absorbed with reports of Queen Elizabeth's visit. Soon he was admonished in a cable from the DEA that he maintain a better balance between messages sent to the Department for official release and those telegraphed to AAP. 'You will appreciate that final responsibility for deciding what is said about expedition must rest with Minister. There is no objection to human interest stories under your name',[7] he was told. Later on he received a cable from Nel, who was obviously keen for him and the expedition to gain good publicity, to say 'Articles excellent headlines send more length.'[8]

The following day, Wednesday, 3 February, Leckie flew Dovers to examine the surrounding terrain and Dovers confirmed Law's opinion that it was a suitable place for the station. Meanwhile the Captain was having difficulty breaking through the fast ice, which averaged 30 to 40 inches in thickness, the top 12 inches being glassy, hard, blue ice. Twice the ship was wedged after charging the ice and had to be winched off. At 10.15 p.m. the sun went down and Law, for once, took time to describe it. 'The scene is quite out of this world. There is a flaming sunset which, just before the sun dropped behind the Antarctic plateau, bathed the icebergs in the bay behind in a rosy glow and cast the ship's shadow far out across the pink tinted ice.'

The two Auster aircraft were fitted with vertical cameras and, during the slow painstaking progress through the fast ice, Leckie, Law, Seaver and Dovers photographed the group of islands near Horseshoe Harbour, the mountain ranges and 250 miles of coast between Scullin Monolith and Stefansson Bay.

The next day, 4 February, Leckie and Dovers made the first landing at Horseshoe Harbour. When asked years later about the excitement he must have felt on this historic occasion, Leckie replied 'I was too busy. I was working flat out to cope with the job that had to be done. But we did feel "we have found a base".'[9] The landing on fast ice had been a risky one and the Auster had broken its tail ski on the rough ice.

Leckie and Dovers reported that there was fast ice as far as the eye could see. Captain Petersen estimated that it might take a week for the *Kista Dan* to break through to Horseshoe Harbour. After discussion with Thompson and Dovers, Law decided that they would continue their program of aerial mapping of the coast and nearby mountains. At the same time they would unload certain stores onto the ice and use the weasels to transport Dovers and some of his men to Horseshoe Harbour where they could establish a shore party and begin to erect the first hut.

On Friday, 5 February, Law rose at 4 a.m. and he and Leckie flew to Horseshoe Harbour and landed on blue, pebbly, highly polished ice, with the skis on the plane clattering and bumping as they ran on towards an iceberg about a third of a mile ahead. As the aircraft showed no signs of stopping, Leckie put the plane into a 'ground loop', which spun it around, putting extra friction to the edges of the skis. This had the desired effect and the Auster came to rest 30 yards away from the iceberg. Law took photographs on the selected site 'before the men got onto it'. Leckie completed the marking out of an airstrip for the aircraft whilst Law inspected the area. Law later recorded 'I thoroughly enjoyed my outing—alone in this glorious wilderness on a fine day—terrific!'

When they returned to the ship the unloading had proceeded and two weasels, each towing a caravan and a man-hauled sledge, had set out, under Dovers' leadership, for Horseshoe Harbour. It was a slow trip, for the weasels had to zigzag to avoid cracks and weak-looking ice. The Auster aircraft directed them from overhead and planks of timber, bolted together, were used to bridge any unavoidable gaps in the ice.

The *Kista Dan*'s progress was also slow. She had been forced to be stationary during the morning whilst the cargo was being unloaded and had become badly stuck for 45 minutes during the afternoon. Later in the day Law had an altercation with the Captain over a request from Dovers to reload some of the cargo they had taken off the ship earlier. Petersen complained that they would 'never get there at this rate [as] he was not being given a chance to push ahead with the ship,' and suggested Law make up his mind whether he wanted the cargo on or off the ship. After an argument in which Petersen told Law that if he were not allowed to 'go through he would give up and go home' and Law pointed out that 'I was not God, I couldn't be perfectly right all the time,' Petersen calmed down and, Law reported, twenty minutes later was joking. They proceeded to put the cargo back on board and Law 'fervently prayed' that Dovers would get through for it would have been very embarrassing for Law, after his trouble with Petersen, if Dovers returned to the ship and asked to have his weasels and caravans hoisted on board.

That evening at about 11 p.m., within half a mile of their goal, the leading weasel in Dovers' party broke through weak ice into the sea. Dovers radioed to Law that the weasel was floating and they would attempt to salvage it. But at 1 a.m. they reported that repeated attempts to rescue it had failed. Law radioed back that he would send in a block and tackle in the morning. Dovers' party finally abandoned their attempt and made camp for the night in their caravans on the ice.

The following morning, 6 February, Law prepared to send the supplies to Dovers but the wind came up and Seaver reported that, with the wind at 35 knots, he doubted that he would be able to control the Auster on the slippery ice. The Captain confirmed Seaver's opinion and the flight had to be cancelled. The wind increased the danger of the ice breaking up and the situation, with Dovers and his men on the ice, had become alarming. Law sent a message to him to use every possible method to get off the ice onto land. At 9.20 a.m. Dovers replied that he would place a man-hauling sledge on the nearest island with 60 mandays rations and endeavour to get the weasel and caravans onto the island. By now the wind was blowing at 45 knots.

At 1.25 p.m. Dovers sent another message, this time informing Law that he had been able to place both caravans onto an island one mile from Horseshoe Harbour and that the weasel which had broken through the pack-ice was now frozen in and could be left indefinitely. In the meantime, the Captain told Law that with the strong wind he could not work the ice and so had carved out a turning circle in it, in case of emergency, and had turned the ship's bow into the wind. Law was pleased with this as it meant the Auster 201 on the deck was safer. But he still feared for the safety of the Auster 200 which had been tied down in the lee of a nearby island.

The storm raged all day Sunday causing great ice movements to port and astern of the ship, piling blocks of broken ice high on each side of the vessel and forcing heavy slabs beneath the hull. The ship began to shudder as the pressure built up around her. 'The question in our minds was,' Law later wrote, '"What will break first, the ice or the ship's hull?"'[10] He was relieved when he noticed that slabs of ice were cracking and sliding up the steel hull and collapsing back in great heaps of jagged pieces. The condition of the ice was a mixed blessing, as Law recorded:

> This is just what we need, provided the ice close inshore does not move out before we have rescued the weasel and aircraft! However, it has to move out, otherwise we cannot land! It would be worth the sacrifice of these vehicles for the advantage of being able to get ashore.

At 7 a.m. the situation was critical. The Captain, worried about the safety of the ship, asked Law to order all his men, dressed in their warmest clothing, to go onto the deck. By now the ice cracking against the sides of the ship had piled up so high that pieces were falling over the bulwarks onto the foredeck. By 8 a.m. the movement suddenly ceased and all on board heaved a sigh of relief. Law, eager to capture the scene for his film, climbed over the side of the Kista Dan and clambered onto the piled ice and photographed the ship. The Captain called out to him that the ice might buckle up at any moment. 'However,' Law recorded, 'the pictures were too good to miss.'

The Kista Dan was now immovably wedged, with huge slabs of ice piled up to deck level or higher. The party was in an invidious position, but they had survived one of the major hazards to an Antarctic ship. Most on board would have read, or been aware of, Shackleton's account of his 1914–16 expedition when his ship, the Endurance, had been destroyed by the pressure ice of the Weddell Sea. But the Kista Dan was safe at last, after withstanding similar pressure.

Later in the day they heard from Dovers that the wind at his island camp was gusting to 70 knots. With nothing more to be done, Law slept almost all day and by the evening there was still no sign that the ship could move.

The following morning, Monday 8, Leckie was able to fly to Dovers and bring him back to report on their situation. The five men had spent a comfortable night in the caravans but Dovers and Schwartz were dismayed at the force of the wind, which Dovers said, was even worse at Horseshoe Harbour than it was at the ship. Dovers told Law he did not want to set up the new station at Horseshoe Harbour for he believed the wind would make it too difficult to erect the full complement of huts. He suggested that the stores be placed on his island camp and he would stay there for a a year with a couple of huts and, next year, they should explore the coast to try and find a better site. Law told him he would not agree to the island proposal at any cost and insisted that he move everything to Horseshoe Harbour.

Meanwhile, the men at the ship had been working during the previous day digging away ice, 'by the absurdly primitive method', Migot wrote, 'of smashing the ice by hand with boat-hooks and spikes and shoving it back out of the way.'[11] Migot was getting more excitement than he had bargained for.

On Tuesday 9, the Captain asked Law to arrange to blast a crack about 10 yards from the edge of the after quarter. Law suggested that the Captain use explosive *under* the ship the way he had seen the Norwegians do on the *Norsel* trip but 'the Captain is not game enough' Law recorded. Blasting was carried out as the Captain had requested, but it failed to free the ship. Later in the morning Law received a report that Dovers had rescued the floating weasel and later on Leckie flew Law to Dovers' island camp.

The island was a dismal place and the morale of the men had been low during the storm. But morale, Law had learned from previous experience, was conditioned by weather, and with no wind and the sun shining, the men were cheerful and optimistic again and quite ready to proceed to Horseshoe Harbour. After a reconnaissance trip to choose a vehicle route to Horseshoe Harbour, Dovers returned and reported that the route provided no difficulties and immediately mobilised his group for the trip.

When Law returned to the ship he found that the Captain had agreed to explode a charge beneath the ship. This attempt was successful and, with the assistance of the ship's winches hauling on ice anchors astern, the vessel was finally freed.

Next day the *Kista Dan* was able to detour to reach a narrow crack which the storm had broken in the fast ice and, following this, she made rapid progress. Law visited Horseshoe Harbour to talk with Dovers and the party, and found them comfortably established in their caravans on the solid rock. 'The scenery in this glorious sunlight was magnificent.' He and Dovers sketched out positions for huts and Law happily recorded that the men's morale was good.

By Thursday 11, the *Kista Dan* pushed through the remaining fast ice, which was thinner than that encountered earlier and, by late afternoon, they turned south towards the entrance to Horseshoe Harbour. This was a critical moment, for they did not know if there would be a reef blocking the entrance to the harbour or if there would be sufficient depth once inside it. Luck was on their side. At 9.30 p.m. they finally reached the centre of Horseshoe Harbour and anchored in deep water. The Captain broke up a circular area of ice to give himself turning room and to face the ship into the icy, 50 knot wind blowing from the plateau. Law, as usual, was worried about the safety of the aircraft on the deck with such a high wind and asked Morgan and Leckie to tighten up the guys holding it. At 11 p.m. he recorded:

Thank God we are safely here—I never expected to get as close to our objective as this! Captain Petersen has done a remarkably fine job and a lot of credit goes to the stout ship *Kista Dan*.

His elation, however, was short lived. At 4.15 a.m. the following morning, Friday, 12 February, Law was awakened by Thompson and Leckie, who told him that both Auster aircraft had been damaged beyond repair. The Captain had been unable to face the ship into the wind and had left the vessel almost broadside to it, which meant that the tips of the aircraft had taken the full force of the storm. Law despondently recorded: 'Fridays are not our lucky days', cancelled all activity and slept till 11 a.m. Thompson, also in bed but not asleep, listened to the 'roar of this tempest' and wrote in a letter to his future wife, 'a strange thing is that because of the absence of grass, trees, sand or snow and the existence of only rock and ice, by looking out a porthole, you can see no evidence of any wind at all.'[12]

Later in the day, in a burst of inspiration, Law asked the RAAF crew if it were possible to make one serviceable aircraft out of the two damaged planes. They told him that the situation looked hopeless, but that they would try. Their one hope of achieving this miracle was Sgt Morgan, the rigger who had carried out most of the rehabilitation work on the Austers.

Before retiring that evening Law composed telegrams announcing their arrival at Horseshoe Harbour, to be sent on to Casey, HRH Queen Elizabeth, who was still on tour in Australia, and Mawson.

On Saturday morning Law asked Captain Petersen to move the ship so the hull abutted solid fast ice. In this position they would be able to begin the unloading onto the ice. The Captain doubted he could do it. After another altercation between Law and Petersen, Petersen made an attempt to move the ship, but the wind swung it around. 'I don't think it was much of an attempt', Law scathingly recorded. Again Law asked to have the ship moved. The Captain made another attempt, this time succeeding, but only gave, Law considered, 'the absolute minimum of what he could get away with.' and concluded '[Petersen] is an objectionable, obstructive, stubborn unco-operative boor! I am still avoiding an open breach but it takes all my self-control to keep my temper.'

If Law thought he was keeping secret the problems he was having with the Captain he was mistaken, for everyone on board, as Leckie later reported, was aware of it. 'You would have had to be blind not to notice it.'[13] Thompson also commented at the time on the atmosphere between Law and Petersen: 'The skipper and Phil are at loggerheads and have been for some time now. They rarely speak to each other and the atmosphere is very strained.'[14]

At 7 a.m. they started unloading the ship and by 5.10 p.m. on 13 February they were finally able to hold the official flag-raising ceremony. Law made the following dedication:

In the name of Her Majesty Queen Elizabeth II and the Government of the Commonwealth of Australia, I raise this Australian flag on Australian Antarctic Territory; and I name the site of this new ANARE station 'Mawson' in honour of the great Australian Antarctic explorer and scientist, Sir Douglas Mawson. God save the Queen.

The men sang the National Anthem, gave three hearty cheers and the gathering was photographed. But there was no time to dwell on this historic moment, and the men continued working until 10.30 p.m.

On Sunday 14 Dovers complained to Law about the 5 a.m. start, maintaining that Law would 'tire out my men'. Law refused to start later, justifying his decision in his diary: 'Thompson and I believe in starting early and thrashing the work while the weather holds—there will be plenty of days when it is too windy to work and the men can catch up on their sleep.' Later in the day Law took some time off to investigate the rock slope behind the station and 'had a most enjoyable ramble.' He found that the area was a paradise for mineralogists: 'even I became fascinated by the rocks,' he later wrote 'and couldn't resist picking up some specimens.'

Law was also thrilled to record that Frank Morgan [the RAAF rigger] 'is a treasure. They have rebuilt Auster 200 using the wings from 201 and all sorts of sundry struts. Leckie was very confident tonight that he would be flying in a few days' time again!'

During the following days the unloading proceeded and the building of the station went ahead:

The three huts were completed and the floors of two others laid; aircraft operations were resumed; seals were killed and skinned for winter dog-food; gravity and magnetic observations, also an astronomical determination of position, were made at Mawson; geological and botanical specimens were collected; and philatelic mail comprising 23,000 letters were stamped.[15]

By Wednesday, 17 February unloading had been completed and the rehabilitated Auster 200, minus the flaps which could not be repaired, was successfully tested by Leckie.

Law's diary entry of Thursday 18 February gives some idea of the range of duties of the men:

Elliott, Thompson, Dalziel, Henderson are helping ashore. Brooks is doing magnetic work, Storer is stamping mail, Stinear is helping erect Brooks's tent and is then going collecting rocks. Gwynn and Shaw are slushies and with Dingle are cleaning out for'ard food store and scrubbing saloon floor. Gwynn then goes ashore to gather lichens and mosses. The RAAF are preparing to fly. Dingle and Morgan then search holds for ANARE goods which might be hidden behind RAAF stores. Duffle is acting as radio man on ship for this flight. Schwartz ... had gone ashore.

On 20 February Law received many congratulatory cables, including one from Casey, Captain J. K. Davis and Brian Roberts of the Scott Polar Research Institute. Law was 'very pleased to receive one from J. K. Davis [who had a reputation for meanness]. He is a nice old boy—fancy spending a couple of pounds on a long cable!'

By 22 February, their eleventh day at Mawson, with the work progressing satisfactorily, Law declared a half-day holiday. That evening the men met for a final dinner and celebration. André Migot noted that, although it was late and there was to be an early start for their departure, 'the Australians could not leave before we had sung "For he's a jolly good fellow" for the benefit of Dr. [sic] Law.'[16]

The *Kista Dan* departed on 23 February. At 5.30 a.m. Law arose and 'called the troops. Farewells were said.' The wintering party stood on the ice, sheltered in the lee of the weasel, to wave a final farewell. Photographs were taken of the historic event, farewells were shouted, the ice anchors were hauled in, the engines started, the propeller beat the water but the ship stayed, stuck fast, in the ice. An hour later the ship was still in the same place and the wintering party had gone back to the huts. 'What an anti-climax', retorted Law, and went to sleep. He awoke at 11 a.m. and the ship finally departed at 11.15 a.m., 'the ship blew its siren and the winter party came out and waved farewell.'

Law was now able to begin the exploration work that had been planned and the *Kista Dan* was heading towards Scullin Monolith where it arrived at 8.30 a.m. on Thursday 25. The ship anchored about a quarter-of-a-mile offshore.

There had been two previous landings on Scullin Monolith, one by Mawson during the 1931 BANZAR Expedition, and another by the Lars Christensen Expedition from Norway in 1937, but neither landing party had been able to obtain an astrofix. If the ANARE's coastal aerial photography they had just conducted between Mawson and Scullin Monolith was to be accurately pinned down, Law needed to obtain an astrofix on Scullin Monolith. He arranged for Bill Pedersen (the Second Officer) and Thompson to take him and two other ANARE members ashore. Thompson, told the story:

> Now this Monolith rises up 1000 feet, sheer out of the water; the rocks at its base upon which the landing was to be effected were smooth, slimy and faced with ice. The temperature was 22° and the spray breaking over the boat froze on Bill and I, (we were both standing) ... With the sea running and the ice and smooth rocks it would have been suicidal, and if the weather got worse, they could never be got off. ... Phil wanted to, but I kept saying No! ... We scrubbed the idea, came back to the ship.[17]

But Law was determined to get the astrofix he needed and at 11.30 a.m. told Thompson he wanted to make another attempt. Thompson continues the story:

I shouted out at him 'Are you bloody crazy', at which he laughed—probably thought I was joking! We went in again much closer than before and right into a narrow cleft in the rocks with the water racing in and out like a millrace. That! was where Phil had set his heart on landing. I said 'No dice' sixteen times and headed the boat out again. We were in a space as wide as your house with precipitous smooth rocks and ice on either side, and this tide rip racing around like mad. No good to me, Bill [Pedersen], Arthur [Gwynn] or Jim [Brooks].[18]

The only comment Law noted in his diary about the second attempt was 'I made one more attempt to land but again allowed discretion to deter me.' The note he had prepared to be placed in a bottle beneath a cairn had they managed to get ashore, he now sadly placed between the pages of his diary. The visit had been disappointing, but he had some photographs and cine shots for his film.

The *Kista Dan* sailed from Scullin Monolith at 4.15 p.m. They were now headed east to the Vestfold Hills, an area which comprises about 200 square miles of ice-free rock on the eastern side of Prydz Bay. There had been only two previous landings at the Vestfold Hills: one in 1935 by the Norwegian Klarius Mikkelsen and the second by the American explorer Lincoln Ellsworth and his Australian adviser, Sir Hubert Wilkins, in 1939. The *Kista Dan* soon encountered heavy pack-ice to the north and east and Petersen stopped the ship for the night. 'I hope the Captain doesn't get the wind up and head for home', Law fretted into his diary that evening.

The following day, Friday, 26 February, was 'a perfect day. Temperature 14.5° at 9 o'clock but calm and sunny.' During the day they sailed through 'a great accumulation of countless icebergs grounded on the Fram Bank off Cape Darnley—hundreds of them in 150 metres of water with a sea bottom planed as flat as a table by their passage.'

In the middle of the thickest accumulation of icebergs, the Captain turned north and ran into open leads, covered with young ice or new sludge. Bill Pedersen later recalled that sometime during this period Captain Petersen told his senior officers 'I don't like it at all—new ice forming fast and so strong that it could carry an elephant seal.'[19]

By 6 p.m. they were in open water, but Law was still worried:

I knew this afternoon as we passed through a lot of new ice that the Captain would declare it time to go home and, sure enough, at 6.30pm he interrupted my dinner to say that he was sorry, but he reckoned we had seen the last of the Antarctic for this year. I said I'd see him after dinner and discuss it.

Thompson's version of the story also gives his personal opinion of the situation:

> In effect, he [the Captain] presented Phil with a fait accompli. He was very much in the wrong; he goes where he is told and only where the safety of the ship is concerned can he do things against the will of the charterer. He should have advised Phil this morning that he considered it too risky to go East and I'm quite sure that Phil would have agreed, because the new ice was forming at an alarming rate, and we should have got to hell out of there.[20]

It is impossible to know if the situation would have been different had Petersen consulted with Law earlier in the day. In any event, the outcome was that Law checked on his itinerary, then went to see Petersen and told him he would like to use up two or three more days and go east to do reconnaissance work in the Vestfold Hills area. The Captain agreed.

That night Law could not sleep. 'I tossed around, turning various possibilities over in my mind and worrying about being blocked off at this stage from exploring Prydz Bay when we were within reach of it.'[21] His premonition was correct. When he approached the Captain the following morning, Petersen told Law he had looked at the charter document and found survey work was not included. He also told Law that he had contacted the owners for advice as to whether the ship was covered by insurance or not for survey work. Law asked him whether, in the meantime, he would stick to the agreement they had made the previous evening. Petersen agreed, but later altered course to the south-east and dropped back to half speed. 'He was prepared to go at full speed last night heading north!' a furious Law wrote in his diary, 'I suspect he intends stalling all day until he gets his message.'

Law did not wait to find out. He approached Petersen at 7.30 a.m. and told him he was not prepared to waste the day in mid-ocean whilst Petersen awaited the reply to his cable. He pointed out to Petersen that Australia was paying £375 per day for the ship, and that half speed would not get him anywhere and he wanted nothing less than three-quarter speed. Petersen did not comment, but pushed the telegraph handle over to three-quarter speed. Law asked to be informed if Petersen altered course or speed. 'I'm afraid that from now on I shall have to play the game tough,' Law wrote.

To add to his bad humour, Law received a message informing him that the Minister had not forwarded Law's messages to Mawson or the Queen. 'I have sent off a stinker [telegram] to Waller [DEA]', Law recorded and concluded, 'These lousy petty shiny-bums in Canberra.' (He was later advised that the Minister had telegraphed Mawson personally and that the Minister did not consider that the circumstance warranted a message to the Queen.)

The battle between Law and Petersen continued throughout the day. Finally Law asked Petersen if he would be prepared to enter the pack-ice if he received approval from the owners. Petersen said he would and, 'at that,' Law wrote, 'I had to be content.' Law and Petersen were enacting the classic situation between Captain and Expedition Leader that had been played out on so many previous Antarctic expeditions.

After lunch the ship encountered some less dispersed pack-ice and, just as Law was thinking 'this is better,' he noticed that the ship had changed course and was sailing NNW. The Captain had not informed him of the change of direction. Law gave up arguing with Petersen and instead sent a cable to the shipping agents, Westralian Farmers Transport Ltd in London, which read:

> Captain Kistadan has refused survey MacKenzie Sea area as requested by me not on grounds of safety to ship but because he states charter does not cover this type of work and insurance would be void stop He has cabled owners for instructions stop Pending reply my time is being wasted at pounds Sterling 375 daily stop As I supplied owners before leaving with my itinerary stating my intention proceeding eastward after landing wintering party I take strongest exception to Captain raising this quibble at this stage stop I consider vessel should be declared off charter for period wasted awaiting owner's instructions.

He sent a copy to the Antarctic Division, delivered another copy to Captain Petersen and returned to his bunk. Forty-five minutes later Captain Petersen came to his cabin, very upset, and told Law his cable was incorrect as he had come out of the pack-ice the previous evening because of the safety of the ship. Law told him 'I am not talking about last night—this morning when I asked you to go south you said you were not afraid for the ship it was because of the insurance.' Law then requested Petersen, as per the clause he had written into the Charter Agreement, 'if ... it is a matter of ship safety would you please let me have in writing your reasons for refusing?' Petersen agreed and left Law's cabin. Sometime later Law was somewhat mollified to notice that the ship was moving faster and on a course further south than had been the case earlier in the day.

Later Petersen returned to Law's cabin and, Law recorded, was 'very courteous and subdued ... and pretended there had been a misunderstanding. He parted in very friendly fashion. Like most bullies he deflates easily.'

The following morning, Sunday, 28 February, Law prepared a document setting out exactly what he wanted done and asked Petersen to give him a written statement if he could not do it. Petersen told Law that 'he had received a cable from the owners stating that the survey was in line with the charter' and agreed to proceed as Law had requested. 'Everything is smooth and pleasant again', Law smugly recorded. On the surface, this may have been so, nevertheless the Second Mate, Bill Pedersen, later recalled that the trip to the Vestfold Hills was made against the Captain's wishes. 'HP [the Captain] was scared and I understand him.'[22]

By 7.30 a.m. they were proceeding south and, at 11.15 a.m., still going south, Law, with obvious elation, wrote 'This is something like it.' So far they had not met with any consolidated pack-ice and there was still a swell coming in:

> It has been a splendid day! We have charged down through Prydz Bay at high speed ... without stopping and are now further south than Casey Range and Mawson. ... I hope we can get close to Vestfold Hills tomorrow and get a good fix! If so I can go home happy.

As if aware of his mood of exultation, that evening there was an aurora, but it only rated a marginal note in Law's diary, 'Aurora! Drapery—brilliant white—south of Zenith', taking second place to the detailed explanation of the 'lovely dinner' they had that evening: 'chicken, green beans, green peas and potatoes; spongecake and tinned blackberries and cream'.

The following morning they were almost level with the Vestfold Hills, but 40–50 miles off the coast. Law still 'entertain[ed] vague hopes of making a landing and getting a fix there.' But it was one of the coldest days they had had yet, with the temperature at 13°F and the sky overcast. By 1.30 p.m. they had encountered pack-ice and were forced to go in an easterly direction. By 3 p.m. they were proceeding through an area of new black ice. 'This great area, three miles wide and of unknown length, was obviously open sea until a few days ago. Everything, though, is now freezing up at a great rate.' Then they hit very heavy pack-ice. With little hope of success they investigated a 'weak looking lead which appeared to run SE from a couple of icebergs'. But they were pleased to be proved wrong, and the lead 'widened out after we reached it and we went on and on.' Finally they saw the Vestfold Hills and 'everything went better and better until we finished up in open water, running straight in to our objective.' They anchored 100 yards off an island at 8.40 p.m. and Law made arrangements with the men for the next day's program.

Law arose at 4.30 a.m. the following morning. The RAAF crew made preparations for a flight and other men were selected and prepared to go ashore. Then a strong wind rose and all their arrangements had to be altered. The ship was forced to weigh anchor and steam out to another anchorage further off-shore and they were 'immobilized here waiting for the wind to moderate.' The frustration of this added delay showed.

'Here we are, after a lot of trouble, needing only a few hours good weather and sunshine, and we are stalled by this lousy weather.' By nightfall the wind was gusting to 70 knots and the ship was dragging its anchors. Law noted, 'all I can do is pray for an improvement tomorrow.'

The French observer, André Migot, was well aware of the mounting tensions and he wrote:

I felt that the Captain's one wish was to turn northwards and head for Heard Island, but poor Dr. [sic] Law was so unhappy at his persistent ill-luck and at the prospect of failure that they agreed that he should have one more day of grace. But it was to be the last, and whatever the weather and whether the work had been finished or not the *Kista Dan* would start for home in twenty-four hours.[23]

Law's prayers were answered and the following morning it was snowing heavily but quite calm. By 5.30 a.m. the shore party was ready but it took an hour, after heating the engine block with a blow torch and priming three cylinders with petrol, to get the motor boat started in the intense cold. They needed the sun to take a position shot, but the sky remained cloudy. 'Two days without any sun at all,' Law moaned, 'just when we want some, more than at any other stage of the trip!'

At 9.30 the Captain had brought the ship back close to the island and the motor boat was successfully launched, with Seaman John Hansen as boatman. The plan was to land Brooks and Eliott on the island to conduct magnetic observations, with Thompson, Gwynn, Shaw and Law to go on to the mainland, two-and-a-half miles further on, to raise the Australian flag. It was 'dead calm, snowing, everything black and white', Law recorded 'snow forming sludge on surface of water, coloured green by algae'. Thompson described the landing:

We landed the first two on the island okay and then shot through into a maze of islands to try and find the coast. We were out of sight of Kista in a few minutes and then the engine broke down. Always the great humourist, by now I'm killing myself laughing, because I couldn't hear the ship on the radio (We had arranged schedules every 15 minutes). Got the motor going; to have it stop four times in the next half hour. Eventually it seemed to settle down and work O.K. but I mistrusted it, and between that and the lack of contact on radio I was rapidly developing ulcers. Get the picture;—Phil is foolhardy, knows nothing of boats and has no conception of their pitfalls and risks; Arthur is in another world, birds, nothing else ... Shaw is a know-all, and dull, but young enough not to have any imagination and has no boat experience at all.

We eventually get to the mainland, where Phil proceeds to run us aground (not seriously) while I'm fiddling with the radio. Howls of anguish and martyrdom from Dick; 'I wonder where the penguins are' from Arthur; 'why don't you do this' from Shaw; and seventy-eight concise, clear, direct, ambiguous and conflicting orders from Phil. We push off and land on some ice across which we are to trek to the shore. I had a flagpole and flag, of course. 'Dick, leap ashore carrying the flag'. ... Phil, of course, was taking it all on his cine camera. That was the reason for the histrionics. We struggled ashore, built a cairn out of rocks, planted the flag on its pole, while Phil took our picture. Then I took photos of him with the flag, and a cine film of the three of them waving their caps like a trio of scat singers.[24]

'We had a lovely placid trip back', recorded Law, 'between the islands and icebergs over the still black glassy water on which patches of snow sludge and pancake were beginning to show.' They dropped Gwynn and Shaw off at the island and Thompson and Law returned to the ship where, much to Thompson's disgust, Law arranged for other members to be taken to the mainland. 'Snowing like mad,' Thompson wrote, '68.30° South, 100 miles between us and the ocean and I'm running ferry trips.'[25]

Visibility had been too poor for an aircraft flight and too dull for the astronomical fix that Law wanted. He persuaded the Captain to postpone leaving until early the next day to give him one more chance for sunshine. 'Tomorrow is our last chance,' he recorded that night. 'I hope to (a) fly the aircraft for photos [and] scintillometer [survey] (b) take sun fix ashore ... If we can do this we shall have accomplished everything we set out to do ... Here's hoping!'

Thursday, 4 March, and the weather was fine. But the day was full of frustrations. The motor boat engine seized and would not run. Law decided to put the survey party ashore in the dinghy. The aircraft cartridge starter jammed and it took almost three hours to get the engine going. But, by 12.30 p.m., when the men had returned from the island, Brooks had successfully obtained the coveted sun observations and finished his magnetic work and Leckie had completed a photographic flight. 'The ship can now sail for Heard I[sland] as far as I'm concerned,' Law recorded and, satisfied, concluded, 'our work is completed and, if I may say so, very well done. I am very very relieved to have finished the work.'

His satisfaction proved to be short-lived. The *Kista Dan* sailed at 1.25 p.m. but, four hours later, the wind force was 8 and the ship only able to do 4 knots. The wind increased during the evening and by 8 p.m. was force 12. At 1.30 a.m. on Friday, 5 March, Leckie woke Law to tell him that the aircraft, lashed down on the deck, had been completely wrecked. The two of them stumbled out to the boat deck to find the Auster lurched over on one side, crumpled and twisted, with the port wing tangled up in the lifeboat davits. 'I was just in time to see the aircraft topple forward on its nose and the starboard wing to crumple in a horrible grinding mess.' Shortly after it disappeared overboard. Their faithful Auster had gone.

The wind had now increased to 90 knots, making a sound, Thompson wrote, like 'a thick solid roaring noise; such a noise that you imagined you could see or feel.'[26] Light after being unloaded at Mawson, *the Kista Dan* rode high out of the water and the Captain could no longer keep it into the wind. She broached and drifted helplessly before the storm. 'From then until daylight it was a nightmare', Law recorded. 'I have never been in anything so frightening and I admit I was really afraid.'

By 2 a.m. the ship was out of control and could only move sideways across wind, crab-fashion:

At one terrifying time [Law wrote] a bergy bit the size of a large two storey house was 30 yards off to port, dipping and plunging wildly in the spindrift and surf and the ship's engines were racing and she was flat on her side trying to turn as the Captain tried to get her clear of the danger.

Another time we were lifted on a large wave and our bows crashed down on a small bergy bit with force that shattered it but shook the ship from stem to stern.

There was nothing Law could do. The ship was completely at the mercy of the elements. 'I have never been so terrified', he wrote years later. 'Never have I experienced, either before or since, terror extending unrelieved over such a long period of time. I don't think anyone on the ship really expected to survive and, over a period of 12 hours, each large roll seemed likely to be the last.'[27]

Law was right. From most accounts, the men did not expect to survive. Bill Pedersen, who later commanded many trips for ANARE, said that this particular situation 'was horrible—the worst in my life!' and, throughout that night, the thought frequently flashed through his mind that what a pity it was his wife would be widowed so early.[28] Thompson, who had been in the Navy and often in 'very very difficult weather ... and under shell fire in which I thought I was in extreme danger' wrote, on Friday, 5 March 1954, 'I have just spent the most horrible day of my life; terrifying would be an understatement.'[29] And Leckie told the other three RAAF men that it might be a good idea if they said a quick prayer. One muffled voice told him 'what in the hell do you think I've been doing for the last two-and-a-half hours?'[30] Migot also described the situation:

Every now and then the ship lay right over on her side, stuck there as if she would never right herself again. Then slowly, very slowly, she raised herself, only to heel over once more on the same side. It was quite agonising, these moments seemed to last for ever, and each time I felt sure the ship would never right herself again—but stay on her side or even turn turtle.[31]

Morning dawned with no improvement and revealed a 'scene of appalling confusion', Migot wrote. 'It looked as if a hurricane had swept through the inside of the ship.'[32] Drawers had slid out and emptied their contents all over cabin floors. Throughout the ship everyone could hear doors banging and furniture crashing. Crockery fell down companion ladders or cascaded through the galley and the ward room:

The ice pack was a seething writhing mass [Thompson wrote] going up and down in the air with the motion of the waves underneath it; the boat deck was a scene of indescribable confusion and wreckage; and covered with snow ... The wind was blowing at about 90mph. Went down to the saloon where I found some of our blokes and some of the Danes sitting there like death warmed up. Their explanation of the picture to me made me feel like it too.[33]

One engineer was so distressed he had to be given sleeping tablets. This particular engineer had been constantly lying down cleaning the strainers for ice slush to get cooling water to the engine. He later had a nervous breakdown, could not work for a year, and never went back to sea again.[34]

At one stage during the hurricane Law went onto the bridge and Captain Petersen turned to him and shouted 'HAVE YOU NOW GOT ENOUGH?'[35]

Conditions did not improve. 'I saw a giant creaming breaker loom up before the port through which I was looking,' Law wrote around noon, 'and crash onto the starboard quarter. ... It was as though an iceberg had struck the ship.'

By lunchtime their situation was eased somewhat when the *Kista Dan* drifted into a tongue of pulverised brash more than a foot thick and the furious seas ceased to lash her and she straightened up. But the danger from heavy ice holing the ship and the threat from icebergs remained acute. 'We go through agony every time she bumps and grinds', Thompson wrote, 'It's a pretty grim prospect as nobody could ever rescue us.' That evening he wrote:

These dark hours are the worst, from now until 4am, the officers can't see where they are going; the Captain has personally been on the wheel from 4pm yesterday until 6pm tonight and now Kristen [the Chief Officer] is there. There is nothing we can do; and everything depends on them.[36]

By Saturday the hurricane had moderated. During all this time Captain Petersen had not slept. He had spent two and a half continuous days on the bridge and Law reflected the opinion of the men on the ship when he later wrote that Captain Petersen 'had shown magnificent seamanship in bringing the ship safely through this hazardous period.'[37]

Early on Sunday 7 progress was resumed and the ship reached the eastern edge of the brash and followed this north. 'It is a relief to be out in open water again', Law wrote.

But the Captain was still unsure of their exact bearings and later the *Kista Dan* ran into heavy pack-ice, too heavy to penetrate. On Monday Law wrote 'we are making good progress but have not much real idea where we are and shan't have until we get a sunshot.' The lateness of the season and prospect of continuing bad weather, together with the amount of new ice everywhere, was causing anxiety to everyone. 'Let's hope we get through OK—it is growing too late in the season to be mucked up and delayed and forced to search for other places to get through.'

On Tuesday yet another violent storm kept them immobilised. Morale on board the *Kista Dan* reached its lowest ebb with the men contemplating the possibility of being beset for the winter. Dan Sweetensen, the ANARE cook, proposed that he take an inventory of the food stocks, but Law, mindful that this action might provoke further apprehension amongst the men, told him he would let him know when he wanted this done. Their anxiety was understandable. The weather was terrible and they were surrounded by pack-ice with no open water visible anywhere. The memory of the recent hurricane in Prydz Bay was on everyone's mind, and the lateness of the season and the rapidly freezing open water showed that they could not afford to remain in the pack-ice much longer.

As it turned out, the storm proved a blessing for it broke up the pack-ice. By Wednesday 10, conditions improved and, at 4.15 p.m., Law jubilantly recorded, they were finally '<u>out of the ice</u> ... we should reach Heard Island on Sunday now.'

Despite continuing bad weather, the *Kista Dan* arrived at Heard Island on Sunday, March 14, picked up the men and, on Monday, sailed for Iles de Kerguelen where they loaded fresh water and, as usual, were generously entertained by the French. 'Eventually we got everyone away amidst much hand shaking and cheering.' The French had given Law two large barrels, over 40 gallons each, of red wine. 'What a bottling party we shall have when we get home!' The next few days were spent reading, resting and interviewing the 1953 expeditioners from Heard Island.

The accomplishments, battles and dangers encountered by the ANARE men on the *Kista Dan* had received only minimal coverage in Australian newspapers, for the media was more interested in the proposed visit of the Queen and Duke of Edinburgh. One journalist did comment that 'a handful of Australians have been taking part, almost unnoticed, in an exploit which, under normal conditions, would have made headline news.'[38]

On Sunday, 28 March, Law was angered by a cable he received from DEA:

> You and all men of Heard Island party will probably be interviewed by press on arrival Melbourne. Such interviews should deal with events, personal experiences and sidelights. Your considered assessment of achievements and value of expedition should be preserved for a report to Minister and may be the subject of a later statement.

'This is typical', Law fumed, 'the first great chance to give the newspapers some serious scientific stuff and I am reduced to nattering about penguins!'

Law cabled a stiffly worded reply to Waller, DEA, Canberra:

> Quite agreeable follow procedure suggested but it appears waste of perfect opportunity to stress serious value expedition instead merely talking penguins and heroics. If Minister can publish leading article on achievement OK but consider an official handout three days later from Canberra would attract little attention.

Law had also asked the DEA about the possibility of paying a small financial bonus to members of the ship's company in recognition of their performance under difficult and sometimes very dangerous circumstances. He received a reply 'Treasury asks whether specific happenings, particularly any resulting in savings for Commonwealth, can be cited to support proposal.' 'Typical!' Law jabbed into his diary. He was tired and suffering from his usual nausea and lethargy: 'flat and lazy—reaction now that all the worry is over I guess.' For once he did not enter into one of his campaigns of attrition with the bureaucracy and let the matter drop. After an otherwise uneventful voyage, the *Kista Dan* anchored at Melbourne at 9 a.m. on Wednesday, 31 March, 1954.

The welcome the party would rightly have expected was not forthcoming. Minister Casey met the *Kista Dan* and informally spoke with Law and Captain Petersen. Many relatives of the returning expeditioners, plus a few reporters and photographers, were on the wharf to greet them, 'but not a great crowd', Law recorded. 'Rather a poor show, as a matter of fact, altogether!' read Law's final comment in his diary.

The 1954 expedition was a landmark in the history of Australia's exploration and scientific endeavour. The men of ANARE had established the first permanent Australian station on the Antarctic continent and, in so doing, had fulfilled the final requirement set down by the Government in 1947 for Australia's involvement in Antarctica. The expeditioners had shown the same spirit of adventure and had undergone the same hardships, privations and life-threatening conditions as had earlier Antarctic explorers.

'Today the Antarctic is a challenge ... to Australian courage and imagination',[39] Casey had stated in 1953 and, under Law's direction, the men of ANARE had accepted the challenge, had shown the courage and imagination, and had triumphed. The tragedy was that Australia barely noticed.

Notes

1. Thompson to author, 9 July 1990.
2. 'New Era Ahead in Antarctic', *Herald*, Friday, 1 January 1954.
3. 'Nine Men Plant Our Flag on a Continent of Ice', *The Age*, Saturday, 2 January 1954.
4. 'Tears, Cheers for Men Sailing to the Antarctic', *Sun*, 5 January 1954.
5. André Migot, *The Lonely South*, Rupert Hart-Davis, London, 1956, p. 131.
6. Migot, op.cit., p. 135.
7. Cable, Series 7, Antarctic Correspondence—Subject Files, Box 20, 7/5, LR (MV) .
8. Ibid.
9. Leckie to author, 22 October 1990.
10. Law, *Antarctic Odyssey*, p. 99.
11. Migot, p. 147.
12. Thompson to Sheelagh Manson, 1954.
13. D. Leckie to author, 22 October 1990.
14. Thompson to Sheelagh Manson, 1954.
15. Law, *Geographic Journal*, vol. 120, 1954.
16. André Migot, op. cit., p. 169.
17. Thompson to Sheelagh Manson, 1954.
18. Ibid.
19. Captain V. Pedersen to author, 4 December 1988.
20. Thompson to Sheelagh Manson, 1954.
21. Law, *Antarctic Odyssey*, p. 137.
22. Captain V. Pedersen to author, 4 December 1988.
23. Migot, op.cit., p. 180.
24. Thompson to Sheelagh Manson, 1954.
25. Ibid.
26. Ibid.
27. Law, *Antarctic Odyssey*, p. 151.
28. Captain V. Pedersen to author, 4 December 1988.
29. Thompson to Sheelagh Manson, 1954.
30. Leckie to author, 22 October 1990.
31. Migot, op.cit., p. 185.
32. Ibid.
33. Thompson to Sheelagh Manson, 1954.
34. Captain V. Pedersen to author, 4 December 1988.
35. Ibid.
36. Thompson to Sheelagh Manson, 1954.
37. Law, *Geographic Journal*, vol. 120, 1954.
38. 'A Dangerous Exploit', *The Toowoomba Chronicle and Darling Downs Gazette*, Thursday ,18 March, 1954.
39. Cited in Swan, op.cit., p. 265.

Epilogue

W HILST THE SETTING UP OF MAWSON STATION IN 1954 WAS THE FUL-
filment of a dream that Law had striven relentlessly towards for
five years, it also marked the beginning of a new career, this
time in exploration.

In the following twelve years Law made twenty-eight visits to Antarctic
and sub-Antarctic regions. A new station, Davis Station on the shores of
Prydz Bay, was set up in 1957 and, in 1959, the American station Wilkes
was taken over for Australia. At the time of his resignation in 1966 he was
busy directing the building of a new station to replace Wilkes, and the
Antarctic Division had grown to seventy permanent staff.

Although much of the extensive Antarctic coastline, approximately
25 000 miles in extent, had been roughly mapped from the sea and the
air, by 1955, two-thirds of it had never been visited by land parties.[1]
During the subsequent ANARE 'summer cruises', 4 000 nautical miles of
the coastline of Antarctica were traversed. The ANARE men, working
from the three established coastal stations, pushed inland with dog
sledges, over-snow vehicles and aircraft to extend the total area mapped
to more than 500 000 square miles of coastal regions and inland mountainous areas.[2]

In 1961 Law was made a Commander of the Order of the British
Empire (CBE), in recognition of his 'substantial contribution to Australian achievement in the Antarctic'.

Law was 55 years old when he resigned from the Antarctic Division
and his resignation ended an era which Antarctic personnel would later
refer to as 'The Law Years'. 'Never again', a later Antarctic expeditioner
and writer commented, 'would ANARE or Australia's Antarctic involvement be so influenced by one individual.'[3]

Law left the Antarctic Division to take up the newly created position
of Vice-President of the Victoria Institute of Colleges (VIC). He had
returned to academia. With this new position he was again faced with the
challenge of building an organisation from scratch. He had to conceive
and build an instrumentality which could develop and co-ordinate the
activities of what, by 1977, totalled sixteen Colleges of Advanced Education.

In 1975 Law was made an Officer of the Order of Australia (AO), two years before he retired in 1977.

On Law's 80th birthday in 1992, the Royal Society of Victoria held a symposium to honour him and his work in Antarctica, education and marine science. The symposium was attended by approximately 250 people. During the evening, whilst Law was on the platform, he received a telephone call, relayed by satellite telephone, from Dr Jim Hasick, the Station Leader at Mawson Station. Hasick talked of things that had remained constant since 1954 including 'the excellent quality of the expeditioners and the strong sense of adventure and desire to experience Antarctica to the full'. He concluded his talk with:

> None of this has changed, Phil. You set the stage, you set the standards. You set the challenges. In 1954 you established Mawson Station; no one could have picked better. Phil you have left us so much.[4]

Notes

1. P. Law and J. Bechervaise, *ANARE, Australia's Antarctic Outposts,* Oxford University Press, Melbourne, 1957.
2. Norman Harding, Division of National Mapping, Department of Minerals and Energy, Melbourne, to Law, 19 January 1973, LP.
3. Quoted in Jonathan Chester, *Going to Extremes, Project Blizzard and Australia's Antarctic Heritage,* Doubleday, Sydney, 1986, p. 273.
4. Dr Jim Hasick, Mawson Station Leader, 'Tribute from Mawson Station, Antarctica', *Education, Antarctica, Marine Science and Australia's Future,* Proceedings of the Phillip Law 80th Birthday Symposium, 29 April 1992, Royal Society of Victoria, Melbourne.

Abbreviations

To save excessive referencing, all quotes by Phillip Law, unless otherwise stated, are taken from interviews with the author, audio tapes, autobiographical notes or his personal diaries.

A	Commonwealth Government Records Australian Capital Territory
AA:CRS	Australian Archives Correspondence Files
AAE	Australasian Antarctic Expedition
AAP	Australian Associated Press
ABC	Australian Broadcasting Corporation
ABC:SHU	Australian Broadcasting Corporation, Social History Unit
AD	Antarctic Division
ADH	Antarctic Division, Hobart
ANARE	Australian National Antarctic Research Expeditions
ANCA	Antarctic Names Committee of Australia
AR	Audio Recording
BANZARE	British-Australian-New Zealand Antarctic Expedition
CBE	Commander of the Order of the British Empire
CSIR	Council for Scientific and Industrial Research
CSIRO	Commonwealth Scientific and Industrial Research Organisation
DEA	Department of External Affairs
EDM	Education Department, Melbourne
EDR	Education Department Report
EPC	Executive Planning Committee
IGY	International Geophysical Year
LD	Law's Diary
LP	Law's Papers in possession of Phillip Garth Law
LR	Law's Records held at Museum of Victoria

MV	Museum of Victoria
NBSE	Norwegian–British–Swedish Expedition
NLA	National Library of Australia
OBE	Order of the British Empire
OIC	Officer-in-Charge
P	Commonwealth Government Records, Tasmania
RAAF	Royal Australian Air Force
S	Series No.
SIOP	Scientific Instrument Optical Panel
UNS	University National Service
VIC	Victoria Institute of Colleges
VD	Voyage Diaries in possession of Phillip Garth Law
YMCA	Young Men's Christian Association

Glossary of Ice Terms [1]

BAY ICE: Fast ice of more than one winter's growth, which may be nourished also by surface layers of snow. Thickness of ice and snow up to about 2 m above sea-level. When bay ice becomes thicker than this it is called an ice shelf.

BERGY BIT: A massive piece of sea ice or disrupted hummocked ice; also medium-sized piece of floating glacier ice. Generally less than 5 m above sea-level, and not more than about 10 m across.

BESET: Situation of a vessel surrounded by ice and unable to move.

BRASH ICE: Small fragments of floating ice, not more than 2 m across; the wreckage of other forms of ice.

CLOSE PACK-ICE: Composed of floes mostly in contact, such that navigation is difficult even for specially constructed vessels and ice-breaker assistance may be required.

CRACK: Any fracture or rift in sea ice not sufficiently wide to be described as a lead. It is usually possible to jump across a crack.

FAST ICE: Sea ice of greatly varying width which remains fast along the coast, where it is attached to the shore, to an ice wall, to an ice front, or over shoals, generally in the position where originally formed. Fast ice may extend 400 km from the coast.

FLOE: A piece of sea ice other than fast ice, large or small. Light floes are anything up to a metre in thickness.

FRAZIL ICE: Fine spicules or plates of ice in suspension in water. The first stage of freezing, giving an oily or opaque appearance to the surface of the water.

GLACIER: A mass of snow and ice continuously moving from higher to lower ground or, if afloat, continuously spreading.

GLACIER TONGUE: An extension of a glacier, projecting seaward, and usually afloat.

GROWLER: A piece of ice almost awash, smaller than a bergy bit.

HUMMOCKED ICE: Sea ice piled haphazardly one piece over another, and which may be weathered.

HUMMOCKING: Process of pressure formation by which level ice becomes broken up into humps and ridges. When the floes rotate in the process it is termed 'screwing'.

ICEBERG: A large mass of floating or stranded ice broken away from a glacier or from an ice shelf. Often of considerable height (in any case more than 5 m above the level of the sea).

ICE BLINK: Yellowish white luminous glare in the sky produced by the reflection on the clouds of pack-ice or an ice sheet which may be beyond the range of vision.

ICEBOUND: A harbour, inlet, etc., is said to be icebound when navigation by ships is prevented due to ice, except possibly with the assistance of an ice-breaker.

ICE CAKE: A floe smaller than 10 m across.

ICE CLUSTER: A concentration of sea ice covering hundreds of square kilometres, which is found in the same region every summer.

ICE COVER: The amount of sea ice encountered; measured in eighths of the visible surface of the sea covered with ice.

ICE EDGE: The boundary at any given time between the open sea and sea ice of any kind, whether drifting or fast. When wind or swell compact the ice edge it may be called a compacted ice edge; when dispersed, it may be called an open ice edge.

ICE LIMIT: The average position of the ice edge in any given month or period based on observations over a number of years.

ICE RIND: A thin, elastic, shining crust of ice, formed by the freezing of sludge on a quiet sea surface. Thickness less than 5 cm.

ICE SHEET: A continuous mass of ice and snow of considerable thickness and large area.

ICE SHELF: A floating ice sheet of considerable thickness. Ice shelves are usually of great horizontal extent and have a level of gently undulating surface.

LEAD: A navigable passage through pack-ice; a lead may still be so called even if covered with young ice.

OPEN PACK-ICE: Composed of floes seldom in contact and with many leads and pools.

PACK-ICE: Any area of sea ice other than fast ice, no matter what form it takes or how it is disposed.

PANCAKE ICE: Pieces of newly formed sea ice usually approximately circular in shape with raised rims, and from one-third to 2 m in diameter.

POLYNYA: A large area of open water, surrounded by sea ice and found in the same region every year. One side is sometimes formed by the coast. Polynyas commonly occur off the mouths of big rivers.

PRESSURE ICE: A general term for sea ice which has been squeezed, and in places forced upwards when it can be described as rafted ice, hummocked ice or pressure ridge.

PRESSURE RIDGE: A ridge or wall of hummocked ice where one floe has been pressed against another.

RAFTING: The overriding of one floe on another, the mildest form of pressure. Hence 'rafted ice'.

ROTTEN ICE: Sea ice which has become honeycombed in the course of melting, and which is in an advanced state of disintegration.

SLUDGE: A later stage of freezing than frazil ice, when the spicules and plates of ice coagulate to form a thick soupy layer on the surface. Sludge reflects little light, giving the sea a matt appearance.

TABULAR BERG: A flat-topped iceberg. Most tabular bergs form by breaking from an ice shelf and show horizontal firm snow layers.

TIDE CRACK: The fissure at the line of junction between an immovable icefoot or ice wall and fast ice, the latter being subject to the rise and fall of the time.

TONGUE: A projection of the ice edge up to several kilometres in length, caused by wind and current.

WINTER ICE: More or less unbroken, level sea ice of not more than one winter's growth originating from young ice. Thickness from 15 cm to 2 m.

YOUNG ICE: Newly formed level ice in the transition stage of development from ice rind or pancake ice to winter ice. Thickness from 5 to 15 cm.

---

1. Taken from Terence Armstrong and Brian Roberts, *Illustrated Ice Glossary*, Scott Polar Research Institute, Cambridge, 1956.

Bibliography

LAW'S RECORDS

The major records of P. G. Law are listed in 'The Records of Phillip Garth Law (1912–)
Australian Science Archives Project', deposited with the National Library of Australia,
Canberra. (As at September 1991, Series 1, 4, 5, 6, 7 and 8 of these records were held at
the Museum of Victoria and Series 2, 3, 9, 10, 11, 12 and 13 were held by P. G. Law.)
Contents of these records are:
Series 1: Personal—Biographical
Series 4: Lectures, Talks and Broadcasts
Series 5: Lectures and Talks—Indexed Sets
Series 6: Manuscripts for Books and Articles
Series 7: Antarctic Correspondence—Subject Files
Series 8: General Correspondence—Subject Files

LAW'S PAPERS

The following records, listed in 'The Records of Phillip Garth Law (1912–)' are held by
P. G. Law. These records, and other papers, are referred to as 'Law's Papers'—LP.
Series 2: Voyage diaries
Series 3: Small diaries and pocket diaries—Overseas Trips
Series 9: Photographs—Antarctic and ANARE
Series 10: Photographs—General and family
Series 11: Photographs—Institutional
Series 12: Scrap-books and Scrap-book materials
Series 13: Audio tapes

ANNUAL REPORTS, ARTICLES AND PAMPHLETS

Commonwealth *Gazette*, no. 122, 12 August 1948.
'Communicating with Antarctica', *ANARE Personal Communications Booklet*, Antarctic Divi-
sion, Department of Science and the Environment, first edition, October 1980.
Education Gazette and Teachers' Aid.
The Educational Magazine, July 1964.
The Grange, Hamilton High School Newspaper.
'The October Meeting was a Winner', *Bohemia*, Melbourne, 1 November 1949, vol.5, no.5.
The School Paper, The Education Department of Victoria.
The University of Melbourne, *Annual Reports, 1939–1946*, Melbourne University Press,
1948.
'Versus Antarctica', *Ski-Horizon*, December 1953, pp. 6–7.
VIC News Letter, December 1977.
100 Not Out, Elsternwick Primary School, no. 2870, 1888–1988.

BOOKS, JOURNALS AND THESES

Armstrong, Terence and Roberts, Brian, *Illustrated Ice Glossary*, Scott Polar Research Insti
tute, Cambridge, 1956.

Attwood, Alan,' Modern Hero of Australian Antarctica, Phillip Law', *Australian Geographic*, Jan.–March 1989, no. 13, pp. 116–17.

'Australians in the Antarctic', *Heritage*, December 1988–February 1989.

Blake, L. J. (ed.), *Vision and Realisation*, vol. 1, Education Department of Melbourne, 1973.

Butterworth, Fay (ed.), *WYTOY, WYSSA, The Antarctic Wives and Kinfolk Association of Australia, An Overview of 25 Years*, Melbourne, 1990.

Calder, Jane, *The Grampians, a Noble Range*, Victorian National Parks Association, Melbourne, 1987.

Chester, Jonathan, *Going to Extremes, Project Blizzard and Australia's Antarctic Heritage*, Doubleday, Sydney, 1986.

Cook, W. F. (Capt.), 'HMAS *Wyatt Earp*, Australian National Antarctic Research Expedition 1947–1948', *Naval Historical Review*, December 1978.

Crowley, F., *Modern Australia 1901–1939*, Wren Publishing Pty Ltd, Melbourne, 1973.

Davies, A. F., *Skills, Outlooks and Passions, A Psychoanalytic Contribution to the Study of Politics*, Cambridge University Press, Melbourne, 1980.

Disher, Garry, *Total War, The Home Front 1939–1945*, Oxford University Press, Melbourne, 1983.

Dow, Hume (ed.), *Memories of Melbourne University, Undergraduate Life in the Years Since 1917*, Hutchinson of Australia, Richmond, 1983.

Garden, Don, *Hamilton, a Western District History*, Hargreen Publishing Company, Vic., 1984.

Garden, Don, *The Melbourne Teacher Training Colleges, From Training Institution to Melbourne State College, 1870–1982*, Heinemann Educational Australia, Victoria, 1982.

Garden, Don, *Victoria, a History*, Thomas Nelson, Australia, 1984.

Geehi Bushwalking Club, *Snowy Mountain Walks*, New South Wales, 1983.

Goldberg, Herb, *The Hazards of Being Male, Surviving the Myth of Masculine Privilege*, New American Library, New York, 1976.

Harris, Stuart (ed.), *Australia's Antarctic Policy Options*, CRES Monograph 11, Australian National University, Canberra, 1984.

Hasick, J., 'Tribute from Mawson Station, Antarctica', *Education, Antarctica, Marine Science and Australia's Future*, Proceedings of the Phillip Law 80th Birthday Symposium, 29 April 1992, Royal Society of Victoria, Melbourne.

Hetherington, John, *Australians, Nine Profiles*, F. W. Cheshire, Melbourne, 1960.

Hudson, W. J., *Casey*, Oxford University Press, Melbourne, 1986.

Huntford, Roland, *The Last Place on Earth*, Pan Books, London, 1985.

Huntford, R., *Shackleton*, Hodder and Stoughton, London, 1985.

Huntford, R. (ed.), *The Amundsen Photographs*, Hodder and Stoughton, London, 1987.

Jacka, Fred and Jacka, Eleanor, *Mawson's Antarctic Diaries*, A Susan Haynes Book, Allen and Unwin, Sydney, 1988.

Johnston, George, *My Brother Jack*, Collins, London, 1964.

Kannuluik, W. and Law P. G., 'Note on the Carbon Dioxide Point in Thermometry', *Journal Scientific Institute*, vol. 25, no. 7, 1946.

Kannuluik, W. and Law, P. G., 'Thermal Conductivity of Carbon Dioxide over a Range of Temperatures', *Proc. Roy. Soc. Vic.*, vol. 58, no. 142, 1947.

Law, A. J., *Modern Teaching*, Robertson and Mullens Ltd, Melbourne, 1934.

Law, P. and Bechervaise, J., *ANARE, Australia's Antarctic Outposts*, Oxford University Press, Melbourne, 1957.

Law, P. G., 'The Australian 1954 Antarctic Expedition to MacRobertson Land', *Geographical Journal*, 1954, vol. 120:490.

Law, P. G., 'The Mawson Story—No. 2, A Powerful, Stubborn and Gentle Man', *Royal Historical Society of Victoria Journal*, 1984, vol. 57, no. 1, pp. 13–18.

Law, Phillip, *Antarctic Odyssey*, Heinemann, Melbourne, 1983.

McCalman, Janet, *Struggletown*, Penguin Books Australia Ltd, 1984.

McClelland, James, *Stirring the Possum, A Political Autobiography*, Penguin Books, Ringwood, 1989.

McKernan, Michael, *All In! Australia During the Second World War*, Thomas Nelson Australia, Melbourne, 1983.

McKinlay, Brian, *School Days*, Robert Andersen and Associates, Melbourne, 1985.
Martel, Leslie F. and Biller, Henry B.*, Stature and Stigma, The Biopsychosocial Development of Short Males*, Lexington Books, Toronto, 1987.
Mawson, Pacquita, *Mawson of the Antarctic*, Longman, London, 1964.
Migot, André, *The Lonely South* (English translation), Rupert Hart-Davis, London, 1956.
Murray, P. R. and Wells, J. C., *From Sand, Swamp and Heath ... A History of Caulfield*, City of Caulfield, Victoria, 1980.
Nance, Lindsay, *Prime Ministers of Australia*, Bison Group, London, 1989.
Rand, Ayn, *The New Left: The Anti–Industrial Revolution*, Signet, New York, 1971.
Robson, L. L., *Australia in the Nineteen Twenties, Commentary and Documents*, Thomas Nelson, Australia, 1980.
Rogers, J. S., *The History of the Scientific Instruments and Optical Panel*, July 1940–Dec. 1946, Commonwealth of Australia, Ministry of Munitions, Ordnance Production Directorate.
Royal Society of Victoria, *Education, Antarctica, Marine Science and Australia's Future*, Proceedings of the Phillip Law 80th Birthday Symposium, 29 April 1992, Melbourne.
Schofield, Ann, *Signposts of Change*, Aird Books, Melbourne, 1987.
Simpson, Frank A. (ed.), *The Antarctic Today*, A. H. and A. W. Reed, Wellington, 1952.
Swan, Keith, *The Shire of Tallangatta*, A History, 1987.
Swan, R. A., *Australia in the Antarctic, Interest, Activity and Endeavour*, Melbourne University Press, Carlton, 1961.
Triggs, G. D. (ed.), *The Antarctic Treaty Regime—Law, Environment and Resources*, Cambridge University Press, Cambridge, 1987.
Trolle-Anderson, Rolph, 'The Antarctic scene: legal and political facts', in G. D. Triggs (ed.), T*he Antarctic Treaty Regime—Law, Environment and Resources*, Cambridge University Press, Cambridge, 1987.
Wainwright, G., 'A Life filled with People', *Melbourne Studies in Education*, Melbourne University Press, Carlton, 1977.
Ward, Russel, *A Nation for a Continent, the History of Australia 1901–1975*, Heinemann Educational Australia, Vic., 1977.
Watt A., *Australian Diplomat, Memoirs of Sir Alan Watt*, Angus and Robertson, Sydney, 1972.
Woods, Graham, 'Rhetoric and Reality, Unintended Outcomes in the Evolution of the Victoria Institute of Colleges', PhD Thesis, La Trobe University, Victoria, 1978.

CITATIONS

Citation for P. G. Law's appointment as a Commander of the Civil Division of the Excellent Order of the British Empire (CBE) on 31 December 1960, LR.

CORRESPONDENCE FILES AND OFFICIAL RECORDS

(Each item quoted in this book is identified fully in endnotes.)
Antarctic Division, Hobart
Department of External Affairs, Canberra
Education Department Records
Elsternwick Primary School Records
Hamilton High School Records

INTERVIEWS (Conducted by author)

Noel Barnard (Law's sister), 6 May 1988 and 11 April 1989.
Dr. Grahame Budd (Physiologist and Party Leader, ANARE), 7 July 1990.
Alan Campbell-Drury (Photographic Officer and expeditioner), 17 October 1989.
Evan Collings (Commissioner Commonwealth Public Service Board), 5 July 1990.
John Fyfield (past student), 2 June 1990.
Dr Fred Jacka (Chief Scientist and expeditioner), 8 August 1990.
Phillip G. Law (numerous throughout 1987–1991).
Geoffrey Law (Law's brother), July 1988.
Nel Law (Law's wife), 26 September 1988.
Douglas Leckie (Pilot), 22 October 1990.

Marjorie Liddelow (Sister), 6 May 1988.
Eric Macklin (Supply Officer and expeditioner), 4 May 1989.
Graeme McKinnon (Geographic Officer and expeditioner), 24 June 1989.
Ian McLeod (Geologist and expeditioner), 5 July 1990.
Ruth McKinnon (Expeditioner's wife), 24 June 1989.
Mr Colin Moodie (Asst. Sec. External Affairs), 7 August 1990.
Bernard O'Brien (past student), 12 June 1990.
Robert Reeve (Photographic Officer and expeditioner), 26 June 1989.
Bruce Stinear (Geologist and expeditioner), 8 July 1990.
Wendy Stuart (Law's sister), 6 May 1988.
Sir Arthur Tange (Secretary, Department of External Affairs), 6 July 1990.
Richard Thompson (Supply Officer and Expedition Lieutenant), 9 July 1990.
Douglas Twigg (Radio Supervisor and expeditioner), 24 June 1989.
Mary Twigg (Expeditioner's wife and member Antarctic Wives Association), 24 June 1989.
Harry Walter (Law's highschool friend), 7 July 1988.

INTERVIEWS (Conducted by others)

ABC SOCIAL HISTORY UNIT AUDIO RECORDINGS:
All audio recordings of Antarctic expeditioners recorded for the 1990 six-part documen-
tary series 'Australians in Antarctica'. Amongst these tapes were six one-hour interviews
with P. G. Law recorded in 1987.

NATIONAL LIBRARY OF AUSTRALIA
Transcripts of interviews conducted with Law in 1975 for the Oral History Project.

LECTURES AND TALKS GIVEN BY LAW
(Unless otherwise noted, copies of these are held in Law's Records, Series 4 or 7, MV.)
After Dinner Speech, CSIROSIP Dinner, 13 November 1987, LP.
'Hazards in Antarctica', Safety Convention, 8 August 1960.
'Nutrition in the Antarctic' The Annie B. Cunning Lectures on Nutrition before The Royal
Australasian College of Physicians in Melbourne on 11 October 1956.
'Character, Leadership and Training', undated.
'Personality Problems in the Antarctic', Paper delivered at 26th Sir Richard Stawell Ora-
tion, Meeting of the Victorian Branch of the British Medical Association, 7 October 1959.
'The Organization of an Antarctic Expedition', undated.
'Planning an Antarctic Expedition', Constitutional Club, Monday, 30 March 1953.
'Some Polar Leaders', undated.
'Tribulations at Sea', Talk given to Shiplovers' Society of Victoria, 11 May 1966.

MAPS
Australian National Antarctic Research Expeditions, 1947–1966. Map produced by Australian Surveying and Land Information Group, Department of Administrative Services
in collaboration with Antarctic Division, Department of Arts, Sports, The Environment,
Tourism and Territories with assistance from Dr P. G. Law, 1989.

MINUTES AND REPORTS
ANARE Voyage Reports.
Leckie, D. W., *A Report on the Participation of the Royal Australian Air Force in the Australian
National Antarctic Research Expedition 1954*, May 1954.
Minutes of Executive Planning Committee, ANARE, 1947–1954. ADH.
The University of Melbourne, Annual Reports 1939–1946, Melbourne University Press, 1948.

NEWSPAPERS
Copies of many newspaper articles are in Series 12 of Law's Papers.
The Age, Melbourne
Argus, Melbourne.

Argus Magazine, Melbourne.
The Australian Women's Weekly, 22 November 1947.
Sun, Melbourne
The Times, London.
The Toowoomba Chronicle and Darling Downs Gazette, Thursday , 18 March 1954.

PERSONAL LETTERS AND DIARIES (other than those in Law's Records)
Alan Campbell-Drury's diaries of voyages and expeditions.
Colin Moodie to author, 1990.
Richard Thompson to Sheelagh Manson, 1954.
Captain Vilh. Pedersen to author, 4 December 1988.

Index

more onerous than anything they ... Australia.

However, back to the story.

I received a message during the morning that Otto Rec, the Labuan by DUKW to help bring dogs ashore, had been by the DUKW against the side of the ship when climb barely able to hold on until dragged up on deck.

Here I was, faced with another difficult ask Gwynn to remain for a further term as doctor was Rec? It was pretty certain bones had been broke broken without complications, no doubt they could they could heal just as well at Heard as in Australia were compound, or there were flesh or arterial injuries to be sent back and Gwynn would then be the doctor at the Island.

I called Gwynn, explained my predicament, to find the extent of the injuries.

They X-rayed Rec and found that he in the bones of the foot. (One was in the heel bone He was lucky at that! Both were clean, there was and there were no superficial injuries. His boot had steel horseshoe on the heel of his boot had broken DUKW to pinned him to the ship's side. Above been badly crushed but not as much as if the Its root the foot, coming third after these two, wh He was getting out of the DUKW He waited until the DUKW was at the crest of the The next swell however was much higher and ot A man higher on the ladder prevented him furth his legs up as high as he could, but it was not

McCarthy, the meteorologist, said and was headed for Heard. He expected the wea blow around about midnight.